COURAGE ON THE BATTLEFIELD

VOLUME II
Canada's Military Heritage

CANADA'S MILITARY HERITAGE ADVISORY BOARD

Senator Hartland deM. Molson, OBE
John A. Aylen, QC
Russell Bannock, DSO, DFC
Robert I. Hendy, QC
Jack McClelland
Denis Whitaker, DSO and Bar

COURAGE ON THE BATTLEFIELD

VOLUME II
Canada's Military Heritage

BY
ARTHUR BISHOP

Foreword by
General A.J.G.D. de Chastelaine
Former Chief of the Defence Staff

McGraw-Hill Ryerson
Toronto   Montreal

Courage on the Battlefield
Volume II Canada's Military Heritage
Copyright © 1993 by Arthur Bishop

All rights reserved. No part of this publication may be reproduced or transmitted in any form or by any means, or stored in a data base and retrieval system, without the prior written permission of the publisher.

First published in 1993 by
McGraw-Hill Ryerson Limited
300 Water Street
Whitby, Ontario
L1N 9B6

1 2 3 4 5 6 7 8 9 10 BG 4 5 6 7 8 9 0 1 2 3

Publisher: Donald S. Broad

Text design: Dianna Little

Original cover design: Michelle Losier

Cover photo design: Dave Hader/Studio Conceptions

Editorial services provided by Word Guild, Toronto.

Photographs from the following sources are used by permission. The author gratefully acknowledges these public and private collections.
• National Archives of Canada • The Canadian Military Institute • The Canadian War Museum • Imperial War Museum, London • Bundesarchiv, Koblenz • Private collections.

Canadian Cataloguing in Publication Data

Bishop, William Arthur, 1923-
    Canada's military heritage

Includes bibliographical references and index.
Contents: v. 1. Courage in the air. — v. 2. Courage on the battlefield. — v. 3. Courage at sea.
ISBN 0-07-551556-3 (v. 2)

1. Canada - History, Military - 20th century.*
2. Canada - Armed Forces - Biography. I. Title.

FC603.B57 1992   355'.00971   C92-094452-3
F1028.B57 1992

Printed and bound in Canada

"Courage mounteth with occasion."
Shakespeare

Contents

Author's Breve: A Selective Salute		xi
Foreword		xiii
Acknowledgements		xv

START-LINE			**1**
THE WAR OF 1812		1812-1814	2
COURAGE ON THE CRIMEA		1854-1856	10
THE INDIAN MUTINY		1855-1859	13
THE BOER WAR		1899-1902	16
	Liliefontein	November 17, 1900	17

WORLD WAR 1		**August 1, 1914 - November 11, 1918**	**21**
1915	Ypres — Gallantry against Poison Gas	April 22-26	23
1915-16	Battle of Attrition		29
1916	*Das Blutbad* — Slaughter on the Somme		
		July 1-December 30	36
1917	Preparation	January-April	45
	Valour at Vimy Ridge	Easter Monday-April 9	48
	Hill 70	April 15-25	59
	Arras	April 13-May 3	65
	Trench Warfare	June-October	68
	Passchendaele	October 30-November 10	74
	Cambrai — First Effective Tank Attack	November 20	86
1918	Final German Thrust	March 21-June 10	89

1918	**CANADA'S 100 DAYS**	**August 4-November 11**	**95**
	Amiens	August 8-22	97
	Breaching the Hindenburg Line		
		August 22-September 2	108
	Collapse at Cambrai	September 27-October 9	126
	Final Pursuit	October 11-November 11	142

	WORLD WAR 2	September 1, 1939-August 14, 1945	155
1941	The Hapless Horror of Hong Kong	December 8-25	157
1942	The Debacle at Dieppe	August 19	167
1943	The Conquest of Sicily	July 10-August 18	184
	The Canadian Campaign in Italy (1)	September 3-December 28	198
	Ortona	*December 20-28*	*207*
1944	*Anzio*	*January 22-May 23*	*211*
	Burma	*February*	*213*
	The Canadian Campaign in Italy (2)		215
	Liri Valley	*May 11-31*	*215*
	Crossing the Gari River	*May 11-13*	*216*
	Assault on the Hitler Line	*May 23*	*219*
	The Melfa River Crossing	*May 24-29*	*224*
1944-45	Europe	June 6-May 7	230
1944	*The Battle of Normandy*	*June 6-August 20*	*231*
	D-Day		*232*
	Build-Up to the Breakout		*241*
	The Falaise Gap	*August 7-22*	*248*
	Breakout		256
	Clearing the Channel Ports	*September 17-22*	*256*
	The Canadian Campaign in Italy (3)		259
	The Rugged Route to Rimini	*August 25-September 23*	*259*
	Breaking the Gothic Line	*August 25-September 2*	*260*
	Slog to the San Fortunato Ridge	*September 2-22*	*263*
	Freeing the Port of Antwerp	September 5-November 28	267
	Market Garden	September 17-26	278
1944-45	The Canadian Campaign in Italy (4)		279
	The Final Phase	*October 1-February 25*	*279*
	The Savio River	*October 19-28*	*280*
	The Last Operation	*December 3-January 7*	*282*
1945	Clearing the Rhineland	February 8-March 19	287
	Crossing the Rhine	March 25-30	296
	Liberation of the Netherlands	March 23-May 5	300
	Build-Up to Capitulation	April 26-May 5	316

KOREA		**June 25, 1950-July 27, 1953**	**321**
1951	Kapyong	April 23-25	324
	Kowang-Hi	November 23-25	326

Epitaph	331
Abbreviations	333
Decorations	333
Designations	333
General	333
Ranks	334
Reference Sources	334
Name Index	337

AUTHOR'S BREVE: A SELECTIVE SALUTE

There never can, nor ever will be, a compleat, definitive compendium of Canadians who distinguished themselves on the battlefield. Mission impossible; they number too many to make that conceivable or practical. In World War 1 alone, 6,679 members of the Canadian Expeditionary Force received the Military Medal, only one of 40 decorations that included the British Victoria Cross, the French Croix de Guerre and the Italian Medaglio Valori, awarded to 15,779 Dominion soldiers in that conflict. Not to mention a few thousand others granted to Canadians for bravery who served with the British and French armies.

Obviously, even a simple name, rank and award listing of all men and women officially honoured for heroism in every war in which Canadians participated, from 1812 to Korea, would fill a small telephone book. By then enlarging those same listings into even the most cursory sketches of deed and data would magnify it into dictionary-size proportions — encyclopedic, boring, dull and unexciting. And would do them all a grave injustice.

My purpose — and in this I was ably assisted by a selection panel which I consider expert by any criterion — was to provide a reflective and representative profile of all Canadians who distinguished themselves so gallantly on the battlefield. It was not easy, but in every case to the best of my ability I tried to be fair. I hope I succeeded.

ARTHUR BISHOP

Foreword

Courage is one of the most admired human virtues, and in wartime it is perhaps *the* most admired. Whether the embodiment of courage is the witnessed act of bravery that leads to an award, the small act of faith that persuades the frightened to take the next step, or the unrewarded act of sacrifice that spares a life or saves the moment, courage is to the battlefield what drama is to the stage. Without the presence of courage, the battlefield is a barren place.

Courage in war conjures up images of the Victoria Cross, the Medal of Honour, the Pour le Mérite and the Legion d'Honneur, and the acts of courage recognised by these decorations epitomize the pinnacle of military bravery and sacrifice. But the battlefield is as extensive as it is murky, and the acts of courage that receive official recognition can only be a small percentage of all the brave events that occur in war. Sadly, perhaps, history only records what is known, and any detailed account of bravery on the battlefield must concentrate on acts that bore witness.

In recounting Canadian acts of courage on the battlefield, from the War of 1812 (when by strict national definition there were no Canadians) to the end of the Korean War (when by the same definition Canadians had existed for 86 years and had fought as such in four wars), Arthur Bishop has selected incidents and actions which demonstrate the fascinating variety and breadth of what it is that constitutes courage.

Thus at the same time as recounting the dashing action that won Captain Hampden Cockburn of the Royal Canadian Dragoons the VC by saving the guns from the Boers at Liliefontein, Bishop also describes the dogged determination of Signaller Harry Gingell of Le Régiment de la Chaudière in France in 1944, cut off from his unit but keeping his radio operating during the 8th Brigade's attack to clear the Channel ports.

Similarly we read of the courage of Private Harry Brown, VC, of Gananoque, at Hill 70 on 16 August 1917, who was despatched to deliver a vital message and persevered through gun fire, the loss of his comrade and a mortal wound to complete his mission. And of Captain Wally Mills of 2 Princess Patricia's Canadian Light Infantry coolly bringing artillery fire down onto his own company position at Kapyong to drive off the attacking Chinese soldiers.

The name "Bishop" in Canadian circles is synonymous with "courage," and it is fitting that Arthur Bishop, the son of Canada's most decorated World War 1 hero, and himself a World War 2 fighter pilot, should so engagingly chronicle the history of courage on the battlefield as he has chronicled the feats of those who flew in his earlier volume, *Courage in the Air*.

Limits have to be placed on any history and this volume takes us to the end of the war in Korea. Canada has participated in one war since then, in which no bravery awards were made, and in numerous peacekeeping operations, in which several were. But recorded or not, the spirit which Canadian Forces personnel carried into the Gulf War, and into peacekeeping operations in the Congo, Cyprus and Sarajevo, has been one fully in keeping with the rich heritage of courage which their predecessors demonstrated during four wars in this century, a heritage which is faithfully recorded in *Courage on the Battlefield*.

General A.J.G.D. de Chastelain, CMM, CD
Former Chief of the Defence Staff

ACKNOWLEDGEMENTS

DND
I am indebted to General A. John G. D. de Chastelain, the former Chief of the Defence Staff, for his very fine Foreword to this book. Thank you — Sir!

CDA
I am particularly grateful to the Conference of Defence Associations Institute — established in 1932 to study the problems of defence and security and to promote the efficiency and well-being of our armed forces — for their contribution and assistance in making this second volume of the Military Heritage Series possible. I would like to acknowledge one of the Institute's chief goals:

To encourage and contribute to the better understanding by the Canadian public of matters relating to national defence, to the security of Canada and to Canada's roles in international security arrangements.

My thanks to CDA President *Ben Shapiro*, Director of Operations *Bill Yost*, and Assistant Director *Ian Cameron*. I am grateful to *Dick Mallot* of the Canadian War Museum for introducing me to the CDA.

DHIST
In establishing a format I throw a much-merited salute to my friend *Carl Christie*, Senior Research Officer of the Directorate of History, who provided so much help with the first volume, COURAGE IN THE AIR. After an early morning meeting in Holly Lane, Ottawa, Carl led me to two invaluable sources which I have used and quoted extensively. In fact, this is the widest use yet made of them. The first of these is a file 713 065 (D1) and (D2), a compilation of virtually every commendation during World War 2 running to some 60 volumes. Because these were written in the field at the time of action they project a spontaneity seldom experienced in researching army files.

The second source was what Carl and I have come to call "The Jackson Papers." This is a *hand-written record* of those army personnel who were decorated in the First World War compiled by Harold Jackson (Lt-Col) who at one time had charge of the War Services Records of the Department of Veterans Affairs.

RESEARCHERS
My thanks to *Strome Galloway*, well-known military historian for his many helpful suggestions and for vetting the final draft. Also to *John Grodzinsky*, historical researcher who helped me with the earlier volume. Another who vetted the manuscript for accuracy and clarification was Dr. *Bill McAndrew* of DHist.

RCMI
Special thanks to the members of the Royal Canadian Military Institute in Toronto, who so willingly proferred suggestions and encouragement.

In particular to *Anne Melvin* the librarian with whom I have spent so many delightful and instructive hours in that fabulous library. No one has been more helpful.

NAC
Micheline Robert of the Documentary Art & Photography Division of the National Archives of Canada, and *Roanne Mokthar*, Reference Archivist, were of great assistance in procuring photographs. My thanks.

MY EDITOR
Thank you *Don Loney* for everything!

MY FRIENDS
A great many friends outside the official military realm, assisted in countless ways. Among them *Clark Wallace, Bud Porter, Peter Worthington*, to name but a few.

MY FAMILY
I would like to thank my family — wife *Cilla*, daughter *Diana*, son *Bill* for their encouragement. They have been helpful in so many ways it is impossible to catalogue them here.

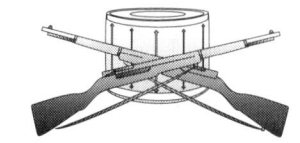

THE WAR OF 1812
1812-1814

Though this conflict was essentially between the United States and England, it was fought on our native soil and the first blood was spilled in defence of our dominion-to-be. As such, to all intents, it produced Canada's first two national war heroes. Though neither was Canadian-born, each gave his life gallantly. In that context the War of 1812 marked, in army parlance, the "start-line" of Canadian courage on the battlefield.

When they first met on the eve of the Battle of Fort Detroit, both protagonists, after clasping hands, stood in awe of each other. Isaac Brock, British governor of Upper Canada, later wrote of Tecumseh: "A more sagacious or more gallant warrior does not exist." The Shawnee Indian chief exalted in turn: "This is a man!" Ironically, neither combatant survived the gory two-and-a-half-year struggle that saw prisoners scalped or burned at the stake, women and children massacred, and houses put to the torch.

Ostensibly, this bitter feud arose over the Royal Navy's blockade of American ships bound for Napoleonic ports and the pressing of their crews into British service on the basis they were deserters. In reality the objective was nothing less than formal conquest. By war's end, territorially Canada had emerged the victor, biting off a huge slice of Maine. But it was a hollow acquisition; under the *Treaty of Ghent* the spoils had to be returned to the United States. On the battlefield, however, that war firmly entrenched the beginning of Canada's military heritage.

(Overleaf) Brock greeting Tecumseh.
(Courtesy Canadian Military Institute)

BROCK Isaac

"Gallant Death Gave Nation Its First Sense of Identity"

When American troops battled the currents of the Niagara River to launch an attack at Queenston on the night of October 12/13, 1812, Isaac Brock, British governor of Upper Canada, was in bed in Fort George five miles to the north. Awakened by cannon fire at Vrooman's Point, he hastily pulled on his uniform, raced for his horse, saddled up, and galloped south with sword in hand towards the sounds of battle.

Major General Sir Isaac Brock (Canadian War Museum)

But by the time he reached the scene dawn had broken; the enemy had scaled the heights and captured the Canadian gun positions that overlooked the field of battle. As the Americans rushed down the slopes to finish off the British, Brock rallied his troops around him. Then, in a charge that proved fatal, he led his men up the hill to engage the American troops, his bright red tunic presenting a tempting target no sharpshooter could possibly miss. A bullet pierced his left breast killing him instantly. But his courage in the face of enemy fire spurred the British to drive the Americans back across the river at bayonet point. Gallant, if foolhardy, Brock's bravery cemented a cornerstone in Canadian history that gave the nation its first hero and sense of destiny at a critical time.

Born at Saint Peter Port on Guernsey, Brock was a lifetime soldier who joined the 8th (King's) Regiment when he was 15 years old and later the 49th, the very unit he led in his charge up the Queenston Heights. Prior to being posted to Canada in 1803, Brock saw active service in the West Indies, in Europe against Bonaparte, and in the Baltic against the Danish and Russian fleets. By 1811, at a time when American-Canadian relations had reached the breaking point, Brock was administrator of Upper Canada and commander of the armed forces with headquarters at Fort Henry. In this capacity he proved to be an able strategist and tactician as well as a shrewd negogiator. He recognized that when war broke out the key to success depended on naval control on the Great Lakes and set about building and outfitting vessels to assure that supremacy. He also had the foresight to befriend the Indians whom he saw as valuable allies, while the Americans, on the other hand, considered them enemies and were bent on their destruction. On June 15, 1812, when the United States declared war against the British, even with the meager forces at his disposal and lack of finances, Brock was far better prepared and ready for battle than his opponents. Although he was under orders to avoid the offensive unless absolutely necessary, he knew that to bring the Indians to his side some immediate action was needed to convince them that the British were serious about the war. His answer was to occupy Michilimackinac Island in U.S. Michigan Territory at the top of Lake Superior. On the morning of July 16, a combined force of British troops and Indian warriors landed and took the island, without a shot being fired. The exploit had the desired effect; Tecumseh, the most powerful of the chiefs, allied his Shawnee tribe with Brock's army. The day before an American force, which had arrived in Detroit a week earlier, in an attempt to control the Great Lakes, crossed the Detroit River and occupied Sandwich with the objective of taking Fort Amherstburg. But the situation soon became tenuous. Indians ambushed a relief supply column. With their resources stretched to the limit, the Americans withdrew to Fort Detroit. Meanwhile, the British at Amherstburg had been bolstered by fresh troops from the main frontier at Niagara and the presence of Brock who took charge. Landing his forces on the American shore on the night of August 15, the next morning Brock, marching at the

The tunic of General Brock, worn on the day he was killed. The sash is said to have been given to him as a token of esteem by Tecumseh. The bullet hole is at his heart. (Canadian War Museum)

head of his troops — "I will never ask [men] to go where I do not lead them" — employed his Indian compatriots in a role designed to terrify the Americans. During the night, in clear view of the Detroit stockade, they played out a war dance waving tomahawks and screaming at the top of their lungs, then repeated the performance in broad daylight. The spectacle unnerved the American commander; fearing a massacre of women and children within the fort he surrendered. Hardly a shot had been fired save for cannon fire from the Canadian shore and the return of American fusillades. Virtually a bloodless victory, the prize was enormous — 2,500 American soldiers captured along with 2,500 rifles, 100,000 cartridges and a ship. A spectacular win for Brock and a significant one for Canada, strategically it left the British in command of the Great Lakes and allowed Brock to concentrate his efforts on the main frontier at Niagara. There, less than two months later, another victory he inspired resulted in his death, but his exploits and valour brought Canada its nationhood. Buried at Fort George, in 1824 Brock's body was moved to the summit of Queenston Heights where a monument erected in his honour dominates the battlefield.

Maj-Gen   Born Oct 6 1789   KIA Oct 13 1812
RefScs: CE 229   FATB 22 181 254–5 278 398 425 427   GB 70 73 76 80 94 115 133 157 196 203 210 1 214 231 2 237 8 253 255 6   SIB 87 98   TIOC 81–4 133–4 141–6 151 163 174–7 180–3 209–10 217–8 231–2 237–40 252–4 307 313–4   TWO1 41–4 55 60 63–6 70 107 256

Brock's telescope, watch, uniform and sash are on display at the Canadian War Museum in Ottawa. Quite visible on his red tunic is the hole made by the bullet that killed him.

TECUMSEH

"Greatest of the Tribal Chiefs Died Helping to Save 'Our Native Land'"

For all his ferocity in battle Tecumseh, the Indian chief whose war-whooping histrionics in battle struck terror into the hearts of his American enemies, was in reality a pacifist by nature who desired nothing more than to seek peace and independence for his people. In fact he abhorred violence and torture, preached against it and did his utmost among his followers to prevent it. A gifted leader, brilliant orator and statesman, the "Leaping Panther" proved to be one of Canada's worthiest warriors. A native of the Ohio Valley, Tecumseh was the son of a chieftain

Tecumseh in battle. (Courtesy Canadian Military Institute)

who died shortly after Tecumseh's birth. By the time he was 15 years old he was battling the immigrant tide; at 16 he was ambushing boats on the Ohio River, and at 22 serving as a raider and scout against the United States army. In his first battle he killed three men, then in true tribal tradition scalped them. But that was the last time he would indulge in such a barbarous practice. During the mêlée, a prisoner had been taken and next day was burned at the stake, a spectacle that appalled and revolted Tecumseh. Displaying the oratory for which he became famous and respected by friend and foe alike, he reproved his fellow braves so eloquently they swore that no prisoner would ever again be tortured or harmed by a Shawnee warrior.

By the time Tecumseh took his place as chief of his tribesmen, he had already siezed upon a policy of coexistence with the Americans. His aim was to create a seperate Indian confederation of all the tribes that could live in harmony with the pioneers. But he reckoned without the greed of the U.S. military and the settlers who were determined to cheat the Indians out of their lands or buy them for little compensation. Though Tecumseh told the Americans he only wanted peace and a fair deal for his followers, the governor of the Indiana Territory suspected that the Shawnee chief might be trying to seek an alliance with the British. In October, 1811, Tecumseh travelled south to enlist others to his confederation which consisted of half a dozen tribes who lived at Prophet's Town on the Tippicanoe River. In his absence, U.S. soldiers attacked Prophet's Town, forcing the Indians to flee across the river to safety. Two days later the Americans sacked the village; they scalped the dead and burned all of the stored crops, leaving the town in ruins. This was supposed to teach the Indians a lesson and put fear into them. Instead it enraged them and set them on the warpath seething with revenge. When Tecumseh returned he vowed that when war started between Britain and the U.S. — it was now imminent — he would cross the Canadian border and side with the British. Thus was formed his alliance with the British general Isaac Brock that contributed to the victory at Detroit in August 1812. All that autumn, and the next spring and summer of 1813, Tecumseh continued to win the admiration and respect of his Canadian allies for his conduct and that of his braves in battle — at Fort Meigs (where he prevented a massacre) and at Fort Stephenson (following which he realized that the fight for his people could never be won).

By this time the situation had changed dramatically. The British lacked the leadership of Brock who had been killed the previous fall. Then, on September 11, 1813, the American fleet, which had been growing steadily since the war began, destroyed the British flotilla in the Battle of Lake Erie opening the way for the reestablishment of a U.S. presence in the northwest. Shortly afterwards, in the face of an imminent American invasion, Fort Amherstburg was dismantled and plans made for a strategic withdrawal eastward by the British army stationed there, to the Niagara frontier. Since the fleet had been destroyed the retreat had to be made overland. This was not Tecumseh's idea of how to wage war. His method was to attack, and he accused the British of cowardice. He wanted to stay and fight. The British commander knew that without the help of the Indians his forces stood a strong chance of being decimated even in retreat. A compromise was finally reached — to make a stand at Moraviatown on the Thames River some 70 miles northeast of Fort Amherstburg. The site offered an excellent defensive position, particularly against mounted troops. On the left was the river; on the right was a large swamp flanked on one side by forest, ideal for Tecumseh's style of fighting even though his ranks had been depleted because several tribes had deserted him to make peace with the invaders. The English general convinced Tecumseh that the added advantage of being this far inland meant the enemy's supply lines would be stretched to the limit. Though Tecumseh agreed, he confided to his tribesmen: "My body will remain on the battlefield."

From the start it was a debacle. On the morning of October 5, the Americans charged and the British broke in disarray and ran. But the Indians continued to fight. As the Americans' horses became mired in the swamp and tangled in the trees the riders dismounted and a furious hand-to-hand combat ensued. Tecumseh, at the head of his warriors brandishing his tomahawk, shrieking his bloodcurdling war cry, urged his braves on. But the U.S. troops — Kentuckians experienced in forest fighting — forced the Indians to give ground. Then, suddenly, Tecumseh was seen to fall, mortally wounded. A single bullet had forever stilled the spirit that had propelled the Shawnees to victory after victory. As they moved his body from the battlefield, word passed down the line that their chief was dead and the fight went out of his tribesmen. In despair and disillusionment they gave up and fled. But in death he became immortal. Steadfast to the last, Tecumseh's sacrifice had not been in vain. By allowing the British to escape and fight another day, he had saved Canada. For his people, however, the ramifications of his loss and their final defeat spelled disaster for their cause. Without his inspiration, the hope of a tribal confederation ended and the fight for independence was gone forever. No prayers were said for Tecumseh, and his body was never found, but a eulogy to his passing was best expressed by the author Norman Gurd who wrote: "Like the shooting star for which he was named, he flamed across the sky and disappeared in the darkness. . . . The country for which he gave his life raised no monument to his memory, but the great chief lives in the hearts of men."

Born circa 1768   KIA Oct 5 1813
RefScs: CE 1794   FATB 105 121 177–80 184 197–206 425   T 27–29
87–109 119 145   TIOC 58–64 66–70 76–7 97–8 159–162 166–7 170 184–6
192 216 307 312–3   TWO1 116 118–20 129–30 188   TSOT 12–17 36–8
46–7 74–5 80 85–9 98–100 133

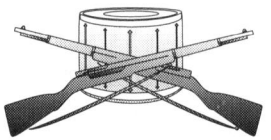

COURAGE ON THE CRIMEA
1854-1856

In July, 1853, Russia began expanding into the Bulgarian territory of the Turkish-Ottoman Empire. To stem the Russian advance, bent on domination of Eurasia, Britain and France went to the aid of Turkey in an action that saw them as allies for the first time in 500 years, landing troops on the Crimean Peninsula in September of 1854. It took two years to defeat the Russians.

BALACLAVA
October 25, 1854

DUNN Alexander Roberts

"Charge of the Light Brigade Hero Won Canada's First VC and Became Youngest Colonel in the British Army"

At six-foot-three, York-born cavalryman Alex Dunn rode so high in the saddle he needed a longer-than-regulation sword with which to do battle (see PA below). In 1854, during the Charge of the Light Brigade at Balaclava, the British Army Hussar wielded his outsized sabre so dextrously and savagely that he single-handedly cut down four Russian Dragoons from their mounts while saving two of his own horsemen from being slaughtered by the enemy. That spirited skirmish earned Dunn the distinction of being the first from the Dominion to win the newly struck Victoria Cross, the British Empire's highest medal for valour.

Toronto-born, he was the son of the Receiver General of Upper Canada. Dunn was educated at Upper Canada College following which he joined the British army serving with the 11th Prince Albert's Own Regiment of Light Dragoons. With the outbreak of war against the Russians, the regiment sailed with the British contingent for Crimea. By October 25, Sebastopol, which had fallen to the Russians, was under heavy British and French seige. That morning Russian cavalry and infantry, 25,000 strong, assaulted Turkish positions in front of the supply port of Balaclava. The British promptly counterattacked. During the mêlée that followed, while retiring from the scene, a horse belonging to one of Dunn's sergeants was so worn out that the cavalryman was unable to keep up and the Russians, quickly singling him out as a straggler, knocked him from his saddle. Dunn rode back to rescue the NCO and was duly attacked by three Dragoons. Prancing, side-wheeling, rearing his thoroughbred, he parried, thrusted, and slashed at his assailants, felling all of them in a matter of minutes. He then went to the aid of another of his men and skewered one more of the enemy to death. In the encounter, however, he lost his steed and had to make his way back to his own lines on foot. Nevertheless, he emerged totally unscathed from the incident.

Subsequently Dunn served in all other major Crimean battles including Inkerman and Sebastopol. Following the cessation of hostilities in 1857, Dunn resigned from the army and returned to Canada. But in June 1858, at the time of the Indian Mutiny, he rejoined to raise and recruit the 100th Foot (later the Leinster Regiment Royal Canadians), with which he sailed to Gibralter. In 1864 he transferred to the 33rd Duke of Wellington's Regiment, joining it in India where he took command in 1866 to become the youngest colonel in the British army. He later served in Abyssinia in the war against Emperor Theodore, where ironically he was killed in a hunting accident in 1868. Dunn had stooped over a ditch to gather some water when both barrels of his gun went off, discharging their load into his side. He was buried at Senafe in Ethiopia, where his remains still rest to this day.

 VC CM & 4 Clasps TM Col Born Sept 15 1833 DA Jan 25 1868
 RefScs: DHist CTV 8 11 CVC 9 RCMIYB-89 19–25 TCW Gen
 TVC Gen VCGC Gen VM 5

Dunn's sword is on display at the Canadian War Museum in Ottawa. The ribbon to his VC was red. At the time that signified an army award. Navy VCs wore a blue ribbon. The two colours were later amalgamated into the purple ribbon for all services. The metal comes from the bronze of the guns captured at the battle for Sebastapol in which Dunn played a notable role.

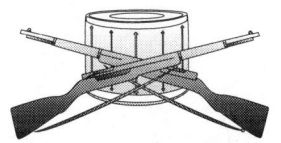

THE INDIAN MUTINY
1855-1859

Resentment over the British East India Company imposing its will on, and interfering with, the Hindu way of life had been boiling steadily for nearly half a century. By 1855 it spilled over into rebellion when a rumour spread that bullets for the new British Enfield rifle (which the men had to bite) were greased with the fat from cows — which the Indians regarded as sacred — and pigs — which they condemned as unclean. One of the earliest results was the fall of Delhi to the insurgent forces. Its recapture, which took place on September 21, became a prime British objective. With the fall of Lucknow in November the mutiny came to an end, but it was not until two years later in 1859 that the last embers of the blaze had been stamped out.

DELHI
September 14, 1857

READE Herbert Taylor

"Action in Saving Wounded during Siege of Delhi Won 'Fighting Surgeon' Canada's Second VC"

Up until a party of rebels began firing from the rooftops of houses onto a Delhi street, the job of assistant-surgeon Herbert Reade of the British Gloucestershire 61st Foot Regiment had been to tend the wounded. With his charges now in mortal danger or, at the very least, facing possible capture, Reade swapped his scalpel for a sword with which to defend them, an action that made him the second Canadian recipient of the Victoria Cross.

Born in Perth, Upper Canada, Reade received his medical training in Quebec City, Lower Canada, and Dublin in Ireland, and was appointed assistant-surgeon of his regiment which he joined on the Peshawar Frontier in India in 1850. On September 14, 1857, at the height of the seige at Delhi, he was attending to wounded soldiers when, at the end of a street, insurgent forces began advancing towards a bank. They established themselves in houses along the thoroughfare, and from the rooftops they opened fire. Drawing his sword, Reade gathered a party of 10 troopers around him and proceeded to dislodge the rebels, all the while under heavy fire. In the engagement two of his group were killed and six others were wounded. Two mornings later, in the final assault on the city, Reade was one of the first to storm the ramparts and, with the help of a sergeant from his regiment, spiked one of the enemy's guns. This attack on the magazine, which earned Reade the sobriquet "Fighting Surgeon," was in part responsible for the final fall of Delhi five days afterwards. Following the Indian Mutiny, Reade rose to the rank of surgeon-general. In 1887 he retired from the army and became Honourary Surgeon to Queen Victoria in 1895. Reade died at Sunnyland, Park Gardens, Bath in Somerset in 1897 at the age of 68.

VC CB A/S S/G Born Sept 2 1828 Died June 23 1897
RefScs: AEW Gen BIM Gen DHist TGM Gen CVC 20-1 VM 9

Herbert Reade (C 33487)

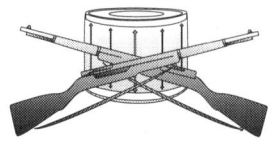

THE BOER WAR
1899-1902

More than 7,000 Canadian volunteers served in the Boer War in South Africa which lasted from 1899 to 1902. It marked the first time the Dominion had acted as a united country to aid England and provide an overseas contingent. Hostilities arose out of a conflict of interests between the Dutch Boers (farmers) and the commercially minded British settlers in the Cape Colony. Late in the 19th century, when gold and diamonds were discovered in the inland Transvaal, the Boers believed Britain was plannning an acquisition of the rich territory, while the British were convinced that the Boers were preparing to drive them out of South Africa and set up a separate republic. War broke out on October 12, 1899. Canadian troops soon demonstrated their superior quality as fighting men; at Sunnyside, in their baptism under fire, they forced the first Boer surrender and also fought in the battles of Liliefontein and Paardeberg. Their part in the conflict was also notable for the fact that that three VCs were awarded in a single action. That participation gave Canada a sense of military maturity and as a result the army militia were beefed up and modernized. New armouries, rifle ranges and a large camp at Petawawa were established. Most importantly, in an international sense Canada's presence in the British Empire was heightened.

WOLFE SPRUIT
July 5, 1900

RICHARDSON Arthur Herbert Lindsey

"Former Mountie Rescued Wounded Comrade under Fierce Fire"

On this date, at Wolfe Spruit some 100 miles south of Johannesburg, as a member of a party of 38 from the Lord Strathcona's Horse, Arthur Richardson, in the face of ferocious enemy crossfire, rescued a wounded comrade whose horse had fallen on him. Richardson became the first in the Boer War to win the Victoria Cross.

Richardson, who was born in Liverpool, England, migrated to Canada when he was 25 years old. He worked first as a rancher, then joined the North-West Mounted Police. At the outbreak of the war he enlisted in the Lord Strathcona Horse with which he sailed to South Africa. At Wolfe Spruit his party became engaged with an enemy force that more than outnumbered them two-to-one and after a brief skirmish were forced to retire. One of the troops, while trying to escape, was shot in the arm and leg. Then his horse, which was also wounded, stumbled and fell on top of him. Seeing the cavalryman's plight Richardson, who was weak from a bout of fever, wheeled about and charged to within 300 yards of the Boer contingent and worked his comrade out from under his disabled mount. Although his own horse had been injured by enemy bullets, Richardson managed to hold his comrade over his saddle and ride back to the camp.

Following the war, Richardson retired from the army and returned to Liverpool, where he died in 1932.

VC Sgt Born 1873 Died Dec 16 1932
RefScs: CSKV 467 CVC 24–5 VM 19

Liliefontein
November 17, 1900

In this rearguard action on the Komati River, during which the Royal Canadian Dragoons were compelled to save two 12-pounder guns of D Battery against a charge by 200 Boers, three of their members were awarded the Victoria Cross. One of the "Liliefontein" guns is displayed at the Canadian War Museum in Ottawa.

COCKBURN Hampden Zane Churchill

"Stood His Ground against Savage Boer Attack"

In the Boer assault on the Royal Canadian Dragoons at Liliefontein to capture their guns, though the enemy came within 70 yards' range, Hampden Cockburn and his party deliberately sacrificed themselves by standing their ground to allow their Canadian comrades to get their artillery away. During the encounter Cockburn was wounded and most of his men were killed, wounded or taken prisoner. But the action helped save the day, and for his coolness and determination under fire Cockburn was awarded the VC.

Born in Toronto, he was educated at Upper Canada College, Rugby College in England, as well as London University and the University of Toronto. At war's outbreak he had a law practice in Toronto which he promptly gave up to enlist in the Canadian Mounted Rifles battalion — later redesignated the RCDs. As a recognition of his services in South Africa, following the war he was appointed a major in the Governor-General's Bodyguard. Cockburn later moved to Western Canada where he died in July, 1913.

VC   Capt   Maj (GGB)   Born Nov 19 1867   Died July 13 1913
RefScs CVC 21-2   DHist   VM 22

HOLLAND Edward James Gibson

"Stole Machine Gun from under the Enemy's Nose"

During the Boer assault at the Komati River, Eddie Holland, who was in charge of the Colt machine gun on the Royal Canadian Dragoons' left flank, managed to hold his attackers at bay until he ran out of ammunition. Then, as the enemy cavalry closed in, he calmly removed the gun barrel — still hot — from its fittings, mounted his horse and, with the weapon firmly tucked under his arm, galloped off just as the Boers reached the gun position. At first they thought they'd captured it, then, when they saw the barrel was missing, they became so infuriated they set fire to the carriage. For his action, the Ottawa native was awarded the VC.

Educated at Model School and Ottawa Collegiate Institute, at age 17 he joined the militia, serving with the 43rd Regiment and the 5th Princess Louise Dragoon Guards from 1895 to 1897. When the Boer War began he transferred to the RCDs (née Canadian Mounted Rifles battalion). Following the war he served in the PLDG again, as well as the Scottish Light Dragoons. In 1914 he was made CO of the Borden Motor Machine-gun Battery which he took to France when WW1 broke out. The following year he returned to Canada and was transferred to the Corps Reserve. He died in 1948 at age 70 in Cobalt, Ont.

VC   Sgt   Maj(WW1)   Born Feb 2 1878   Died June 1948
RefScs: CVC 28   DHist   VM 25

TURNER Richard Ernest William

"Badly Wounded — Rallied Men to Save the Guns"

When the Boers charged at Liliefontein, Dick Turner ordered his troops to dismount and hold the line with the exhortation "Never let it be said that Canadians had let their guns be taken." Though seriously

Richard Turner (PA 6315)

wounded in the neck, and also suffering from a badly shattered arm, Turner rallied his men so effectively the Royal Canadian Dragoon guns were saved, a feat for which he received the VC.

Turner, who was born and raised in Quebec City, also won the DSO during the South African conflict. His later military career was equally distinguished. From 1905 to 1907 he was commanding officer of the 10th Queen's Own Canadian Hussars. From 1907 to 1912 he was commander of the Eastern Townships Cavalry Brigade. During WW1 he commanded the 3rd Brigade, then took command of the Second Canadian Division in 1915 and briefly commanded the Canadian Corps in 1916. He was then made general officer of Canadian troops in the British Isles. He was knighted in 1917. Following the war Turner continued to serve his country in various capacities and was one of the founders of the Royal Canadian Legion of the British Empire Service League. He died in the city of his birth in 1961 at age 89.

VC DSO LdeH CdeGwP OWEoR   Lt/Gen   Born July 25 1871   Died June 19 1961

RefScs: CE 2203   CVC 30–1   DHist   OEDSCC 96–7   VM 23

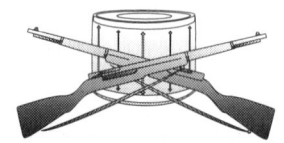

WORLD WAR 1
August 1, 1914-November 11, 1918

When WW1 broke out in August 1914, Britain, France and Russia were allied against Germany and Austria. The Canadian army consisted of only 3,110 men under arms with a militia of approximately 47,000. But thousands more flocked to the colours, and after mobilization and basic drill-training at Camp Valcartier, the first contingent of the Canadian Expeditionary Force, 31,000 strong, left Quebec City at the end of September in the greatest fleet of transports to cross the Atlantic up to that time. On reaching England, the Canadians endured a long miserable winter of training in the mud and drizzle of Salisbury Plain where the men had to fight an epidemic of flu and spinal meningitis. The first Canadian troops landed in France in December and had their baptism of fire near St. Eloi and the Polygon Wood. During the next four years they served in nearly every major battle, and in 1918 formed the spearhead of the thrust that finally broke the deadlock on the Western Front that resulted in the German capitulation. By the time the conflict ended the Canadian army had grown to a force of 418,052 with more than 60,000 killed in action and 150,000 wounded. The record achieved by the Canadian Corps earned the country the right to sign the peace treaties separately and to sit at the League of Nations. With that status the Dominion's nationhood had been established.

(Overleaf) Canadians in the front lines near Givenchy. (PA 2468)

YPRES — *GALLANTRY AGAINST POISON GAS*
April 22 - 26, 1915

By April, 1915, Canadian troops had occupied the centre section of the Ypres salient in Belgium, the only bulge in the Allied line stretching from Switzerland to the English Channel. On April 22, in an effort to break the stalemate and capture the Channel ports, the Germans introduced the vilest, most wicked weapon unleashed on a battlefield: poison gas. After an intense artillery barrage, they released 160 tons of chlorine vapour into a light east wind. As the yellow-green clouds drifted into the trenches, the French defences on the left flank crumpled and their troops fled leaving a four-mile-wide gap in the Allied line that placed the Canadians, and the British to their right, in jeopardy. As the Germans advanced the Canadians, called "Clodhoppers" by the enemy, stood their ground and counterattacked to try and close the gap. Then, on April 24, the Germans launched another gas attack, this time against the Canadians. But despite desperate fighting and the choking effects of the poison gas, the Dominion troops held on until reinforcements arrived. In its first appearance on the Western Front, the Canadian Contingent had established itself as a formidable fighting force that earned it the name "Salvation" army. But the cost was high. One in every three troops was killed, a total of 6,035 lives lost.

ST. JULIEN
April 23

FISHER Frederick

"Died Saving Gun Batteries from Capture"

When Frederick Fisher reached the front line in the St. Julien sector on this second day of the Second Battle of Ypres, he found that several Canadian gun batteries were in imminent danger of being captured. Setting up up his own machine gun in front of them, he warded off the enemy until the Canadians could escape. But during the action he lost his entire troop of four men and had to return to St. Julien to recruit four others. However, while moving back up to the front line, he lost these men as well. He set up his machine gun again and carried on alone fending off the German attack until he was himself killed. For his bravery and determination in the face of enemy fire Fisher was awarded a posthumous Victoria Cross.

A native of St. Catharines, Ont., Fisher was educated in Montreal where he attended McGill University. An ardent sportsman, he excelled at tennis, football, swimming and shooting, and was an active member of the Montreal Athletic Association. When WW1 broke out he enlisted at age 18 in the 5th Royal Highlanders of Canada. Fisher has no known grave, but his name appears on the Menin Gate Memorial at Ypres.

VC L/C Born Aug 3 1896 KIA Apr 23 1915
RefScs: CVC 36-7 VM 30-1

ROTHESAY Frank

"Took Complete Charge"

When his platoon commander was struck down, Frank Rothesay of the 4th Battalion took charge and led his men to the foremost German positions which came under fierce enemy artillery and machine-gun fire. Subsequently, when all the company officers were either killed or wounded, he took complete charge and remained at his post.

MM Sgt
RefScs: DHist 713 065 (1)

YPRES
April 24

HALL Frederick William

"Died Trying to Save Life of Another"

At nine o'clock in the morning, members of the 8th Battalion of the Canadian Expeditionary Force, in a trench close to Ypres, could hear groans from a soldier lying wounded and helpless in No-Man's Land. Frederick Hall, a sergeant-major with the "Little Red Devils," immediately organized a rescue, and with two others climbed over the top to be greeted by heavy and accurate German gun fire. His two comrades were wounded and all three scrambled back into the trench. Hall, however, decided to attempt a second rescue but this time he insisted on making it alone. Despite bullets whizzing and ricocheting around him, he reached the wounded man who was unable to move. Hall squeezed himself under him and lifted the inert body onto his back. He was in the act of crawling back to the trench when, as he raised his head to check his direction, a bullet struck him in the head. For this individual act of heroism, Hall was posthumously awarded the Victoria Cross.

Born in Belfast, Ireland, Hall moved to Canada several years before WW1 where he worked in Winnipeg. In 1914 he enlisted with the 106th Battalion, later transferring to the 8th with which he went overseas as part of the First Canadian Contingent. Hall has no known grave, but his name is etched in the Menin Gate Memorial at Ypres.

VC S/M   Born April 21 1885   KIA April 24 1915
RefScs: CVC 38–9   VM 34–5

BELLEW Edward Donald

"First Canadian Officially Awarded VC in WW1"

As battalion machine-gun officer of the 7th Canadian Infantry Battalion, Edward Bellew single-handedly held his position until he was forced to surrender. That morning when the Germans counterattacked, the battalion's right flank was put out of action. With one other machine gun operating, Bellew warded off the assault until reinforcements arrived. But these too were destroyed by the enemy. Then the other Canadian gunner was killed. Bellew kept firing until his gun failed. Then, as the Germans rushed his position, he seized a rifle, smashed the machine gun and, fighting to the last, was taken prisoner. For his action Bellew won the Victoria Cross, the first officer of the Canadian Expeditionary Force to be officially gazetted for the decoration (see PA below).

Born in Bombay, India, he was educated in England and attended the Royal Military College at Sandhurst. Before moving to Canada he served with the Royal Irish Regiment. Prior to enlisting in the Canadian army in August 1914, Bellew worked for the Public Works Department of the Canadian government in B.C. When he was repatriated he returned to B.C. where he became engaged in surveying and construction work. He eventually retired to Monte Creek and died at Kamloops in 1961.

VC Capt   Born Oct 28 1882   Died Feb 1 1961
RefScs: CVC 170–1   VM 34–5

Bellew did not know that he had won the VC until he saw an announcement in a Vancouver paper after his release from the prisoner-of-war camp. The distinction of being the first Canadian to win the VC in WW1 has generally been credited to Michael O'Leary. Born in Ireland he served in the Royal North-West Mounted Police for just over a year. He resigned in 1914 to rejoin his regiment, the 1st Battalion Irish Guards, with which he won the decoration. Without belittling his valour, his Canadian background — a year as a Mountie — hardly qualifies him as a "Canadian" war hero.

April 25

SCRIMGER Francis Alexander Carron

"Shielded Wounded Officer with His Body"

During the afternoon a farmhouse which served as a first-aid dressing station for the wounded of the Royal Montreal Regiment suddenly became the target of a German artillery barrage and was set on fire by an incendiary shell. Located just outside battered Ypres, the only road leading away from the farmhouse was impassable, so the wounded — with the help of the Canadian Army Medical Corps staff — had to swim across a moat that surrounded the building. But one man was in such bad shape that swimming was out of the question. As splinters from the shells fell all around, Francis Scrimger, the medical officer in charge, stood over the patient shielding him with his own body. He then dragged him to the moat out of danger from the fire and curled himself over and around the man's head and shoulders to protect him from flying shrapnel until help arrived later in the day. For this act of valour Scrimger was awarded the Victoria Cross.

Born in Montreal, Scrimger received his M.D. from McGill University in 1905 and then took post-graduate studies in Europe. When WWI broke out he became the original MO of the 14th Battalion of the Royal Montreal Regiment with which he was serving when he won the VC. He eventually became chief surgeon of No 3 Canadian General Hospital at Boulogne in France. Following the war, he returned to Montreal as assistant-surgeon at the Royal Victoria Hospital and in 1936 he was made surgeon-in-chief. He died in Montreal in 1937.

VC Lt/Col Born Feb 7 1880 Died Feb 13 1937
RefScs: CVC 34–5 VM 36–7

Francis Scrimger (PA 6771)

Canadians in the front lines near Givenchy. (PA 2468)

Battle of Attrition
May 1915 - July 1916

*B*y the summer of 1915 the war on the Western Front had stalemated into one of attrition. After the Second Battle of Ypres there followed sporadic frontal attacks on both sides without any result other than the slaughter of tens of thousands of men. Conditions were appalling. The troops lived in the squalor and dankness of the trenches, sometimes knee-deep in water and mud. In battle, attacking soldiers charged across shell-torn ground and through tangled barbed-wire to be unmercifully cut down by machine-gun fire. Those who reached the enemy redoubt fought hand-to-hand, stabbing with their bayonets. It was a gruesome business made all the more odious by the Allied commanders' conviction that success lay in persistence, larger armies, and more guns and ammunition. While plans were being laid for major offensives, the intermittent forays continued. One such isolated struggle, in which the Canadian First Brigade took part, was typical. In June, in an attack on the German trenches near the French town of Givenchy, the Canadians suffered 400 casualties and were forced to give up the ground they had initially gained.

Near Givenchy
May 20/21

Cameron Herbert Thomas

"Severely Wounded Rescuing Injured while under Fire"

On this night, Herbert Cameron, a sergeant with the medical corps, was the first to volunteer to rescue the wounded in an orchard freshly captured by the Canadian infantry and still under heavy German shelling. Despite the difficulties, he managed to marshall a party of eight to carry out the task under the most arduous and dangerous conditions. In the process he was himself severely injured. After recovering from his wounds he returned to action in 1918, eventually earning an officer's commission.

DCM Sgt
RefScs: DHist TP

Frederick Campbell (C 11195)

GIVENCHY
June 15

CAMPBELL Frederick William

"Boer War Veteran Warded Off German Counterattack"

During the Battle of Givenchy, while advancing on a German trench captured by the Canadians, Frederick Campbell of the 1st Battalion, Canadian Expeditionary Force, had all his machine-gun crews wiped out except for himself and a lone private. When they reached the position, because the tripod from the Colt weapon was missing, Campbell mounted it on the private's back and opened fire on the advancing German infantry. Campbell got off 1,000 rounds, sufficient to temporarily disperse the enemy counterattack before he became so badly wounded that he and his comrade were forced to retire. For the action he received a Victoria Cross. He died from his wounds four days later.

A native of Mount Forest, Ont., after receiving his education Campbell took up farming and subsequently became a Public School Trustee and Director of the Mount Forest Agricultural Society. During the Boer War he served with the 30th Rifles receiving the Queen's South African Medal with four Bars. He was buried in Boulogne Eastern Cemetery in France.

VC SAM & 4 Bars   Lt   Born June 15 1867   DoW June 19 1915
RefScs:CVC 40-1   VM 38-9

April 5-7

BLINKO Alfred Ralph

"Helped Stem German Advance"

When the Germans attacked along the position held by the 29th Battalion, Alfred Blinko was given charge of the Lewis machine-gun section. In the face of an intense enemy artillery barrage, he skillfully moved the unit forward to the front line where for two days he held off the enemy attacks. His leadership was instrumental in stemming the German advance. Several months later Blinko was wounded in the same area and was taken out of action to recover from his wounds before returning to the front.

MM   Cpl(Act)
RefScs: DHist JP

HILL 60
April 26

NELSON Claude

"Mortar Bombadier Kept Up Relentless Fire while under Attack"

During a German bombardment, Claude Nelson of the 34th Battalion calmly fired his mortar intermittently on enemy positions with telling effect. That evening, though the shelling intensified, Nelson continued to train his fire on the Germans, harassing them until his ammunition was exhausted.

   MM Pte
   DHist JP

June 15/16

HOBSON George

"Extricated Wounded from Certain Death"

After two men in his battalion had been wounded in their efforts to dig a trench, an officer and six men were wounded by a high-explosive shell. Hobson picked up the one remaining gun and succeeded in extricating the entire party from the field; they would otherwise have perished. On the following day Hobson participated in an attack on the German trenches and was one of the first in the advance. In the subsequent retreat he rendered invaluable assistance in getting his men back safely to their own lines.

   DCM Cpl
   RefScs: DHist JP

GIVENCHY AND HILL 63
November 7 and December 15

JOHNSON Ernest Charles

"Won DSO for Disregard of Danger"

On November 7 and December 15 at Givenchy and Hill 63 respectively, Charles Johnson of the Fort Garry Horse led attacks on German positions with such determination and disregard for his own safety that, although he was only a temporary captain, he was awarded the DSO. The following year he was wounded only a few days before the attack on Vimy Ridge. Although he was invalided back to England, he returned to the Western Front the following July.

    DSO   Capt (Temp)
    RefScs: DHist JP

October 13

McGIBBON Peter

"Worked Tirelessly Tending the Wounded"

Peter McGibbon serving with the British Imperial Army was in charge of a first aid station. On this date he stayed at his post working tirelessly for 14 hours non-stop. He also led a stretcher-bearing party twice into the lines at enormous risk. Due to his efforts a great many lives were saved.

    MC   Lt
    RefScs: DHist JP

Smashing barbed wire with trench mortar shells. (PA 1380)

1916

January 14

MATHESON Guy Maclean

"Displayed Great Coolness"

When his company sergeant-major was wounded, Guy Matheson, a sergeant with the 25th Battalion, calmly took his place. Although injured himself he carried the CSM and another wounded soldier to safety. He then took charge of the wiring parties, a task he completed with great coolness under extremely dangerous conditions. For these actions he earned the Military Medal. Matheson, who was later promoted to lieutenant and then major, subsequently won both the MC and the DSO in later actions.

DSO MC MM   Sgt (Maj)
RefScs: DHist TP

April 5/6

CLEMENT James Fergus

"Established Communications Post, Held Off Enemy Attack"

When communications between the right and left flanks of the 31st Battalion broke down due to concentrated enemy shelling, acting Sergeant James Clement, on his own initiative, took a party forward and established a post. During the night the Germans incessantly tried to rush the position but Clements and his men hung on. In the morning when they retired to their lines, Clements found a sergeant lying wounded in the line of fire. With the help of one other soldier they carried the injured man to safety.

MM   Sgt(Act)
RefScs: DHist JP

April 26

MacDONALD Cyril Hayden

"Repaired Cable Lines during Shelling"

During a German shelling on the 1st Brigade front, when all lines to the ammunition dump had been smashed by cannon fire, Cyril MacDonald, with the help of another comrade, succeeded in repairing them at the height of the enemy barrage. MacDonald had previously distinguished himself during the Second Battle of Ypres. For this latest action and his previous conduct under fire he received the MM.

MM Cpl
RefScs: DHist JP

June 6

CURTIS Waller Basil

"Dressed Wounded during Shelling"

Intense shelling by the Germans failed to deter Waller Curtis from going about his duties dressing the wounded. In fact he ignored it even when, while bandaging one man, several others around him were killed.

MM   Pte
RefScs: DHist JP

DAS BLUTBAD — SLAUGHTER ON THE SOMME*
July 1 - December 30, 1916

In late August of 1916, the Canadian Corps which by then consisted of three divisions (with another on its way from Canada) under Lieutenant-General Sir Julian Byng, moved from the muddy fields of Flanders to the Somme, a part of the French countryside aptly called Santerre, a contraction of sang terre — land of blood. There it joined in the offensive that had begun on July 1. During the months that followed the "Byng Boys" so distinguished themselves in the Somme battles, among them Courcelette and the Desire, Regina and Stuff trenches, that British Prime Minister Lloyd George was moved to write that "The Canadians played a part of such distinction that thenceforward they were marked out as storm troops. . . . Whenever the Germans found the Canadian Corps coming into the line they prepared for the worst." At the end of the year the rains had turned the battlefield into a quagmire and the offensive bogged down to a halt. By that time between the Allies and the Germans 836,000 men had been killed, 24,029 of them Canadians. And the Allied line had advanced only a pitiable six miles.

*German for "The Blood Bath."

POZIÈRES RIDGE
September 9

CLARKE Leo

"Fought Off Enemy Platoon of 20 Riflemen"

Leo Clarke was in the process of securing a newly captured German trench on the ridge when the position was suddenly engulfed by furious machine-gun fire. This was swiftly followed with an attack by more than 20 Prussian infantrymen. Standing his ground, Clarke emptied his revolver at the onrushing enemy. Then, with a German rifle left in the trench, he again opened fire. One of the German soldiers lunged at Clarke wounding him in the knee with his bayonet, but Clarke shot him dead. Bleeding profusely, Clarke nevertheless continued to fight, killing four more Germans and capturing another. For his feat he received the award of the Victoria Cross.

Born in Waterdown, Ont., Clarke spent his early years in England, his parents' homeland, but later returned to Canada to live in Winnipeg. At the outbreak of WW1 he was working as a surveyor in the Canadian north. Clarke returned to Winnipeg to enlist in the 27th Battalion, arriving in England with the CEF in June 1915 where he transferred to the 2nd Battalion to be with his brother. The pair were in action only a few yards from each other during the combat that won him the VC. (See PA below.) Clarke was killed a few weeks later and was buried in Étretat Churchyard, 16 miles north of Le Havre in France.

VC   Cpl(Act)   Born Dec 1 1892   KIA Oct 19 1916
RefScs: CVC 44-5   VM 40-1

This marked the first time the VC had been presented by a Governor-General of Canada. The Duke of Devonshire handed the decoration to a family representative at a ceremony attended by 30,000 people.

Over the Top! (PA 648)

COURCELETTE
September 15/16

BRADLEY Francis James

"Held His Ground despite Appalling Conditions"

Holding down a support trench close to the final objective near Courcelette, the position of Francis Bradley's platoon had become virtually untenable. But although harassed by wicked ground fire, mortars and shelling, through his own example Bradley encouraged his men to hold their ground. His coolness under fire was largely responsible for the yardage gained and held. For this action, Bradley was awarded the Military Medal.

DCM MM Sgt
RefScs: DHist JP

September 16

KERR John Chapman

"Led Valiant Hand-Grenade Charge despite Wounds"

At Courcelette, one of the two main German defence systems in the Somme, the British used tanks for for the first time, a factor that helped decide the outcome in favour of the Canadians. Spectacular though this was, the most conspicuous action was by Canadian infantryman "Chip" Kerr who, that morning, had been selected as chief bayonet-man to lead a hand-grenade attack on one of the enemy trenches. When his unit had advanced to within 30 yards, a German sentry hurled a grenade at Kerr who threw up his right arm to shield himself from the blast. It saved his sight but the explosion blew off part of his right forefinger and wounded him in the right side. Nevertheless, he remained at the scene as the fracas settled into a grenade-throwing duel between trenches. But when this promised to become nothing more than a stationary exchange, and with the supply of grenades running low, Kerr decided to take the initiative. Climbing out of the trench he moved along a manmade embankment until he drew within close range and in full view of the Germans. Despite loss of blood he was still full of fight and began tossing grenade after grenade into the midst of the crowded defenders. He then opened fire with his rifle. All the while he directed the aim of his grenade throwers, forcing the enemy to seek shelter in a nearby trench bay. He then jumped in after them followed by his Canadian "bombers" and bayonet-men. When he reached the dugout the Germans surrendered and Kerr marched 62 prisoners back to his own lines. For his deed Kerr received the Victoria Cross.

Born in Fox River, N.S., after leaving school Kerr and his brother homesteaded at Spirit River, Alta. When WW1 broke out they packed up and set out for Edmonton to enlist, having left note that read: "War is Hell, but so is homesteading." Kerr was serving with the 49th Canadian Infantry Battalion when he won the VC. He died in 1963 at Port Moody, B.C., where he lived after the war, at age 76.

VC   Pte   Born Jan 11 1887   Died Feb 19 1963
RefScs: CVC 46-7   VM 42-3

WYTSCHAETE
September 16/17

CAMERON James Miller

"Led Daring Raid against Enemy Dugout"

During the night James Cameron led two raiding parties against enemy positions and personally chased several Germans from their dugouts, taking two of them prisoner. Cameron was subsequently wounded but, under heavy fire, helped others injured to get back safely to their own lines.

MM   Sgt
RefScs: DHist JP

October 2

HOLMES Waller John

"Bayonet Charge Inflicted Heavy Enemy Casualties"

Waller Holmes of the 5th Canadian Mounted Rifles was on a reconnaissance when he located an enemy bombing post. He immediately collected a party of his own men and, working around the left side of a trench, led them in a bayonet charge inflicting heavy casualties. He then spotted another enemy position and led a second attack. For his actions he was awarded the MM. Commissioned in the field, he later received the MC.

MC   MM   CSM
RefScs: DHist JP MCb 150

COURCELETTE

October 3

BURRAGE John Alfred Harcourt

"Set Up Cable Line under Fire"

With all communications cable lines practically out of commission, John Burrage was given the job of running a new one to the front trench. No easy task — he came under incessant enemy fire. But despite the merciless German rifle and machine-gun fire, he not only established it quickly and efficiently but kept it repaired and maintained it throughout the day.

    MM Sgt
    RefScs: DHist JP

October 3/4

EMREY Desmond Joseph

"Established Jumping-Off Trenches under Gruelling Conditions"

In the absence of any available officers, Sapper Sergeant Desmond Emrey successfully laid out a new jumping-off trench in advance of the 6th Field Company's front line. Then, risking German machine-gun and rifle fire, he rendered valuable assistance in constructing several other jumping-off trenches. For these actions he was awarded the MM. Later, as a commissioned officer, he won the MC.

    MC MM Sgt(Lt)
    RefScs: DHist JP MCb 38

October 8

BURNS George Herbert

"German Red Cross Flag-Bearer Aided Canadian Stretcher-Bearer"

When his company was practically wiped out, with wounded lying everywhere, George Burns, of the 43rd Battalion, moved into the open to attend them. When rescue parties were organized to bring back the casualties Burns stayed with those remaining, fully exposed to enemy fire. Seeing his plight the Germans sent out one of their men bearing a Red Cross flag to stand by him while Burns finished dressing and treating the rest of the wounded left on the battlefield.

MM   Cpl
RefScs: DHist JP

One of the roads to Bapaume, Battle of the Somme. (PA 884)

REGINA TRENCH
October 8

RICHARDSON James Cleland

"Will I Gie Them Wund?"

During the attack on the Regina Trench, the 16th Canadian Infantry Battalion became bogged down by severe German gun fire and a strong barbed-wire entanglement. In trying to break through casualties were heavy, among them the commanding officer. Piper Jimmy Richardson, who had asked and obtained permission to join in the fighting, now suggested to the company sergeant-major that a marching tune from his bagpipes might be the moving force needed to turn the battle back in the Canadians' favour. The CSM told him to go ahead. Richardson then climbed "over the top" and paraded up and down in front of the barbed-wire piping a Highland martial air. It did the trick. Inspired by his dauntless example, Richardson's comrades charged forward with renewed venom and vigour that soon brought about the capture of their objective. Later, after participating in the assault, Richardson was detailed along with others to take a wounded Canadian infantryman as well as some enemy prisoners back to his own lines. Halfway there he realized he'd left his bagpipes behind. Against strong advice not to do so, Richardson insisted on returning to recover them. He was never seen or heard of again, but for his gallantry and inspired example he was awarded a posthumous Victoria Cross.

Richardson was born in Bellshill, Scotland, and moved to Canada before WW1 where he became an electrician before enlisting in the Canadian army.

VC   Pte   Born Nov 25 1895   KIA Oct 8 1916
RefScs: CVC 120–1   VM 44–5

AVERLOY
November 15

BRISTOW Albert Edward

"Cool-Headedness Prevented Stampede"

On this date during the afternoon while reloading was taking place, the railhead of the town came under heavy German shelling. But for the cool-headedness of Albert Bristow of the 4th Division, a stampede of horses and consequent congestion might have taken place with resultant casualties. Bristow not only looked after his own section but prevented general chaos by calmly taking charge.

MM Sgt
RefScs: DHist JP

November 8

MOSES Omand Forest

"Helped Take Enemy Gun Post"

Wounded two days earlier, Omand Moses of the 38th Battalion took part in a dashing attack on a German gun position which earned him the MM. This enemy strongpoint contained three machine guns, but the assault was so furious that all the guns were captured and numerous Germans taken prisoner. Later Moses was raised to officer rank and received the MC. During his war service he was wounded twice.

MC MM Cpl(Lt)
RefScs: DHist JP MCb 246

MIRALDMOUND
November 20

COWLING Thomas

"Rescued CO after Three Attempts"

When attempts by three different stretcher-bearer teams failed to rescue the battalion commanding officer, several of them having been hit by German sniper fire, Thomas Cowling and a comrade were given the assignment. It took them three tries. On the first two they were driven back by with withering enemy fire, but on the last go they succeeded. Cowling received the MM for the feat and later in the war, as an officer, was awarded the MC.

MC MM L/Cpl(Lt)
RefScs: DHist JP MCb 70

November 20/21

CASTLE Alfred John

"Commanded Bombing Raid on German Trenches"

When two bayonet-men from his bombing squad became wounded by hand grenades thrown from a German trench they were raiding, Alfred Castle quickly reorganized his party and pursued the attack. Having attained their objective, Castle then supervised the withdrawal, made difficult due to heavy casualties. That successfully accomplished, he then returned to the trench to assist a second Canadian combing squad, along with their wounded, safely back to their own lines.

MM   Sgt
RefScs: DHist JP

PREPARATION
January - April 1917

By the beginning of 1917 the Canadian Corps, now four divisions strong, had moved north from the Somme to the Artois Plain entrenching itself on a line running from Ecurie to Souchez. A brief respite followed while plans were laid for another Allied offensive. This one called for an attack by the French between Reims and Soissons combined with British diversionary attacks around Arras. The Canadian share of the British assault was to be the seizure of the formidable German fortification of Vimy Ridge in what would become the most perfectly organized and successful battle of WW1. Meanwhile, the monotonous stand-off continued, sporadically broken by the Canadians who had inaugurated reconnaissance raids behind enemy lines. These forays served the purpose of capturing prisoners, gathering information and keeping the Germans on edge. They also boosted the fighting morale of the Dominion troops who showed themselves particularly adept at this style of warfare — a forerunner of the commando raids of WW2.

NORTH OF ARRAS
December 20, 1916

ADAMS Read Thomas Payne

"Decorated for Leadership"

Read Adams received the Military Medal for his role as a leader of a bomber section in an attack against a German support trench. On reaching his objective he secured a footing in the trench taking several enemy soldiers prisoner. His "courage and bravery" were cited as examples of his "gallantry and devotion" to duty.

    MM Cpl
    RefScs: DHist JP

January 7, 1917

DeLAURIER Melbourne Ross

"Repelled Three Enemy Attacks"

German shelling had kept two Lewis guns in Melbourne DeLaurier's unit busy when the spare ammunition drums were demolished. While the unit awaited for replacement magazines to arrive, the men saw the Germans rise from their trenches and advance on their own position. But under DeLaurier's exhortations and inspired leadership the force repelled three different enemy attacks. Finally, by the time fresh ammunition arrived, a party of six Germans had crept forward, but this time it was not for an assault. They went over the top to carry back their wounded.

    MM Sgt
    RefScs: DHist JP

GUYENCOURT
March 27

HARVEY Frederick Maurice Watson

"Captured Enemy Machine Gun in Head-On Attack"

In an attack on this French village, Frederick Harvey, a cavalry officer with the Lord Strathcona's Horse, single-handedly captured a German gun position to seize the enemy trench for his regiment. When the Strathconas started their attack as dusk fell, a party of Germans ran forward to a trench at the outskirts of the town, protected by barbed-wire. Opening fire with rifles and a machine gun, they inflicted heavy casualties on the Canadian horseman. In the face of this intense fire, Harvey, who was in command of the leading troop, hastily dismounted and sprinted straight at the machine-gun position firing his revolver as he ran. When he reached the wire entanglement, he hurdled it, shot the German gunner dead, and grabbed the gun. As a result the Strathconas were able to quickly occupy the trench and subsequently capture the town. For this audacious feat Harvey, who had already been awarded the Military Cross, received the Victoria Cross.

Born in Athboy, Ireland, during WW1 he attained the rank of brigadier with the Canadian army and became District Officer Commanding for Alberta. Following the war he made his home in Calgary.

VC MC Brig Born Sept 1888
RefScs: CVC 48-9 VM 46-7

ZOUAVE VALLEY
March 27-30

HORIE Harold Wilson

"Courier Carried On under Fire"

As a despatcher, Harold Horie seemed oblivious to danger. During these three days he ran messages through the Zouave Valley from one position to another all the while dodging bullets and shrapnel which he treated with imperious contempt. Officially this work, which earned him the MM, was described as "excellent."

MM   Pte
RefScs: DHist   JP

VIMY RIDGE AREA
April 4

CARTENACH James Sterling

"Annihilated German Sentries on Defence Probe"

With the attack on Vimy Ridge scheduled for four days' hence, Canadians were busy probing the German defences. On one such foray James Cartenach accompanied an officer to the enemy trenches. There he succeeded in killing two enemy sentries. This action enabled his officer to acquire the information he had be assigned to gather without interference.

MM   Sgt
RefScs: DHist JP

VALOUR at VIMY RIDGE
Easter Monday - April 9, 1917

The key to a successful attack and capture of the elevation that dominated the Artois Plain between Thelus and Avion, and the outskirts of Lens, lay in meticulous planning and careful preparation. Its execution called for perfect timing and the highest degree of coordination between infantry, cavalry and artillery. It also required the most intense advance bombardment possible. The Germans were well and firmly dug in on the ridge; the slopes defended by an interlacing and elaborate honeycomb of trenches, dugouts and tunnels heavily protected by barbed-wire, machine guns and mortars. All previous attempts to capture the rampart had failed.

With the help of aerial reconnaissance pictures, which triggered the heaviest air fighting of the war,* the planned assault was laid out on

Vimy Ridge Memorial (C 7492)

a scale model. Troops were drilled over terrain which, with the use of coloured flags and tape, simulated the ground over which they would advance. At the same time they were schooled in the exact positions of enemy guns, trenches, dugouts, mines, barbed-wire defences, machine guns and mortars. Meanwhile, the Canadians brought up 983 heavy guns and howitzers into position.

The preliminary bombardment began on March 20. By April 2 this had so intensified that the Germans called the period "the week of suffering." In fact, during that time the majority of their work-horses had been killed and most of their artillery put out of action. By the evening of April 8, all Canadian units were in place and next morning at five-thirty, in driving snow and sleet and under a barrage of artillery fire, the four divisions of the Corps, acting in concert for the first time, began their assault on Vimy Ridge. An hour later they had taken the first line of trenches and by mid-afternoon were, with the exception of two positions captured three days later, in command of the crest. More than 4,000 prisoners were taken, some of them found chained to their machine guns.

The victory, which historian George Nasmith called "perhaps the most brilliant success of the war on the British Front," marked a national coming-of-age for the Dominion. It also revealed that the Germans held the Canadian soldier in the highest repute. Prior to the battle, a captured German headquarters document read: "The Canadians are known to be good troops and are, therefore, well suited for assault. **There are no deserters to be found amongst the Canadian.**"**

*See Bishop's *Courage in the Air*, page 14
**Emphasis is the author's.

MONTGOMERIE James Baird Thorneycliffe

"Led Company after All of His Officers Became Casualties"

Baird Montgomerie of the 42nd Battalion had already proved his mettle as a fighting man at the Second Battle of Ypres and the Somme. So it was natural that he was picked to lead the first wave of his company in the attack on "The Ridge." When that wave was held up by machine-gun fire, he quickly disposed of the enemy nest and led his men forward. Subsequently all the officers of his company became casualties. Montgomerie took charge and reorganized it. It was due to his leadership that all the unit's objectives were reached on schedule. Montgomerie received the MM for his day's work. Later in 1918, by which time he had been commissioned in the field, he added the MC to his laurels.

MC MM   L/Cpl(Lt)
RefScs: DHist JP MCb 234

MORLEY Leonard

"Took Charge of the Moppers-Up"

Leonard Morley of the 10th Battalion was in the vanguard of the fighting when he suddenly discovered the sergeant in charge of mopping-up the operation had been severely wounded. Switching helmets — figuratively — Morley took command of the "moppers-up" and finished the job. By this time all the officers in his company had either been killed or wounded, so he assisted the senior NCO in consolidating the ground gained. Morley won the MM at Vimy Ridge but that was only the start of an illustrious combat career. Later, as an officer, he was decorated with the MC and Bar.

MC & Bar MM Cpl(Act) Lt
RefScs: DHist JP

STANLEY Frank Charles

"Harassed Retreating Germans"

Though injured four days previously, Frank Stanley of the 29th Battalion was in the thick of the fighting at the head of his platoon from the start. Stanley was particularly effective in using his men to harass the Germans in retreat.

MM Pte
RefScs: DHist JP

STANLEY Harold Poole

"One of the First to Enter Enemy's Lines"

Leading his company up the ridge, Harold Stanley of the Royal Highlanders of Canada was one of the first to penetrate the German lines. Having consolidated his position, he then led his men in repulsing an enemy counterattack. Though suffering two serious wounds, he remained at his post for seven hours until relieved.

DSO Lt
RefScs: DHist JP

HOSKING Ernest Lawrence

"Laid Down Communication Cables under Vicious Fire"

A veteran of the Ypres and Somme fighting, Ernest Hosking and four linesmen carried communications cable under heavy German rifle and shell-fire into the freshly captured enemy front-line position. There they were able to open up communications to notify headquarters that the objective had been reached. Shortly afterward Hosking was wounded. After reporting that the post was in good working order he retired to have his injuries dressed.

MM   Cpl
RefScs: DHist   JP

MacDOWELL Thain Wendell

"Stilled Two Gun Posts — Took 75 Prisoners"

Thain MacDowell won the Victoria Cross shortly after dawn when, during the assault on the ridge, he knocked out a pair of machine-gun nests and took 75 Germans prisoner. MacDowell felled the first post with a hand grenade while he and two runners advanced on an enemy dugout. As he attacked a second position, the gunner ran for cover. However, MacDowell immediately gave chase and killed him. On reaching the trench he called down to the Germans to surrender. When they refused he jumped into the ditch and rounded a corner to find himself at the entrance to the main room of the subterranean fortress and facing a formidable body of enemy soldiers. Pretending he had a considerable force with him, he shouted fake orders to his men to come forward and open fire. The ruse worked. The Germans threw up their hands in surrender. This marked the second time MacDowell had been decorated for bravery. During the Somme battles he had been awarded the Distinguished Service Order.

Born in Lachute, P.Q., MacDowell was educated in Brookville, Ont., and graduated from the University of Toronto. Enlisting in the 38th Canadian Infantry Battalion, he served with that unit overseas. Following the end of WW1 he became an executive with several mining and chemical companies and from 1923 to 1928 acted as private secretary to the Minister of National Defence. He later made his home in Toronto. In 1960 MacDowell died in the Bahamas at age 79.

VC DSO   Capt Lt/Col(Ret)   Born Sept 16 1880   Died Mar 29 1960
RefScs: CVC 50-1   VM 48-9

At 8:00 a.m. MacDowell filed the following report: "Objective reached but am afraid not fully consolidated. The mud is very bad and our machine guns are filled with mud."

It was written on a German report form!

DRYDEN John Cameron

"Steadied His Men while Working under Fire"

John Dryden, a sapper with the 3rd Divsion Engineers, was charged with the supervision of building a communications trench from the previous Canadian front-line position to the objective post. This was undertaken under constant German fire and shelling. But by his example Cameron kept his men calm and unnerved, helping to bring the job to a successful completion.

MM   Cpl
RefScs: DHist JP

ALLAN Robert James

"Decorated for Coolness under Fire

Robert Allan won his Military Medal for his calm composure under fire and the handling of his men, setting an example to all those around him. He was instrumental in flushing out the German trenches and assisting in the consolidation of his company's objectives.

MM   Cpl(Act)
RefScs: DHist JP

CHAPMAN Thomas Baird

"Engaged Enemy Machine Gun at Close Quarters"

To enable his unit to take its initial objective, Thomas Chapman was forced to engage an enemy machine gun which stood in their way at close quarters. Almost immediately both the officer and sergeant in charge were killed, compelling Chapman to take command of a considerable number of men. But with great proficiency he reorganized them and led them on to overcome their second objective.

MM   Cpl
RefScs: DHist JP

MILNE William Johnstone

"Put Pair of Machine Guns Out of Action"

A native of Wishaw, Scotland, William Milne was a member of the 16th Canadian Infantry Battalion during the storming of the ridge. When his company came under heavy German machine-gun fire, the troopers sought refuge in shell-holes. Suddenly a series of explosions could be heard in the direction of the enemy gun. Milne sprang from his shelter and signalled the others to advance. Inching forward on his hands and knees to within throwing range of the machine-gun crew, he lobbed several hand grenades into the position putting it out of action. Later he repeated the performance by silencing a second machine-gun nest. For the feat he received the Victoria Cross. But the award had to be made posthumously. Later in the day he was killed in action. Milne's name appears on the Vimy Memorial in France at the top of the ridge.

VC   Born Dec 21 1892   KIA April 9 1917
RefScs: CVC 52-3   VM 50-1

CAVE Gerald Richard

"Performed Scout Missions with Exceptional Aplomb"

Gerald Cave, throughout the fighting, performed his scout duties as if the shelling and gun fire around him were meant for somebody else. Time after time he went back and forth, to and from advanced positions, obtaining valuable information on German positions. In addition he took part in three raids on the enemy trenches. At Vimy he won the MM. Later he received a Bar to the decoration.

MM & Bar   Pte
RefScs: DHist JP

BAVERSTOCK William

"Cited for Bravery in Three Battles"

After assisting in the clearing of the initial German trenches, by the time his company moved up the ridge William Baverstock and two other NCOs were all that was left. Nevertheless, they carried on "unceasingly and indefatiguably" until reinforcements arrived. Baverstock received the MM for his actions at Vimy but his previous exploits at both Ypres and the Somme were recognized in the same commendation.

MM Sgt
RefScs: DHist JP

SIFTON Ellis Wellwood

"Silenced Machine-Gun Nest Allowing His Battalion to Advance"

After overwhelming the first line of trenches on Vimy Ridge shortly after dawn, the Canadians met their first stiff resistance while assaulting the second line of defence. As a member of C Company of the 18th Canadian Infantry Battalion, Ellis Sifton, a native of Wallacetown, Ont., was among those held down by one of several machine-gun nests lodged in concrete fortresses safely tucked away from the merciless artillery barrages. Peering through the snow and sleet, Sifton spotted the barrel of the weapon on top of a trench parapet. Without waiting to study the situation further he rushed towards it. Leaping into the trench, he charged the gunners with his bayonet, killing them all, and took command of their gun. With the gun now taken out of action the advance of the 18th Battalion was allowed to continue. Meanwhile, however, Sifton came under attack from a group of German soldiers from down the trench whom he fended off with his bayonet and rifle butt until help arrived. But it was too late. One of his victims, who lay dying, summoned up enough strength to lift his rifle and take aim on his protagonist. His shot killed Sifton instantly. Sifton's body was buried in Lichtfield Crater Cemetery, half a mile east of Neuville-Saint-Vasst in France, not far from where he fell.

VC L/Sgt Born Oct 12 1891 KIA April 9 1917
RefScs: CVC 54-5 VM 53-4

JASPER Tate

"The Cheerful Messenger"

During the first two days of the battle, Jasper Tate of the 62nd Battalion had the unenviable chore of running messages back and forth between headquarters and the front lines. But Tate carried out these excursions so cheerfully it seemed as if he actually enjoyed them. He also appeared to realize how important they were to the campaign because no matter how intense and heavy the German shelling and machine-gun fire he always managed to get through — and always with a smile. It was no surprise to his comrades who recalled his similar action in September on the Somme.

MM Pte
RefScs: DHist JP

WALLACE William

"Led Party 400 Yards Behind Enemy Lines"

On that wet morning Bill Wallace of the 75th Battalion had to lead his party 400 yards behind the German front-line trenches to achieve their objective. Wallace was subsequently wounded, and these injuries permanently affected his health. After serving for many years as advertising manager of the *Toronto Star* and *Star Weekly*, Wallace died in December 1947 at the age of 53.

MC Lt
RefScs: MCb 343

April 10

PATTISON John George

"Immobilized Nest of Machine Guns Single-Handedly"

On the second day of the battle, John Pattison's company found itself beaten back each time it tried to attack a German stronghold. Pattison decided to take matters into his own hands. Single-handedly he ran to-

Bill Wallace (Private Collection)

wards a nest of machine guns that time after time had halted the 50th Canadian Infantry Battalion in its tracks. Using shell-holes for cover he reached a point 30 yards from the nests before stopping. Then, standing up in full view of the gun crews, he threw three hand grenades at the position. These landed with such accuracy that the resulting explosions immobilized the guns and stunned the gunners. Before they could reorient themselves, Pattison charged full tilt towards them brandishing his bayonet. By the time his companions caught up with him he had killed all five Germans. This action resulted in the Canadians capturing and consolidating their objectives; Pattison consequently received the Victoria Cross. However, he never lived to wear it. He was killed in an attack on a generating station at Liévin near Lens that June.

Born in Woolwich, England, Pattison moved to Canada in 1906 where worked for a public utility company in Calgary. He enlisted in the Canadian army in 1916. Pattison was buried at La Chaudière Military Cemetery at Vimy. In his honour, a mountain in Jasper Park, Alta., is named after him.

VC Pte   Born Sept 8 1875   KIA June 3 1917
RefScs: CVC 58-9   VM 54-5

April 12

BOON Charles Edward

"Led Determined Bombing Assault"

Only a day after he was wounded in battle, Charles Boon of the 51st Battalion was decorated for bravery under fire while leading a bombing section against a German position coded the "Pimple." During the daring attack, through sheer determination he overcame a stubborn enemy defence and after a bitter fight consolidated the position.

MM   Pte
RefScs: DHist JP

April 14

DURNFORD Harry George

"Quick Thinking Earned a Military Medal"

While clearing Le Fulle Wood, the officer in charge of Durnford's unit was wounded by German fire. Durnford, a sergeant with the 49th Battalion, took over. In double-quick time he seized a strategic position under heavy fire and subdued a nest of enemy snipers. His quick thinking under pressure, which resulted in the consolidation of the ground gained, earned him the MM.

MM   Sgt
RefScs: DHist   JP

Author's Note
I first saw the Vimy Memorial from 20,000 feet in the cockpit of a Spitfire over German-occupied Western Europe on a clear evening late in May 1944, only two weeks before D-Day. An orange brilliancy from the setting sun in the west cast a majestic glow on that magnificent monument that could be seen for hundreds of miles. It seemed to blazon like a beacon of hope for those below that freedom from the barbarism of Nazi oppression was close at hand.

When, years later, I visited it on foot I was no less in awe. In fact, that momentous symbolic structure drove me to my knees.

HILL 70
April 15 - 25, 1917

In what was the severest fighting they had experienced, during a bitter 10-day battle, the Canadian Corps overran Hill 70, a strategic position at the northern approach to Lens, and captured the western part of that city. But the hard-fought victory had been costly. The Corps had sustained 9,198 casualties.

April 15-18

O'ROURKE Michael James

"Stretcher-Bearer Worked under Fire to Rescue Wounded from No-Man's Land"

Michael O'Rourke, a stretcher-bearer with the 7th Canadian Infantry Battalion, won the Victoria Cross for rescuing the wounded and tending to them under heavy machine-gun and rifle fire, as well as severe shelling, during this four-day period. On several occasions he was knocked down and partially buried by enemy shelling. Seeing a comrade who had been blinded stumbling around in No-Man's Land, O'Rourke jumped out of his trench and, in full view of the enemy, brought the man back while being heavily sniped at. On another occasion he ran forward in the face of machine-gun and sniper fire to rescue a wounded man. Later, when the battalion line of advanced posts was retired to the line and consolidated, O'Rourke again went forward under enemy fire to rescue a badly crippled Canadian soldier who had been left behind. During this time he worked unceasingly, dressing the wounded and bringing them food and water. The VC was O'Rourke's second decoration. He had previously been decorated with the Military Medal at Mouquet Farm on September 16, 1916, during the Battle of the Somme.

Born in Limerick, Ireland, O'Rourke retired to Vancouver where he died in 1957. His picture hangs in the Canadian War Museum in Ottawa.

VC MM Pte   Born Mar 19 1878   Died Dec 6 1957
RefScs: CVC 66-7   VM 62-3

April 16

BROWN Harry

"Delivered Critical Message despite Mortal Wound"

The day after the Canadians captured Hill 70, the Germans launched a massive counterattack. With all wires cut between the 10th Canadian Infantry Battalion and its headquarters, Harry Brown, of Gananoque, Ont., and another runner, were despatched to deliver a message calling for artillery support to smash the assault. The other runner was killed and Brown had his arm badly shattered. But, despite his wound and intense enemy fire, he managed to reach the close support lines. By that time he was so weakened and spent that he stumbled down the dugout steps and collapsed. But he regained consciousness long enough to deliver the missive with the words: "Important message" before passing out again. Carried to a dressing station, Brown died several hours later. In carrying out his mission he had saved the loss of the battalion's position and prevented countless casualties. He earned the posthumous award of the Victoria Cross. Brown was buried at Noex-les-Mines Communal Cemetery, four miles southeast of Béthune in France.

VC   Pte   Born May 1898   KIA Aug 16 1917
RefScs: CVC 58-9   VM 58-9

August 18

HOBSON Frederick

"Boer War Veteran Single-Handedly Stopped Enemy Counterattack"

During a strong German counterattack on the 20th Canadian Infantry Battalion position on Hill 70, a forward Lewis machine-gun post received a direct hit from an enemy shell. The blast buried the gun and killed all but one of the crew. Though he was not a gunner, Frederick Hobson dashed from his trench over to the post, dug the weapon out and helped the gunner to man it. By this time the enemy were advancing towards him and the gun jammed. Hobson left the gunner to clear the stoppage and then rushed ahead to face the Germans. With bayonet thrusts and by clubbing them with his rifle butt, he killed 15 of the enemy before a bullet ended his own life. By that time the Lewis gun was back in action and reinforcements had arrived that beat the enemy off. For this single-handed feat, Hobson received the Victoria Cross posthumously.

Born in London, England, during the Boer War he served with the Wiltshire Regiment. Hobson's burial place is unknown but his name appears on the Vimy Memorial.

VC   Sgt   Born Sep 23 1875   KIA April 18 1917
RefScs: CVC 64-5   VM 64-5

Frederick Hobson (C 33053)

LEARMONTH Okill Massey

"Wounded Company Commander Stayed in the Line to Direct Battle"

Though wounded three times and under acute artillery fire, company commander Okill Learmonth of the 2nd Canadian Infantry Battalion continued to direct the defence against a concentrated German counter-attack until he had to be pulled out of the battle. The incident took place August 18, only three days after the Canadians had overrun Hill 70. Learmonth rallied his men from the parapet of his trench and when hand grenades were hurled at him he picked them up and threw them back. Finally, when he could fight no longer, he asked to be laid out in the dugout where he still carried on, issuing instructions. He soon had to be taken from the field to a hospital where he died of his wounds. But on the way he insisted on stopping at battalion headquarters to give a comprehensive first-hand verbal report of the situation on the line. For his valour under fire, Learmonth, who had previously been decorated with the Military Cross, was awarded the Victoria Cross.

A native of Quebec City, at the outbreak of WW1 in 1914 Learmonth was on the staff of the Quebec Provincial Treasurer's Department. Enlisting as a private in the Canadian army, he was commissioned in June 1916. His name is commemorated in Quebec City by Learmonth Avenue and the Okill Learmonth Chapter of the Imperial Order of the Daughters of the Empire. His portrait hangs in the Canadian War Museum in Ottawa. Learmonth was buried in Noex-les-Mines Communal Cemetery.

VC MC   Born Feb 22 1894   KIA Aug 18 1917
RefScs: CVC 68-9   VM 66-7

August 21

HANNA Robert

"In Face of Vicious Fire Captured Critical Machine-Gun Post"

On August 21, 1917, during the second phase of the Hill 70 fighting, a stubborn German machine-gun post held up a Canadian advance, repelling three attacks and killing all the officers of a 29th Canadian Infantry Battalion company. Robert Hanna, a sergeant-major, found himself in charge. Though the nest was heavily protected by barbed-wire as well as rifle fire and the machine gun itself, Hanna decided the position had to be taken if the assault was to succeed. Collecting a party of men, he rushed through the wire entanglement at their head, personally bayoneting three of the enemy gunners and braining a fourth with a blow from his rifle butt. For this courageous action, in which the enemy post was captured and the machine gun silenced at a critical time in the Canadian foray, Hanna received the Victoria Cross.

Born in Kilkeel, Ireland, he came to Canada in 1905 and was engaged in logging in B.C. when WW1 broke out in 1914. That November he enlisted in the Canadian army. Following the war Hanna returned to B.C. where he ran a logging camp. In 1938 he moved to Mount Lehman, B.C., to take up farming. He died there in 1967.

VC Sgt/M Born Aug 1887 Died June 15 1967
RefScs: CVC 70-1 VM 68-9

Green Crassier
August 22 and 24

KONOWAL Filip

"Spirited Individual Action Overcame 16 of the Enemy in Two Days"

On two different days of hand-to-hand fighting, Russian-born Filip Konowal, a corporal with the 47th Canadian Infantry, killed 16 German soldiers all by himself. The objective was the Green Crassier near Lens at the height of the Hill 70 battles. Consisting of an immense expanse of coal slag-heaps thrown up by bursting land mines, it was infested with machine-gun nests. To silence them the German gunners had to be ferreted out from tunnels, craters, dugouts and cellars. Konowal was an expert at this kind of close-in combat; he had served five years with the Russian army where he had become a bayonet instructor. In one cellar he bayoneted three German soldiers, then attacked seven others in a crater, killing them all. At one machine-gun post, which was inflicting heavy casualties on the Canadians, Konowal rushed forward, charged into the emplacement, killed the crew and brought the weapon back to his own lines. On another occasion, once again all by himself, he attacked another machine-gun position killing all three of the crew. He then destroyed the gun and the emplacement with explosives. But in this final assault of his two-day combat spree, Konowal was wounded and had to be taken out of the line. For his dauntlessness in the face of danger he received the Victoria Cross.

Born in Podolsky, Konowal left his native Russia for Canada in 1913 and lived in Ottawa, where, a year later, he enlisted in the army. Following the war Konowal returned to the capital city where he was employed as a member of the Parliament Buildings staff. Later he retired to Wrightsville, P.Q., where he died in 1959. A portrait of Konowal hangs in the Canadian War Museum in Ottawa.

VC   Sgt   Born Sept 15 1888   Died June 3 1959
RefScs: CVC 72-3   VM 70-1

ARRAS
April 13 - May 3, 1917

Following the victory at Vimy Ridge, the British and Canadians continued the attack on the Arras front even though the objectives were limited. The chief aim was to relieve the pressure on the French who had launched the main assault in the Aisne along the southern part of the Hindenburg Line. Nevertheless, on May 3, the Canadians achieved a minor breakthrough with the capture of Fresnoy.

VIMY VILLAGE
May 3

COMBE Robert Grierson

"Braved Enemy Barrage and His Own Guns to Reach Objective"

Three miles from Vimy Village, Robert Combe's company had advanced within 200 yards of its objective, a German trench near Acheville, when the company was struck down by a heavy artillery barrage. Men collapsed by the dozens, blown to pieces or crushed by the weight of uptorn earth. Combe was the only officer in the unit to survive. With his company now a tattered remnant of what it had been minutes earlier, he nonetheless rallied the depleted force forward through intense enemy fire. Ahead they faced a new hazard — an ironic one — barrage from

Robert Combe (C 33100)

their own guns. Under Combe's inspired leadership they persevered, although by the time they reached the German trench there were only five men left. Assisted by a few Canadians from another company, they made their way along the trench attacking with captured German hand grenades, having exhausted their own supply. Eighty prisoners were marched back to the Canadian lines and 250 yards of trench had been taken. But the fight continued and, in the ensuing mêlée, Combe was killed by a bullet from an enemy sniper. For his actions that day he received posthumously the award of the Victoria Cross.

Born in Aberdeen, Scotland, Combe emigrated to Canada in 1906 where he operated a drugstore in Melville, Sask. In 1915 he enlisted in the Canadian army going overseas the following year where, after a short illness, he joined the 27th Canadian Infantry Battalion in France. Combe has no known grave but his name is inscribed in on the Vimy Memorial and a life-size painting of him hangs in the Peace Tower in Ottawa. Also in his honour, a lake in northern Saskatchewan bears his name.

VC   Lt   Born Aug 5 1887   KIA May 3 1917
RefScs: CVC 56-7   VM 56-7

FRESNOY

AMES Maurice Roland

"Silenced Enemy Machine Gun, Led Capture of Host of German Prisoners"

Leading a platoon in an attack on the town, Maurice Ames of the 32nd Battalion was primarily responsible for silencing a German machine gun holding up the advance. After the final objective was reached he led a patrol against the enemy defences in which his section captured two German officers and 50 other ranks. He then maintained his post until driven back by his own shell-fire, an operation in which he was wounded. This was the second time he had been injured in battle. On this occasion Ames was awarded the MM. Later a Bar was added to the decoration for bravery in the field.

MM & Bar   Sgt
RefScs: DHist JP

May 4

BIGGS Percy Armstrong

"Stretcher-Bearer Worked Tirelessly to Attend to Wounded under Fire"

At the height of the fighting, stretcher-bearer Percy Biggs of the Medical Corps, though constantly under the duress of heavy German shelling, dressed the wounded and carried them to shelter until his battalion was relieved. Then, as he was on his way back, word was received that the Germans had launched a fresh assault. Briggs decided to return to the battlefield. For the rest of that day he continued to work tirelessly attending to the wounded and carrying them to shelter all the while under heavier enemy shelling and fire than before. In the citation to his MM he was commended for his "spirit of devotion to duty [which was] most inspiring."

MM   Pte
RefScs: DHist JP

IN FRONT OF VIMY RIDGE
May 4 - 7

BROWN William Allen

"Escorted Parties to Forward Positions"

During this period William Brown was responsible for leading parties to and from a captured German trench. On one occasion, due to heavy casualties requiring immediate attention, he was forced to guide a medical officer to the trench in broad daylight, a risky operation in the face of heavy enemy fire. This daring feat earned Brown the Military Medal.

MM   Sgt
RefScs: DHist JP

TRENCH WARFARE
June - October 1917

Following the spring battle, there were no major Canadian campaigns until the fall. Meanwhile, the situation stagnated into trench warfare with the occasional reconnaissance or raid "over the top." Conditions were unbearable. Discomfort from the rain, mud and rodents was added to by the ever-present danger of being blown up by mines set off by the enemy in tunnels dug under the trenches.

June 3

MacLACHLAN Roy Hansford

"Held Off the Enemy until Out of Ammunition"

By the time his bombing platoon reached its objective, Roy MacLachlan was left with the realization that with his platoon commander and all his NCOs put out of action he, as a lance corporal, was now in charge. Garrisoning the survivors with himself positioned in the centre to direct consolidation of the position, he was able to fend off German hand grenades, mortar fire and shelling attacks for 10 hours until, with all his ammunition gone and the defenders reduced to four, he was forced to withdraw.

    MM L/Cpl
    RefScs: DHist JP

COULERIE

EILER Lorne Sinclair

"Absolutely without Fear"

When Lorne Eiler of the 10th Field Company reached his objective, having taken command of his platoon when its commander became a casualty, he found his men isolated and severely pressed by German counterattacks. But he successfully beat them off and then withdrew his unit to establish contact with the rest of his company, fighting all the way. The commendation for his MM stated that he was "absolutely without fear," with some justification. Promoted to officer rank, he later won the MC.

    MC Sgt
    RefScs: DHist JP MCb 97

July 25

HARDY John

"Led Men Forward, Aided Wounded, Acted as Runner"

Early in the morning the Germans began an intense artillery barrage. During this time John Hardy of the 58th Battalion helped his officers move troops forward to the front line under the heavy bombardment. Hardy led one party up to the line by himself then, having completed the task, returned to aid a man who had been wounded. He then, with the shelling still in progress, brought back a message to battalion headquarters.

    MM Pte
    RefScs: DHist JP

NEAR LENS
August 13 and 15

GRANT Alexander Robert

"Held Off Multiple Enemy Counterattacks"

On the 13th of the month, Alexander Grant was in charge of a patrol which, despite heavy German opposition, had gained its objectives. In the process he took a prisoner who provided valuable information on the enemy's positions. Suddenly the platoon had to withstand a heavy counterattack. The unit held its ground until, seeing the flank on his left being driven back, Grant ordered a withdrawal. Two days later he took charge of a bombing squad. He again showed his leadership in repelling a series of German counterattacks until orders arrived for the unit to retire to its former position.

    MM Sgt KIA Oct 18 1918
    RefScs: DHist JP

August 15

HAMMERT Nathan Thomas

"Put Enemy Machine Gun Out of Action, Took Charge of the Line"

When a German machine gun temporarily held up an advance, Nathan Hammert charged it and put it out of action with his own Lewis gun. He then led his section on to its objective, where with no officer in sight, he took charge of that part of the line. Organizing its defence, he succeeded in repulsing two enemy counterattacks and securing the position for the company.

    MM   Lt(Temp)
    RefScs: DHist JP

August 21

FYLES Charles Douglas

"Kept Germans at Bay for an Hour"

Under assault by a squad of 50 Germans, Charles Fyles, a lance-corporal with the 29th Battalion, quickly organized a machine-gun party to repel them. Then he swung into action training his gun on the enemy force, holding them at bay for an hour until reinforcements arrived.

    MM   L/Cpl
    RefScs: DHist JP

September 5/6

McGUIGAN Stewart Parrel

"Used Grenades to Silence Enemy Machine Gun"

Placed in charge of an outpost, Stewart McGuigan was ordered to advance his position where he could protect Canadian night patrols. This he accomplished with no fuss and no casualties. Once established, however, he discovered a German machine gun, a threat to the patrols. McGregor crept forward from his position and, by lobbing hand grenades, he put the weapon out of commission and the crew along with it. This allowed the patrols to carry out their reconnaissance without harassment.

MM   Sgt(Act)
RefScs: DHist JP

September 15

JAMES Robert Eustace

"Instant Reaction Saved His Men from Grenade Explosion"

On this date, Robert James was put in charge of attacking patrols and immediately set up his position in front of the German lines. There his unit was attacked for eight straight hours. The position was heavily damaged by shelling and bombing, and by evening had become untenable. With the help of one of his troops he began bombing the enemy with Mills hand grenades. However, one of them fell in the midst of the post. Reacting instantly, James picked it up and tossed it out of harm's way before it could explode and cause casualties among his own men. Though it was gruelling and hair-raising combat, James and his comrades managed to inflict heavy casualties among the Germans. When the position could no longer be held he supervised the evacuation, managing to get the survivors, as well as the wounded, back to a supporting post.

MM   Cpl
RefScs: DHist JP

IN FRONT OF PASSCHENDAELE RIDGE
October 2

EVANS Walter Allen

"Conveyed Ammo through Enemy Barrage"

Walter Evans, a bombardier with the 2nd Division, had charge of a convoy ordered to bring ammunition forward to a gun battery. The Germans got wind of this and brought down a fierce cannon barrage along the road to the front lines. Undaunted, Evans brought his vehicles through and delivered his cargo.

MM   Cpl
RefScs: DHist JP

POLYGON WOOD
October 10

BENT Philip Eric

"Come on the Tigers!"

Just prior to the opening of the British fall/winter offensive, Philip Bent, a Canadian serving with the British Leicestershire Regiment, won the Victoria Cross for his coolness under fire while securing a position of essential importance in the campaign to come. On this date, the Germans attacked through the Polygon Wood in Belgium forcing back Brent's right flank and the battalion on his left. Due to the resulting confusion, coupled with intense artillery fire, the situation quickly became critical. Bent rallied a platoon held in reserve, along with other troops from various companies and details, and organized a counterattack. Charging forward at the head of his men, he inspired them with the shout: "Come on the Tigers!" But as he advanced toward the German positions, he was cut down by enemy bullets.

Brent, who was born in Halifax, had earlier been decorated with the Distinguished Service Order in June 1917. In October 1914, he had enlisted in the Royal Scots and the following month was granted a temporary commission in the Leicestershire Regiment with which, as a lieutenant-colonel, he was awarded the VC, posthumously.

VC DSO   Lt/Col   Born Jan 3 1891   KIA Oct 10 1917
RefScs: CVC 78-9   VM 72-3

October 19

CAMPBELL Malcolm

"Graded Road by Ignoring Shelling"

Malcolm Campbell was in charge of an infantry party grading a road which ran past a gun battery. They were exposed to heavy German shelling, but Campbell exhorted his men to ignore it. By disregarding the barrage, he kept his party on the job and completed the task. A month later he set a similar example while supervising repair work on a railway line under enemy fire, and with similar results.

MM Sgt
RefScs: DHist JP

PASSCHENDAELE
October 30 - November 10, 1917

*W*inston Churchill later described it as "a forlorn expenditure of valour and life without equal in futility." But over the strong objections of Canadian Corps commander General Sir Arthur Currie that the battlefield was too muddy for an attack without horrendous losses, on October 26 the British commander General Sir Douglas Haig launched an assault in the Ypres sector. The Canadians' objective was the capture of the crossroads village of Passchendaele, the outskirts of which the First and Second Divisions entered in a driving rain on October 30. There they held on for five days, often in waist-deep mud and constantly harassed by a violent hail of German shelling until reinforcements arrived. By November 6, the entire town was in Canadian hands, but the cost

Disabled tank in badly shelled area at Passchendaele. (PA 2195)

had been horrific: 16,000 casualties, all for a bloody, paltry ground-gain of four-and-one-half miles. A shocking, senseless slaughter and sacrifice. Canada's Calvary.

October 26

HOLMES Thomas William

"Stifled Pillbox Position Single-Handedly"

At the outset of the assault to capture Passchendaele, the Canadian right flank was held up by heavy machine-gun and rifle fire from a German pillbox. Heavy casualties resulted and the advance bogged

Thomas Holmes (PA 2352)

down, whereupon Tommy Holmes, an 18-year-old private with the 4th Canadian Mounted Rifles, leapt forward on his own volition to attack the blockhouse with hand grenades. Despite heavy enemy fire he hurled two of the missiles into the stronghold killing and wounding a pair of gun crew. Returning to his unit for a moment to pick up more grenades, Holmes rushed back again in the face of more gunfire, hurling two grenades into the entrance of the pillbox forcing its 19 occupants to surrender. Miraculously, he was not even scratched and his battalion was now allowed to advance. For this incredible deed, which saved his countrymen countless live, Holmes received the Victoria Cross. When he arrived back in Canada on leave he was accorded a hero's welcome.

Born in Montreal, Holmes moved to Owen Sound, Ont., where he took his education. In 1915 he enlisted in the Canadian army, going overseas with the 4th CMRs. Following WW2 he became a chauffeur with the Toronto Harbour Commission where he was employed for 14 years until poor health forced him to retire. Holmes died in Toronto in 1950.

VC   Sgt   Born Oct 14 1898   Died Jan 4 1950
RefScs: CSGWW 325   CVC 80-1   VM 74-5

SHANKLAND Robert

"Inspired His Men to Capture and Hold Key Position"

Robert Shankland, of Winnipeg, was in the vanguard of the attack on Passchendaele. Already the recipient of the Distinguished Conduct Medal for bravery in action at Sanctuary Wood in June 1916, he was about to add further distinction to an already exemplary war record. As an officer with the 43rd Canadian Infantry Battalion, Shankland led his troops in the capture of the Bellevue Spur, one of the main German trench lines of defence. Despite heavy casualties he rallied his force to maintain command of the position and repel a heavy enemy counterattack. Then, temporarily taking leave of his command, he reported to battalion advanced headquarters on the frontal situation from an overall brigade standpoint. This proved highly accurate and invaluable to the success of the battle. Shankland then returned to take over his command under severe fire until relieved. For his example, which inspired all ranks, coupled with his gallantry and skill, he was awarded the Victoria Cross.

A native of Ayr, Scotland, Shankland emigrated to Canada in 1911. He enlisted in the Canadian army when WW1 broke out. Following the war he lived in Vancouver, where he died in 1968.

VC DCM   Lt   Born Oct 10 1887   Died Jan 28 1968
RefScs: CVC 74-5   VM 76-7

Pine Street, renamed Valour Street, in Winnipeg, is the only thoroughfare to boast three Victoria Cross recipients. In addition to Shankland, they are Leo Clarke and Frederick Hall.

O'KELLY Christopher Patrick John

"Led Series of Attacks and Counterassaults to Consolidate Position"

On the morning of the capture of the German Bellevue Spur Line trench position (see Shankland), Christopher O'Kelly, in charge of A Company of the 52nd Canadian Infantry Battalion, led his troops to the assistance of the 43rd Battalion which was under heavy enemy counterattack. This officer, who a month before had been awarded the Military Cross, advanced his force 1,000 yards, sweeping the brow of the position and catching the German flank head-on. Driving the enemy infantry before them, his men cut them down as they charged. But now they ran into stubborn resistance from German pillboxes. However, in a series of well-planned and well-executed assaults, O'Kelly directed the capture of six of the strongholds, taking 100 prisoners and 10 of their machine guns. Later, in the afternoon, O'Kelly rallied his company to repel a strong counterattack and take more prisoners. Then that night he led a foray which netted his unit a German raiding party, made up of one officer, 10 men and machine gun. For this series of actions that, through his leadership and daring, helped consolidate the Spur Line position for both battalions, O'Kelly received the Victoria Cross.

Born in Winnipeg, O'Kelly joined the Canadian army in 1915. In 1922 he drowned accidently at Lac Seul, Ont.

VC MC   Capt   Born Nov 18 1895   KA Nov 15 1922
RefScs: CVC 81-2   VM 78-9

October 29 - November 2

BINGHAM Owen

"Concern for His Men Was Paramount"

During this five-day period, Owen Bingham, of the 78th Battalion, was a driving force in the success achieved by his platoon. Whenever a German assault seemed imminent he would maneuver his men into a strategic position. It was said of him, "His only thought was the security, comfort and welfare of his men." Throughout he showed a total personal disregard to the danger from heavy enemy shelling to which his trenches were subjected. His determination and spirit did much to steady his men under the stress of embittered fighting. Bingham was described as being "of the greatest assistance to his platoon during the attack and consolidation that followed."

MM   Sgt(Act)
RefScs: DHist JP

October 30

CAMPBELL Glidden

"Continued to File Reports though Wounded in the Face"

When all the senior officers in his unit became casualties, after the objective had been captured, Glidden Campbell took over command of his sector of the front line. Campbell was himself wounded in the face but he carried on. His frequent reports were so accurate that they enabled the German counterattacks to be broken up. Campbell, in some pain, stayed at his post unto the battalion was relieved.

MC   Capt(Temp)
RefScs: DHist JP

PASSCHENDAELE VILLAGE

MacKENZIE Hugh

"Sacrificed Himself to Enable Capture of Enemy Pillbox"

During the attack on the village itself, all the officers and NCOs of a company of the Princess Patricia's Canadian Light Infantry were cut down by machine-gun fire from a German pillbox on the crest of a hill. But although the surviving men in the unit could not advance, they also refused to retreat. Surveying the situation, Hugh MacKenzie left a corporal in charge of his machine guns and made his way through heavy enemy fire to the forward position. Taking command he detailed several small parties to circle around the flanks of the stronghold and attack it from the rear (see Mullin). To draw fire away from them, MacKenzie led a frontal assault directly up the slope leading to the fort. As they charged forward the men were met by a deadly fusillade from the pillbox. Ironically, at the moment of its capture, MacKenzie was felled by a bullet through the head. For his valiant action he was awarded a posthumous Victoria Cross.

Born in Liverpool, England, MacKenzie emigrated to Canada before the outbreak of WW1 in 1914 at which time he joined the army to become a member of the 7th Canadian Machine-gun Company. With this unit, in addition to winning the VC, he also received the Distinguished Conduct Medal. Whereabouts of his grave are unknown, but MacKenzie's name is inscribed on the Menin Gate Memorial at Ypres.

VC DCM   Lt   Born Dec 5 1885   KIA Oct 30 1917
RefScs: CVC 94-5   VM 80-1

Passchendaele Ridge

KINROSS Cecil John

"Armed Only with a Rifle, Silenced Machine Gun Manned by Six"

Shortly after the assault on the ridge, the 49th Canadian Infantry Battalion came under an intense German artillery barrage. Then machine-gun fire halted the advance. Cecil Kinross made a careful study of the situation and then decided to attack the nest head-on. Stripping off all his equipment except his rifle and cartridge belt, he dashed forward in full view of the enemy gunners. Undaunted, he charged into the emplacement, killing the crew of six, and seized and destroyed the gun. Inspired by his example and courage, his company renewed its advance covering a distance of 300 yards. Kinross continued to fight all day until, against overwhelming odds, he was severely wounded and had to be evacuated from the battlefield. For his determination and bravery he was awarded the Victoria Cross.

Born in Stirling, Scotland. Kinross later came to Canada and took up farming at Lougheed, Alta. In 1915 he enlisted in the Canadian army, and after the war returned to Lougheed where he died in 1957.

VC Pte   Born Feb 17 1891   Died June 21 1957
RefScs: CVC 84-5   VM 84-5

GRAF AND MEETCHEELE

MULLIN George Harry

"Silenced German Pillbox in Lone Frontal Attack"

George Mullin was one of those detailed to work their way around an enemy pillbox that was inflicting severe casualties on the Princess Patricia's Canadian Light Infantry (see MacKenzie). But Mullin, a gunner with the unit who had won the Military Medal earlier in the year at Vimy Ridge, decided to rush the stronghold head-on. Blasting it with hand grenades, he crawled on top of the emplacement and, aiming his revolver through the gun aperture, shot the two machine gunners dead. He then ran to the entrance of the pillbox and forced the garrison of 10 men to surrender. Mullin received the Victoria Cross for his audacious feat and went on to survive the war.

Born in Portland, Oregon, he moved to Canada at an early age with his parents who settled in Moosomin, Sask., where they took up farming. Graduating from school, Mullin joined the Canadian army in 1914. Following WW1 he returned to the family farm. He also served with the Militia. During WW2, he joined the Veterans Guard of Canada. After that conflict ended Mullin moved to Regina, where he became sergeant-of-arms for Saskatchewan. In 1953 he represented the province at the coronation of Queen Elizabeth II. Mullin died 10 years later at age 80.

VC MM   Pte   Maj(M)   Lt   Born Aug 15 1892   Died April 5 1963
RefScs: CVC 86-7   VM 82-3

October 30/31

PEARKES George Randolph

"Mountie to Major-General to Minister"

George Pearkes held nearly every senior Canadian army post it was possible to attain, topping his career as Minister of National Defence. During active service he was wounded five times. As a soldier he earned such respect from his men that one of them said "I would have followed him to hell if I had to."

Born in Watford, England, after graduating from college Pearkes moved to Alberta where, for a time, he homesteaded. In 1911 he joined the

George Pearkes (PA 2364)

Royal Canadian Mounted Police and served in the Yukon until 1914. When WW1 broke out he enlisted in the 2nd Battalion of the Canadian Mounted Rifles as a private. Posted to France, he was engaged in every major battle in which the Canadian Expeditionary Force took part. During the Somme battles in 1916 he was awarded the Military Cross. It was during the battle of Passchendaele, as commander of the 5th Canadian Mounted Rifles Battalion, that he won the Victoria Cross. About to lead his troops against a German strongpoint, he was struck in the left left thigh by shrapnel. He later said: "There seemed to be a little uncertainty among the men around me, whether they should go on when I'd been hit." For a brief moment Pearkes had visions of being carried away on a stretcher. The thought appalled him. "I said to myself: 'This can't be. I've got to go on for a while . . . wounded or not.'" Pearkes clambered to his feet. His leg felt stiff from his wound, but he was able to drag himself forward, the rest of the company following.

Taking a forward positon, Pearkes and his troops held out against heavy counterattacks for two days, enabling the Canadians to advance and reach their objectives. At nightfall of the second day, the survivors, who by this time had been reduced to a handful, were finally relieved. Subsequently, for his part in the battle of Amiens in 1918, Pearkes was awarded the Distinguished Service Order.

When the war ended he stayed in the army. In 1922 he was made General Staff Officer at Royal Military College, Kingston, Ont., a post he held until 1933. From 1935-38 he was Director of Military Training. During WW2, Pearkes was given command of the First Canadian Division. Then when the Japanese entered the war, he took over as Commander-in-Chief, Pacific Command. After the war ended Pearkes retired from the army, ran for Parliament, was elected, and subsequently became Minister of National Defence. He retired from politics in 1960 and for the next eight years held the post of Lieutenant-Governor of British Columbia.

VC CB DSO MC KGStJ USoM CdeG(F) Maj/Gen Born Feb 26 1888
RefScs: CVC 88-9 VM 86-7

PASSCHENDAELE RIDGE
October 31

GOODWIN Wilder Penfield

"After Evacuating His Men Returned to Tend the Wounded"

Wilder Goodwin of the 64th Battery Canadian Field Artillery was in charge of a party stacking ammunition when they were caught in a heavy German artillery barrage. Several of the men were wounded. Goodwin got his group out and then went back to the position to attend the injured. This resulted in his men rallying round him to carry their wounded comrades to a field dressing station.

MM Sgt
RefScs: DHist JP

NEAR PASSCHANDAELE

McDONALD Joseph Gerrad

"Stayed Behind to Care for the Casualties"

That night, a section of the line to which Joseph McDonald of the 116th Battalion was attached, came under such heavy shelling that the company was withdrawn. Because of the number of casualties, McDonald stayed behind to help the stretcher-bearers. He dug out some of the wounded, dressed them and dragged them to safety. In the process he was hit twice by exploding shells. However, the two senior NCOs had been killed so McDonald took complete charge of the situation.

    MM Sgt
    RefScs: DHist JP

PASSCHENDAELE
November 5

ANDERSON Alexander Davidson

"Ran Guns into Battery Post through Mud and Shell-Fire"

Alexander Anderson, who was acting sergeant-major of the guns, suddenly found himself in command of building a road to run six cannon into the battery position, all the while under heavy German shell-fire. Although the obstacles and the incessant enemy gun barrages made the job seem insurmountable, all six guns were in place by November 6. In one instance it became necessary to dismantle a carriage which was bogged down in the mud up to the axle hubs. Rain and shelling failed to deter the party from pulling it out. Anderson was cited for his initiative and determination.

    MM S/M (Act)
    RefScs: DHist JP

VINECOT
November 6

BARRON Colin Fraser

"Solo Sortie Silenced Machine-Gun Nemesis"

Three machine guns at a German strongpoint known as "Vinecot" formed one of the last pockets of resistance preventing the complete Canadian occupation of Passchendaele Village. Guarding the Godberg Spur trench, they were inflicting heavy casualties. While Canadian riflemen countered the fire, the situation had reached a standstill. To break the stalemate Colin Barron, a corporal with the 3rd Canadian Infantry Battalion, inched his way forward on his stomach to the position. When he was close enough he hurled several Mills bombs into the nest. Rushing it, he found most of the gun crews were dead. He turned his rifle on several more, taking prisoners. He then turned one of the captured guns on the retreating enemy. For the exploit Barron was awarded the Victoria Cross.

A native of Baldavie in Scotland, Barron moved to Canada in 1910 where he became a railroad worker in Toronto. When WW1 broke out, he enlisted with the 3rd Battalion with which he went overseas. During WW2 he re-enlisted, serving with the Royal Regiment of Canada at home, in Iceland, and Great Britain. Following the cessation of hostilities, he was employed on the staff of the Don Street Jail in Toronto. Barron died in that city in 1958 at age 65.

VC Lt   Born Sept 20 1893   Died Aug 15 1958
RefScs: CVC 90-1   VM 888-9

November 6/7

GILBERT William McCombe

"Heroism under Air Attack"

William Gilbert did not take his responsibilities as a section leader lightly. His first and greatest concern was always the safety of those in his charge. On this particular instance he skillfully directed his men to their front-line post. They had no sooner secured this position when they were attacked by German aircraft. Gilbert coolly ordered his men to take cover from the strafing and bombs, thereby keeping casualties to a minimum.

MM   Cpl(Act)
RefScs: DHist JP

BUTTON Edward William

"Buried Alive, Rescued, Rejoined His Platoon"

Edward Button was a member of the Lewis gun section of his platoon moving forward in support of the 1st Battalion. While advancing through a heavy barrage, he and the corporal in charge were both wounded and Button and the Lewis gun were buried under dirt and debris. The NCO rescued Button by extricating him along with their machine gun. Though Button was in considerable pain, he nevertheless helped the corporal clean the weapon. That accomplished, they were able to rejoin their platoon before it reached its objective. Once the position was secured Button refused aid for his injuries and continued to fight.

MM   Pte
RefScs: DHist JP

November 10

BUCKNAM Norral

"Masterful Leadership"

In the early morning of the last day of the battle, Norral Bucknam led a storming party along the road to Passchendaclc to a dominating point in the front line. On arriving they encountered stiff German resistance but this they managed to overcome, taking six prisoners in the process. Though wounded in the fracas, Bucknam continued to direct his men and consolidate the position against an enemy counterattack. In the citation for his action he was hailed for his "masterful leadership."

MM   Sgt
RefScs: DHist JP

CAMBRAI — FIRST EFFECTIVE TANK ATTACK
November 20, 1917

In the aftermath of the capture of Passchendaele the Canadian Corps returned to the Lens front and to trench warfare stalemate, with one notable exception — the tank assault on the textile town of Cambrai. The elimination of the usual artillery bombardment took the Germans by surprise and the Allies easily occupied the Hindenburg Line and reached the open countryside beyond. But it was no breakthrough. The British lacked tank reserves and the metal monsters, along with the troops, bogged down in the Flanders mud. Nevertheless, the Canadian Cavalry Brigade covered themselves and the Newfoundland Regiment with distinction in the defence of Masnières against an enemy counterattack.

MASNIÈRES
November 20

STRACHAN Harcus

"Led Cavalry Charge to Wipe Out Enemy Gun Battery"

When his squadron leader was cut down in his saddle by enemy bullets and the Fort Garry Horse Regiment was brought to a standstill, Harcus Strachan immediately took command. Riding at the head of his troopers through a ring of German machine-gun posts, he charged a gun battery killing seven of the gunners with his sword. With the battery silenced, he rallied his men and fought his way back at night through the enemy's line bringing in 15 prisoners. His fearless leadership, for which he was awarded the Victoria Cross, not only resulted in putting a gun battery out of action and the death of the gunners as well as many German infantrymen, but also three telephone communication lines were cut two miles back of the enemy's front position.

Strachan was born in Borrowstounness in Scotland but came to Canada in 1908. In 1915 joined the Canadian Cavalry. On reaching the Western Front, in May 1917 he distinguished himself in a courageous raid on several German gunposts south of St. Quentin for which received the Military Cross. Following the end of WW1, Strachan went into the banking business but remained active with the militia and reserves. When

Harcus Strachan (PA 6744)

WW2 started he was back in uniform and in 1940 was given command of the Edmonton Fusiliers. Following the cessation of hostilities, Strachan returned to banking, later retiring to Vancouver.

VC MC   Maj   Lt/Col(WW2)   Born Nov 7 1889
RefScs: CVC 76-7   VM 92-3

March 12/13

MacDONALD Erik Whidden

"Flawless Raid Result of Meticulous Organation and Planning"

On this night Erik MacDonald of the 106th Battalion pulled off a faultless raid behind enemy lines as a direct result of meticulous organization and planning in the 48 hours beforehand. No detail was overlooked. His men were able to penetrate the German lines through gaps in the barbed-wire fences on which they had been fully briefed. Not only did the party inflict heavy casualties on the enemy as well as destroying guns and equipment, but invaluable intelligence was also obtained. For the foray MacDonald received the MC. But that was only the start of an illustrious military career in which he was decorated with the DSO three times as well.

DSO & Two Bars MC   Maj(Act)   Lt/Col(Temp)
RefScs: DHist JP DSOb 659

March 16/17

GOODWIN Leo Francis

"Led Inexperienced Men into Battle"

On the morning of the 16th, when Leo Goodwin's company commander was killed, the 38th Battalion lieutenant took charge. He had three officers with him, none of whom had anything but the barest battle experience. On hearing the beginning of a German artillery barrage, Goodwin started towards the front lines. On the way he came across a working party of 20 whom he recruited for his company. On reaching their destination, he distributed the men, most of whom had not yet fired a gun in anger, to various positions along the line. He then walked up and down the trench talking to each one to bolster their courage. The result was that in the ensuing fighting they gave a very fine account of themselves.

MC Lt
RefScs: DHist JP MCb 122

FINAL GERMAN THRUST
March 21 - June 10, 1918

At 5:00 a.m. on March 21, through a blanket of heavy white fog, 64 German divisions attacked the Allied line on a 54-mile front between St. Quentin and Arras. As part of a three-pronged drive, it aimed at splitting the British and French armies and gaining a quick victory before the American presence on the Western Front could be felt. It succeeded in advancing to within 10 miles of Amiens and reaching the Marne River 40 miles from Paris, but it failed in its objective. By the beginning of June the drive had petered out and the Allies were counterattacking all along the line. Furthermore, the Americans by this time had two million men in France, many of them in action. Though Passchendaele, so heavily fought for, and several other points had to be surrendered, the Canadian Corps sector around Lens and Vimy held firm, preventing the Germans from enlarging their northern salient.

GROUGIE
March 21

DE WIND Edmund

"Died Holding Down Post Alone while Wounded Twice"

A native of Ireland, Edmund De Wind received the Victoria Cross for his bravery the first day of the German offensive in holding down a British machine-gun post at the Race Course Redoubt near Grougie. Though he was twice wounded he maintained his position practically single-handed for seven hours until reinforcements arrived. On two occasions De Wind went over the top in the face of heavy machine-gun and rifle fire to clear out an enemy trench by killing its occupants. Back at his post he continued to repel attack after attack until, mortally wounded, he collapsed and died.

De Wind was born in Comber, County Down, and came to Canada in 1910. Joining a banking firm he lived in Toronto, Ont., Yorkton and Humboldt, Sask., and Edmonton, Alta. In 1914 he joined the 31st Canadian Battalion and from September 1915 to April 1917 served in that unit as a machine gunner on the Western Front. He was then commissioned to the 15th Battalion of the Royal Irish Rifles with which he won a posthumous VC. His name appears on the Pozières Memorial in France, and in 1948 Mount de Wind in Alberta was named in his memory.

VC   2nd Lt   Born Dec 11 1883   KIA March 21 1918
RefScs: CVC 168-9   VM 94-5

BOIS DE MOREUIL
March 30

FLOWERDEW Gordon Muriel

"Routed Two Lines of Enemy in Old-Style Cavalry Charge"

From the start of the German offensive, the Canadian Cavalry Brigade had been called upon to fight a series of rearguard actions. With the introduction of the tank and the deployment of rapid-fire machine guns, these horse-mounted skirmishes, though becoming outdated, had lost none of their élan. Such was certainly the case when the brigade was ordered to seize the Bois de Moreuil. As Gordon Flowerdew's squadron of the Lord Strathcona's Horse rounded the corner of the wood on the gallop to cut off the retreat of the enemy on the eastern side, they suddenly faced two lines of German infantry. Some 60 men formed each line and machine guns were positioned in the centre and on the flanks of both. Immediately the Germans saw the Canadian cavalrymen they opened fire. Flowerdew ordered Frederick Harvey, who had won the VC at Guyencourt the year before (see Harvey), to execute a diversionary movement with his troop. Then, with his remaining men, Flowerdew charged the German lines head-on. It was one of the last such cavalry assaults in history and one reminiscent of the Charge of the Light Brigade. Flowerdew led his horsemen through the first line, across the intervening space, then through the second line. As they slashed across the German positions the Canadians cut down the enemy with their sabres as they rode. Then they wheeled about and rode back through both lines at full tilt inflicting more casualties. But Flowerdew's squadron had also suffered heavily: 70 percent casualties in killed and wounded. The fury of the charge, however, had totally demoralized the Germans who broke and fled in disorder. Shot through both legs during the attack, Flowerdew died the next day. However, his inspired leadership and complete disregard for his own safety earned him a posthumous Victoria Cross.

Born in Billingford, England, Flowerdew emigrated to Canada in 1903 where he lived at Duck Lake, Sask. In 1914 he enlisted in the British

Gordon Flowerdew (C 3344)

Columbia Horse and later transferred to the Strathconas. Flowerdew is buried at Namps-au-Val British Cemetery near Amiens in France.

VC Lt Born Jan 2 1885 KIA March 30 1918
RefScs: CVC 96–7

Gavrelle
April 27

McKEAN George Burdon

"Captured Enemy Block in Daring Lone Attack"

While leading a raiding party in the Gavrelle Sector near Vimy Ridge, George McKean's progress was bogged down by fierce fire from hand grenades thrown from a block in the enemy trench and by fire from a machine gun behind it. Three times his party from the Royal Montreal Regiment ran out of hand grenades and three times McKean sent back to his forward line for more ammunition. But their efforts failed to dislodge the stubborn trench block. Though it was well protected by barbed-wire as well as the machine gun, McKean decided to capture it single-handedly. Running forward to the right of the block, he leaped over it head-first landing on top of a German rifleman. Then another enemy soldier rushed at him with his bayonet. McKean shot him through the body with his revolver and then killed the man lying underneath him. This action enabled his party to take command of the position. Once again McKean sent back to his front line for a fresh supply of hand grenades and, while waiting for them, engaged the enemy in hand-to-hand combat. When the grenades arrived McKean attacked a second enemy block killing two enemy soldiers, capturing four others and drove what remained of the garrison, including a machine-gun section, into a dugout. He then destroyed the dugout and its occupants. For these feats McKean was awarded the Victoria Cross.

Born in Wellington, England, McKean was in Montreal when WW1 started and there enlisted in the RMR which became a part of the 14th Canadian Infantry Battalion. In addition to the VC, McKean also won the Military Medal and the Military Cross for heroism under fire. He survived the war only to be killed by a freak accident in 1928 in a sawmill he operated. A portrait of McKean hangs in the Canadian War Museum in Ottawa.

VC MC MM   Lt   Born July 4 1888   Died Nov 28 1928
RefScs: CVC 100–1   VM 100–1

NEUVILLE-VITASSE
June 8/9

KAEBLE Joseph

"Halted Enemy Attack Shooting from the Hip"

On this night, Joseph Kaeble (see PA below) of the 22nd Canadian Infantry Battalion stood at his trench parapet post, his drum-fed Lewis machine gun shouldered at the ready. The heavy German barrage on the Canadian position at Neuville-Vitasse in the Arras sector signalled that a German attack would begin as soon as the shelling stopped. Kaeble was well and ably prepared for the enemy assault. He knew his job and he knew his weapon. He had already been decorated for courage under fire with the Military Medal, and he was a crack shot which was just as well — the Lewis gun had a short range of fire. As soon as the German artillery bombardment halted, 50 enemy infantrymen charged the position. In no time at all, except for Kaeble and one other, the rest of his section had become casualties. Kaeble jumped over the parapet to face the oncoming infantry and, holding his weapon at his hip, emptied one drum after another at them. Although wounded several times by fragments from shells and grenades, he continued to fire, stopping the German advance by his determined stand. Finally he fell back into the trench mortally wounded but still firing. While lying on his back he let off his last rounds over the parapet and, before losing consciousness, shouted to his comrades: "Tenez bon, mes vieux, ne les laissez passer, il faut les arrêter." ("Keep it up boys, don't let them through! We must stop them!") Kaeble never knew that, as a result of his brave action, the Germans were already in retreat. Nor did he ever learn that his deed had earned him the Victoria Cross.

Kaeble was born in St. Moise, P.Q. Leaving school at age 17, he worked in a lumber camp until he was old enough to join the Canadian army in 1915. He is buried in Wanquetin Communal Cemetery Extension, seven miles from Arras.

VC Cpl Born May 5 1893 KIA June 9 1918
RefScs: CVC 104–5 VM 104–5

The family name was Keable, but the spelling "Kaeble" is used in the records and has become official.

1000 DAYS

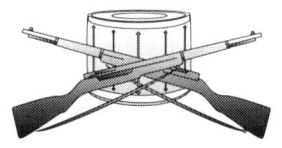

CANADA'S 100 DAYS
August 4 - November 11

By June the Allied forces had been coordinated under the leadership of Marshal Ferdinand Foch. The Americans were finally in the field in force; the British army had undergone a thorough reorganization; and tanks had been established as a major weapon. Plans were laid for one final assault to end the war. To spearhead it the Canadian Corps was placed in the vanguard. In 100 days it advanced from the Amiens salient to Mons, the site of the first major British engagement of World War 1. During that period the four Canadian divisions defeated no fewer than 47 divisions, nearly a quarter of the entire German strength.

(Overleaf) Canadian infantry begin their advance across No-Man's Land.
(C 46606)

AMIENS
August 8 - 22, 1918

*K*ey to the success of the initial assault of the Allied offensive were deception, utter secrecy and surprise. To the Germans, the Canadians' sudden appearance on the line spelled imminent attack. On August 7, the day before the launch of the campaign, part of the Corps went north to the Ypres sector. Having established a viable visibility, the contingent then moved south to join the rest of the divisions who were lurking in the Gentilles Wood near Amiens. At 4:20 a.m., without the customary artillery bombardment but supported by tanks, the Canadians charged forward on a front 8,500 yards wide. The ensuing onslaught so shattered enemy morale that chief of the Prussian staff, General Erich Ludendorff, called August 8 the "black day of the German army." By nightfall, the "shock troops," as the enemy labelled them, had advanced 14,000 yards, captured 8,000 prisoners, 100 guns and countless supplies of ammunition. By August 22 the Canadians had overcome 10 German divisions, occupied 27 towns and villages, and had penetrated a distance of 14 miles. Having fulfilled that primary function, the Corps then moved north to Arras to spearhead the battles of Cambrai and the Hindenburg Line.

AMIENS
August 8

CROAK John Bernard

"Though Wounded Led Spirited Charge against Enemy Stronghold"

On this first day of the Allied offensive, John Croak (see PA below) of the 13th Canadian Infantry Battalion became separated from his platoon east of Amiens. Encountering a German machine-gun nest, he overwhelmed it with hand grenades, captured the gun, and took the crew prisoner. Shortly afterwards he was wounded, but when his platoon ran up against another strongpoint he insisted on charging the enemy's position. The first to reach the German trench, Croak led his men in capturing three machine guns, and bayoneting the enemy and forcing the entire garrison to surrender. However, during the action Croak was again wounded, this time so severely he soon died of his wounds. For his courageous leadership, which inspired the men of his platoon, Croak was awarded the Victoria Cross.

Born in Little Bay, Nfld., Croak attended school in Glace Bay, N.S., where he later worked in the mines. He is buried in Hangar Wood British Cemetery in France.

VC   Pte   Born May 18 1892   KIA Aug 8 1918
RefScs: CVC 106–7   VM 106–7

Though he enlisted under the name "Croak" it is spelled "Croke" on his birth certificate. Most records spell it "Croak."

HANGARD WOOD

GOOD Herman James

"Busy Day for a Battling Highlander"

It was a busy day for Herman Good. A native of South Bathurst, N.B., he was in action almost from the moment the 13th Canadian Infantry Battalion surged forward in the vanguard of the Amiens offensive. His first feat was a solo affair. Near Hangard Wood, Good attacked a nest of three German machine guns all by himself, killing some of the crew and taking the rest prisoner. His next exploit he shared with three other Highlanders. Later that day, when the battle had penetrated deep into the German lines, Good discovered an artillery battery of 5.9-inch cannon that was hammering at the Canadian advance and pounding positions to the rear. To assault it with only three others from his platoon on first reflection would seem insane, but Good reckoned that the enemy gunners would not be trained in hand-to-hand combat, and even though his party would be overwhelmingly outnumbered, the position could be overcome by their experience in close-in fighting. Surprise as much as anything played a large part. Attacking at point-blank range, the Canadians forced a quick surrender from the artillery crews and captured three heavy guns. For his conspicuous bravery and determination that day, Good received the Victoria Cross.

At the time WW1 broke out, Good was engaged in lumbering operations in the Bathurst area. Following the war he became the game, fish and fire warden for the district. He died in in 1969 at age 81.

VC   Cpl   Born Nov 29 1887   Died April 18 1969
RefScs: CVC 108–9   VM 108–9

Herman Good (PA 6663)

MINER Harry Garnet Bedford

"Despite Severe Wounds Fought to the Death"

Before the Amiens offensive took place, Harry Miner had already been decorated for bravery under fire. The French had awarded him the Croix de Guerre for his actions in the Lens fighting of 1917. But his finest hour, albeit his last, was yet to come. During an attack by B Company of the 58th Canadian Infantry Battalion at Demuin east of Amiens, Miner, though severely wounded in the head and shoulder, refused to retire from the battle. Instead, he led his platoon in an assault on the middle of the German outpost trench lines. Then, when a machine gun held up the advance, he single-handedly attacked, killed all the crew and turned the weapon on the enemy. Subsequently Miner and two others overwhelmed a German grenade post, bayoneting two of the garrison and putting the rest to flight. However, during the action Miner was mortally wounded by a German stick grenade and died later in the day. For his courageous example and fearless leadership, Miner was awarded a posthumous Victoria Cross.

Born in Cedar Springs, Ont., Miner joined the Canadian army in 1915. He is buried in the Crouy British Cemetery at Crouy-sur-Somme in France.

VC CdeG(Fr)   Born June 24 1891   KIA Aug 8 1918
RefScs: CVC 122-3   VM 110-1

MÉHARICOURT

BRILLANT Jean

"Led Three Different Attacks before Succumbing to His Wounds"

Shortly after the Amiens attack got underway, the left flank of Jean Brillant's 22nd Canadian Infantry Battalion company was held up by a German machine gun at Méharicourt near Amiens. Brillant dashed forward and captured it, killing two of the enemy gunners in the process. Though wounded in the assault, he refused to leave his command. Later in the day his company was again halted by machine-gun fire. Organizing two platoons, he led a rush on the German post in which 150 men and 15 machine guns were captured. Accounting for 15 of the enemy himself, Brillant was wounded a second time but again insisted on staying at his post. He subsequently attacked a field gun that was firing at his men over open sites. After advancing 600 yards Brillant was wounded once more but continued on for another 200 yards before collapsing into unconsciousness from exhaustion and loss of blood. He died of his wounds on August 10 and was awarded a posthumous Victoria Cross for his determination and leadership under fire.

Brillant was born in Assametquaghan, P.Q., graduated from St. Joseph University N.B., and joined the Canadian Militia serving with Les Fusiliers de St. Laurent. In 1915 he enlisted for overseas service with the 189th Battalion which later merged with the 22nd in France. Brillant is buried in Villers-Bretonneux Military Cemetery at Fouilloy in France. In Montreal, Jean Brillant Avenue is named in his memory and a statue erected in his honour at Brillant Park. The Jean Brillant Branch of the Canadian Legion, Rimouski, P.Q., is also named after him.

VC   Lt   Born March 15 1890   DoW Aug 10 1918
RefScs: CVC 110-1   VM 112-3

AMIENS

BRADY Michael Lewis

"Wounded Three Times — Kept Fighting"

Michael Brady, a lieutenant with the 13th Battalion, though wounded early in the day continued to lead his men in a charge against the enemy. Then, while rushing a German machine gun by himself, he was wounded again. Still he refused to leave the field and made a fresh assault on the German positions using hand grenades which cost the enemy numerous casualties. Then Brady was wounded a third time and forced to leave the field. This heroic performance was officially cited as an "admirable . . . example to his men."

    MC Lt
    RefScs: DHist JP

AMIENS
August 8-11

TAIT James Edward

"Following Heroic Actions, Died Directing His Men in Battle"

During this period, James Tait of the 78th Canadian Infantry Battalion, who had already been awarded the Military Cross at Vimy Ridge, added further to his laurels by winning the Victoria Cross. Though the initial advance of the British offensive had been checked by intense enemy fire, Tait rallied his company forward. A concealed machine gun, however, began to cause heavy casualties. Seizing a rifle and bayonet, Tait dashed forward alone and killed the German gunner. Inspired by his example, his men rushed the position, capturing 12 machine guns and 20 prisoners, an action that cleared the way for Tait's battalion to advance. Later, when the Germans counterattacked under an intense artillery barrage, Tait was mortally wounded. Nevertheless, he continued to encourage and direct his men until he died. It was this dedicated leadership and daring that earned him a posthumous VC.

Tait was born in Kircudbrightshire, Scotland. Upon emigrating to Canada, he was employed by a government survey party in the Kettle River

James Tait (PA 6710)

District of the Canadian North-West Territories when WW1 broke out. Enlisting in Winnipeg, he went overseas in September 1916, joining the 78th Battalion in France in time for the Vimy attack. He is reported to have been buried at the Fouquescourt British Cemetery in France.

VC Lt Born May 17 1886 KIA Aug 11 1918
RefScs: CVC 116–7 VM 120–1

WARVILLERS
August 9

ZENGEL Raphael Douglas

"Efforts Helped Secure Battalion's Position"

On this second day of the Amiens assault, Raphael Zengel, an NCO with the 5th Canadian Infantry Battalion, was leading his platoon in the advance east of Warvillers when vicious German machine-gun fire

Raphael Zengel (PA 6796)

mowed down troops on his flank leaving a gaping hole in the line. Zengell ran forward on the double some 200 yards ahead of his own men, tackled the enemy gun alone, killed the gunner and the officer in charge, and dispersed the rest of the crew. Later in the day, when the battalion was held up by heavy machine-gun fire, Zengell directed his unit's fire with deadly accuracy on enemy positions. Suddenly he was knocked unconscious by an exploding shell. However, he soon came to and coolly continued to issue firing orders to harass the enemy. His efforts helped bring the day's actions to a victorious conclusion. For the confidence he inspired in his men, with total disregard for his own safety, he received the Victoria Cross. This was his second decoration. On November 11, 1917 — his 23rd birthday — his exploits during the bloody battle of Passchendaele earned him the Military Medal.

Born in Fairbault, Minn., Zengel moved to Canada at an early age. When WW1 started he was working on a farm in Virden, Man., and in December 1914 he enlisted with the 45th Canadian Infantry Battalion. On arriving in France, he was transferred to the 5th. After the war he lived in Rocky Mountain House, Alta., later moving to Errington, B.C.

VC MM   Sgt   Born Nov 11 1894
RefScs: CVC 118-9   VM 114-5

AUBRERCOURT

PYMAN Colin Keith Lee

"Aggressive Leadership Won Bar to DSO"

Colin Pyman had already won the DSO. Now, after two solid days of fighting as second-in-command of the 2nd Battalion, he was severely wounded within 50 yards of reaching the objective. Previously when his unit had become weakened due to heavy casualties, he collected new troops and after a vigorous fight placed then in the gaps in the line. He was then instrumental in capturing a German field gun and a taking a number of prisoners. On another occasion he threw out a protective flank that enabled the advance to continue. For his deeds he was awarded a Bar to his DSO but he never lived to wear it. He died of his wounds the next day.

DSO & Bar   Lt Col   DoW Aug 10 1918
RefScs: DHist JP   DSOb 86

BRERETON Alexander Picton

"Solo Attack on Enemy Machine-Gun Nest Saved His Platoon"

Alexander Brereton of the 8th Canadian Infantry Battalion found his platoon caught in open country exposed to a next of German machine guns with no way to find cover. He knew that unless some drastic action was taken the whole platoon could be wiped out. Seizing the initiative, Brereton sprang forward alone and attacked the closest enemy post. There he shot the gunner and bayoneted another soldier who tried to man the gun. His fierce attack so completely unnerved the Germans that nine of them threw up their arms up in surrender. By his single action Brereton, without any regard for his own safety, had saved his unit from total annihilation. His bravery earned him the Victoria Cross.

Brereton was born in Oak River, Man., and prior to enlisting in the Canadian army had worked on a farm. Following WW1 he returned to farming, later acquiring a large ranch of over 600 acres at Elnora, Alta. During WW2 he served as a quarter-master sergeant with an army unit at Red Deer, Alberta.

VC Cpl Sgt(WW2) Born Nov 13 1892
RefScs: CVC 112–3 VM 116–7

August 12

DINESEN Thomas

"Twice Decorated for the Same Action"

Danish-born Thomas Dinesen was awarded two medals for bravery for the same action in which he was engaged in 10 hours of desperate hand-to-hand combat. A private with D Company of the 42nd Canadian Infantry Battalion, Dinesen time and again led assaults on German positions, wielding his bayonet and using his rifle butt as a club. During the day's fighting, Dinesen charged the enemy lines five times by himself, single-handedly putting a host of machine guns out of action and accounting for 12 enemy killed with his rifle and bayonet, and with hand grenades. For his resolute grit he received both the Victoria Cross and French Croix de Guerre.

To reach the Western Front Dinesen had shown almost as much determination as he displayed once he arrived there. Born in Tungstad, and a graduate civil engineer from the Polytechnic School in Copenhagen, Dinesen tried to enlist in the British and French armies but both of them turned him down. In 1917 he went to the United States and tried to join the U.S. army with the same negative result. Finally, through the Canadian Recruiting Office in New York City, he was accepted as a private with the Black Watch (Royal Highland) Regiment of Canada. When he went overseas he was assigned to the 42nd Battalion. Following WW1 Dinesen moved to Kenya where he became a farmer and civil engineer until 1925. He then returned to Denmark to pursue a literary career from his home in Vaenger, Hilleroed.

VC CdeG(Fr) Lt   Born Aug 9 1892
RefScs: CVC 124–5   VM 122–3

PARVILLERS
August 12/13

SPALL Robert

"Gave His Life to Repel Enemy Attack"

For sacrificing himself to stem a German two-day counterattack, Robert Spall, an NCO with the Princess Patricia's Canadian Light Infantry, won a posthumous Victoria Cross. His platoon, entrenched at Parvillers, had become isolated. Spall picked up a drum-fed Lewis machine gun, climbed the trench parapet and opened fire, inflicting severe casualties on the enemy. He then returned to the trench to direct his unit's fire from a mere 75 yards' range. Later, as the counterattack persisted, Spall picked up another Lewis gun and once again climbed the parapet. This time his fire stopped the Germans in their tracks. But in the action, an enemy bullet ended his life.

Born in Suffolk County, England, Spall came to Canada with his parents when he was two years old. Just prior to the start of WW1, he worked in an office in Winnipeg. In August, 1915, he joined the 90th Winnipeg Rifles later transferring to the Princess Pats. Spall has no known grave, but his name is inscribed on the Vimy Memorial in France.

VC Sgt   Born March 5 1880   KIA Aug 13 1918
RefScs: CVC 126–7   VM 124–5

August 13/14

CANTIN Alfred Henry

"Prompt Action Saved Many Lives"

During the attack north of Parvillers this night, a German trench mortar position wiped out an entire detachment of the 7th Field Company. Alfred Cantin, in a spirited charge, led his men against the post and quickly overcame and captured it. The commendation to the DCM which he was awarded for the action was terse but accurate. It stated, "His prompt action saved many lives."

    DCM Sgt
    RefScs: DCMb 43   DHist JP

DAMERY

August 15

MEADOWS Cecil Herbert

"Led Audacious Bombing Charge"

Leading a squad of bombers through a gap in the German lines, Cecil Meadows of the 52nd Battalion successfully captured five enemy machine guns. He then cleared the way for the platoon behind to advance and was himself the first to enter the village. On realizing the objective, with another comrade Meadows kept following the Germans until they turned and took a stand. But even though he was wounded, Meadows refused to be carried from the field until night fell. Meanwhile, he was able to furnish a report of inestimable value noting enemy strength, positions and weapon dispositions.

    DCM Sgt
    RefScs: DCMb 185   DHist JP

EAST OF ARRAS
August 20-29

HILL Cecil Henry

"Constantly in the Thick of It"

During the week Cecil Hill of the 49th Battalion was in the midst of the action constantly. In one instance he led his men into the face of German machine-gun and rifle fire right up to within 500 yards of the enemy trenches into which they hurled hand grenades causing havoc and inflicting heavy casualties. For his determination and aggressiveness, Hill not only received the MC but was also credited with being responsible for the battalion reaching all its objectives.

MC Lt
RefScs: DHist JP MCb 146

BREACHING THE HINDENBURG LINE
August 22 - September 2, 1918

From the Arras front, the Canadians were again placed in the vanguard of a renewed British assault, this time against the formidable Hindenburg Line. Key to success was the capture of the Drocourt-Quéant Switch Line which joined with the other German trench lines. The attack, which began on August 26, was successful from the start. Among the towns falling to the Canadians were Monchy-le-Preux and Bapaume. By September 1, the "Switch"* had been reached and by noon was in Canadian hands. The advance had gained them three miles and the capture of 8,000 prisoners as well as a horde of guns of all types. Two days later the Corps had reached the heavily fortified Canal du Nord Line. The Allies had finally achieved a breakthrough. With their defences broken the Germans were in full retreat. Victory was not far off.

---

*With Teutonic efficiency the German trenches were interlocked, and in addition to telephones, lights, store-rooms and other facilities, they also had a mini-rail system as a means of transporting ammunition, shells, supplies and even troops. Thus evolved such terms as "Switch Line" and "Spur Line."

Monchy-le-Preux
August 26

Rutherford Charles Smith

"Captured 70 German Prisoners in a Single Day"

Charles Rutherford had already won the Military Medal at Passchendaele as well as the Military Cross at Parvillers during the Battle of Amiens. Then, at the start of the Hindenburg Line offensive, he added the Victoria Cross to his row of ribbons when he single-handedly took 45 Germans prisoner. An officer with the 5th Canadian Mounted Rifles,

Charles Rutherford (PA 53784)

Rutherford was well ahead of his troops during the advance on Monchy-le-Preux when he came upon a fully armed party of enemy soldiers outside a machine-gun pillbox. Coolly drawing his revolver, he marched forward and told them they were surrounded. His bluff worked; the 45 Germans, which included two officers and three machine-gun crews, promptly surrendered to him. Rutherford then ordered them to halt the gun fire from another pillbox. They quickly complied, allowing his men to advance and take charge of his prisoners. Later, when Rutherford saw one of his assault parties pinned down by heavy machine-gun fire, he led an attack on the emplacement capturing another 35 prisoners. That Monchy-le-Preux fell that afternoon was largely due to Rutherford's quick thinking, daring and leadership.

Born in Haldimand Township near Colborne, Ont., he worked on the family farm there until enlisting in the army in 1916, later transferring to the 5th CMR. After the war he became a charter member of the Lieutenant Charles Rutherford VC Branch of the Royal Canadian Legion serving as its president. In 1939 he was made postmaster of Colborne; then, with the start of WW2, he joined the Veterans Guard of Canada which supervised German prisoners. Rutherford also served as Guard to the Duke of Windsor in the Bahamas. After the war ended he returned to the post office in Colborne, then opened a dry-goods store in Keswick, Ont. He retired in 1978 and returned to Colborne. In 1989, at age 97, Rutherford died at the Rideau Veterans Home in Ottawa. At the time of his death he was the only surviving Canadian VC WW1 recipient.

VC MM MC   Lt   Born Jan 9 1892   Died June 11 1989
RefScs: CL J/A 89   CVC 128-9   VM 126-7

Rutherford was known for his innate modesty which at times seemed stretched to the extreme. His granddaughter, Mary Ellen Cain, said: "He never talked about his war experiences unless he was asked. Except for Remembrance Day and special occasions, he kept the Victoria Cross in a dresser drawer with his socks."

INGLES Charles James

"Wounded in the Arm — Remained in Command of His Men"

During the morning, Charles Ingles was wounded in the the arm while leading his company forward through heavy German artillery and machine-gun fire. Twice he organized parties to clear out enemy machine-gun nests. Despite his injury, he insisted on staying at his post through the afternoon and night, and during that time commanded defences of the company's portion of the line against counterattack. "His example," the citation to his DSO read, "was an inspiration to his men."

DSO   Maj
RefScs: DHist JP   DSOb 47

August 26/27

COCKERAM Alan

"Wounded Twice, Led Platoon in Daring Raids and Counterattack"

As Alan Cockeram's platoon came within sight of its objective, it was suddenly met with wicked German machine-gun crossfire. Taking two of his men with him, Cockerman rushed forward, personally annihilating the enemy gun crew. He then noticed a booby-trap that had been attached to the gun. Pulling it off, he heaved it backwards whereupon it exploded on impact with the ground. He then took possession of the gun. During this operation he was wounded by enemy fire but continued to lead his unit. Later in the day, on a reconnaissance with two of his NCOs, he ran into a German squad, all of whom were killed by the trio. Next morning the enemy counterattacked in force. Cockram led his platoon into the open, engaging in bitter hand-to-hand fighting, during which he personally accounted for numerous Germans killed. He was again wounded, this time severely. But his "marked fearlessness" resulted in the attack being repulsed.

Following the war he was engaged in the mining business and also served as Conservative Member of Parliament for York South, Toronto.

DSO   Lt   Died Sept 10 1957
RefScs: DHist JP   DSOb 47

EAST OF ARRAS
August 26-28

AFFLECK John Ernest

"Won Bar to MC for Courageous Work with Wounded"

Earlier at the front, John Affleck of the 9th Field Ambulance was awarded the MC for rescuing a wounded officer while exposed to enemy fire, an action which saved the man's life. During these first two days of the Hindenburg Line battles, he won a Bar to his decoration for his level-headed, energetic efforts in attending the wounded. On several occasions he had to bring his stretcher-bearers close to the German trenches to dress the injured and carry them back to safety.

MC & Bar   Capt
RefScs: DHist Jp   MCb 37

BRIGGS John Alfred

"Blown Off His Feet — Carried On"

John Briggs of the 10th Field Ambulance was another medical officer who defied harassment from German shelling and gun fire to take care of the wounded. In fact, he was blown off his feet by an exploding shell and badly bruised. That didn't stop him; he kept right on with his work, attending to injuries and supervising the stretcher-bearing.

MC   Maj(Act)
RefScs: DHist JP   MCb 37

SOUTH OF THE SCARPE

EWING Royal Lindsay

"Leadership Captured the Jigsaw Wood"

During an operation south of the Scarpe which resulted in the capture of the Jigsaw Wood, Royal Ewing's "initiative and absolute disregard for personal danger" earned him a Bar to the DSO. As commander of the 42nd Battalion, his leadership and gallantry under fire ensured the attainment of the objective on which rested the success of the entire brigade.

DSO & Bar MC Maj
RefScs: DHist JP   DSOb 33

NEUVILLE-VITASSE, HARCOURT, CHÉRISY
August 26-29

ELLIOTT Onvil Ard

"Dogged Determination Saved Lives"

As the infantry advanced, Onvil Elliott of the 5th Field Ambulance followed closely with his men to render medical assistance where needed. Frequently he had to pass through heavy German artillery barrages. However, he stayed in touch with his battalion establishing collecting posts as far forward as possible. His dogged determination and untiring efforts were responsible for saving countless lives. For his actions he was awarded the DSO. Some weeks later he won a Bar to the decoration for rescuing two wounded men under fire.

DSO & Bar Maj
RefScs: DHist JP   DSOb 32

VALERY RIDGE
August 27/28

HANSON Harold Stewart

"Won DSO for Persistence"

Harold Hanson of the 43rd Battalion had earlier been awarded the MC. In an action at Valery Ridge he won the DSO for his persistence. In the capture of the village his company seized four German field guns, but the cost was high. That night, with only 30 men left, Hanson had to beat off five enemy attacks. Next day he led his men, now only eight in number, in the capture of a bridge. Though enemy resistence was stubborn, he managed to hold onto it until relieved by fresh forces.

DSO MC Capt(Act)
RefScs: DHist JP DSOb 41

CHÉRISY
August 28

VANIER Georges-Phileas

"Future Governor-General Lost Leg in Capture of Town"

On the afternoon of August 27, 1918, Georges Vanier was given command of the 22nd Battalion. The following day, at half-past twelve, he led a charge on the village of Chérisy. The town was captured by the Canadians but in the battle Vanier suffered broken ribs, and his right knee was so badly shattered the leg had to be amputated. Vanier had already won the MC and Bar, had been given the French Legion of Honour as well as being mentioned in despatches for bravery in battle.

On January 11, 1919, he was officially gazetted with the DSO. In part the citation read: "For conspicuous gallantry and devotion to duty . . . this officer took charge of the battalion and led it with great skill to the attack and capture of a large village."

Born in Montreal, Vanier attended Loyal and Laval colleges and was called to the Quebec Bar in 1911. He enlisted in the army in 1915, and after WW1 became founding officer of the "Van Doos" — the Royal 22nd Regiment. Later he entered the diplomatic service and represented Canada at the League of Nations in London. When World War 2 broke out he was serving as Canadian minister to France and in 1943 was appointed minister to all governments in exile in London. Vanier returned to France in 1944 as Canadian ambassador and served in that capacity until his retirement in 1953. In 1959 he was installed as Governor-General, a post he held until his death in 1967 in Ottawa, at age 78.

DSO MC & Bar MiD Legion deH (Fr) Maj Born April 23 1888 Died March 3 1967
RefScs: CE 1894 DHist Bio JP DSOb 107 V 49-82

Georges-Phileas Vanier (C 63530)

Fresnes-Rouvroy Line
August 28

Clarke-Kennedy William Hew

"Though Wounded and Bleeding Stayed in Shell-Hole to Direct His Battalion"

On the second day of the attack on the German Fresnes-Rouvroy Line, "CK" Clark-Kennedy, in command of the 27th Canadian Infantry Battalion, was badly wounded in the leg. Though bleeding profusely

William Clarke-Kennedy (PA 3909)

and in intense pain, the Boer War veteran who on August 27 had led the initial charge on the enemy trenches, refused to be evacuated from the battlefield. Using a shell-hole as his command post, he continued to direct his men until, realizing his exhausted troops could advance no further, he established a strong defence line. This not only saved countless lives but made it possible for the fresh troops to resume the forward attack. For his valiant action Clarke-Kennedy, who already wore the Distinguished Service Order, the Croix de Guerre and had been mentioned in despatches four times, received the Victoria Cross.

A native of Dinsky, Scotland, Clarke-Kennedy served in the South African War with the Imperial Yeomanry and the Rhodesian Horse. In 1902 he was transferred by the Scottish life insurance company he worked for to its Canadian office in Montreal. When WW1 broke out in 1914, he enlisted in the Royal Highlanders of Canada. Clarke-Kennedy returned to the insurance business after the war, retiring in 1945. He died in Montreal in 1961 at age 81.

VC DSO CdeG(Fr)   Lt/Col   Born March 3 1880   Died Oct 25 1961
RefScs: CVC 138-9   VM 128-9

HENDECOURT
August 31

MILNE James

"Fierce Defence Caused Complete Enemy Route"

When all of the officers of his company had become casualties, James Milne of the 2nd Battalion was left in charge. The Germans began an attack on his positions near Hendecourt. Milne read the situation so perfectly and led his men so fiercely that the attacking force was completely routed. He was later commended for his coolness and ability which "inspired his men with great confidence in a critical situation."

MC   Lt (Temp)
RefScs: DHist JP

Vitry-en-Artois
September 1/2

Nunney Claude Joseph Patrick

"Inspired His Comrades by His Own Fearless Example"

Claude Nunney had already been decorated twice, once at Vimy Ridge in April 1917 and again in an action at Avion the same year, when he won the Victoria Cross during the attack on the Drocourt-Quéant Switch Line. On September 1 and 2, 1918, in the vicinity of Vitry-en-Artois, when the Germans laid down a heavy artillery barrage and counterattacked, Nunney, a private with the Canadian 38th Infantry Battalion, left his post at company headquarters to scramble forward through the bombardment. Running from one outpost to another he encourage his men by his own fearless example. It no doubt helped to save a critical situation. The enemy counterattack was repulsed and the Canadians resumed their advance. During the assault Nunney, though by then severely wounded, continued to display the same initiative urging his comrades forward. He died from his wounds 16 days later on September 18.

Born in Hastings, England, Nunney emigrated to Canada where he lived near Cornwall, Ont. When the war started he enlisted in the army. He is buried at the Aubigny Communal Cemetery Extension in France.

VC DCM MM   Pte   Born Dec 24 1891   DoW Sept 16 1918
RefScs: CVC 141-1   VM 129-30

Nunney's medals are on display at the Cornwall Armoury.

Drocourt
September 2

Bradfield Reginald Henderson

"Won DSO for Determined Leadership"

Reginald Bradfield of the 75th Infantry Battalion had already been awarded the MC. On this date, for his "determined courage and leadership" in an attack against the Germans near the Drocourt-Quéant

Switch Line, he received the DSO. Leading his men through heavy enemy fire over 500 yards of open ground, they overcame a German stronghold, took 150 prisoners and captured 18 machine guns. Bradfield then led what remained of his company forward and established a position in a captured trench. From there the unit was able to bring heavy fire to bear on a German trench.

DSO MC   Lt
RefScs: DHist JP   DSOb 12

ARRAS

METCALF William Henry

"Directed Tank Charge in Face of 17 Machine Guns and Bomb Clusters"

When a tank attack was held up at Arras on September 2, 1918, William Metcalf of the 18th Canadian Infantry Battalion raced in front of the vehicle and directed it with flags. All the while 17 German machine guns were trained on the tank and the enemy also bombarded it with clusters of explosives. The battalion historian later wrote in amazement: "How Metcalf escaped being shot to pieces has always been a wonder to me." Metcalf was wounded, however, but continued to lead the way for the tank crew until he was ordered to take refuge in a shell-hole where he had his wounds dressed. His bravery should have come as no surprise; he had already been awarded the Military Medal for gallantry on the Somme in October 1918. For his extraordinary feat during the Battle of Arras, he received the Victoria Cross.

An American born in Waite Township, Maine, Metcalf joined the Canadian army shortly after the start of WW1. Following the war he returned to the U.S. He died in Lewiston, Maine, in 1968.

VC L/Cpl   Born Jan 29 1885   Died Aug 8 1968
RefScs: CVC 132–3   VM 134–5

DROCOURT-QUÉANT SWITCH LINE

BROWN Percy Wells

"Awarded MC for 'Splendid Work'"

During the attack on the Drocourt-Quéant Switch Line, Percy Brown's company captured its position but shortly afterwards the company commander was killed. The 50th Battalion captain quickly took over and under heavy artillery fire reorganized the unit. But then Brown was temporarily incapacitated when he was struck by shrapnel. Though wounded, he recovered sufficiently to lead his men forward, capturing a number of machine-gun works along with 250 German prisoners. Once again Brown led his men in an advance under extremely heavy enemy shelling, taking all objectives before he led the company back to its captured position. The citation to his MC stated laconically: "He did splendid work."

MC   Capt(Act)
RefScs: DHist JP   MCb 39

VILLERS-LEZ-CAGNICOURT

KNIGHT Arthur George

"Led Three Individual Charges Alone"

During his three years on the Western Front, Arthur Knight of the 10th Canadian Infantry Battalion became known for his individual prowess as a combat soldier. During the Battle of Passchendaele in November, 1917, he was awarded the Croix de Guerre. On September 2, 1918, he was leading an attack on the German trenches at Villers-lez-Cagnicourt when his section was slowed down by a wall of enemy fire. Knight dashed forward alone, bayoneting several German machine gunners and mortar crews, and forced the remainder to flee in confusion. He then brought up a Lewis machine gun which he fired at the retreating enemy, causing heavy casualties. As his platoon advanced Knight noticed some 30 German infantry trying to escape into a tunnel running off the trench. Once again, all by himself, he ran ahead killing an officer and two NCOs, and captured 20 others. Later he once more single-handedly routed another party of Germans trying to hold up his section's advance. Knight was soon fatally wounded and died the next day. For his heroic actions he was awarded a posthumous Victoria Cross.

Born in Sussex, England, Knight emigrated to Canada in 1911 and worked as a carpenter in Regina. When WW1 broke out he joined the army and served overseas at the front from 1915 until he was fatally wounded. He is buried in Dominion Cemetery at Hendecourt-lez-Cagnicourt in France. Knight and Sussex Crescents at Coventry Place in Regina are named in his honour.

VC CdeG(Fr) Sgt   Born June 28 1886   DoW Sept 3 1918
RefScs: CVC 130-1   VM 132-3

PECK Cyrus Wesley

"Received VC for Phenomenal Leadership under Fire"

Here at Villers-lez-Cagnicourt also, Cyrus Peck, lieutenant-colonel of the 18th Canadian Infantry Battalion, won the Victoria Cross for bravery and leadership under intense enemy fire. On September 2, 1918, when his unit ran up against heavy German resistance, Peck personally reconnoitered the area in the face of a fierce fusillade of bullets from German machine gunners and snipers. Returning to his battalion, he reorganized it, arranged to cover his flanks, and moved forward. Then, under a thundering enemy artillery barrage and murderous machine-gun fire, he intercepted the supporting British tanks, and from his own knowledge of the situation, steered them in the proper direction enabling them to reach their objective. He thus also paved the way for his own battalion to move ahead. Of the feat the battalion historian recorded: "I do not know how the Colonel escaped being riddled by bullets." But Peck led a charmed life. In addition to the VC, during WW1 he was awarded the Distinguished Service Order and was mentioned in despatches five times.

Born in Hopewill Hill, N.B., Peck moved to Skeena, B.C., where he became a broker representing salmon canning, saw mill and towing interests before joining the army. After the war he became Member of Parliament for Skeena and later sat for the Islands in the B.C. Legislature. He also served as Aide-de-Camp to two Canadian governors-general. Peck died in Sydney on Vancouver Island in 1956 at age 85.

VC DSO MID(5) Lt/Col Born April 26 1871   Died Sept 27 1956
RefScs: CVC 134-5   VM 136-7

East of Arras

GRAHAM Edwin Ernest

"Gallant Padre Succoured Wounded and Dying under Fire"

From the day the battle started Edwin Ernest Graham, a chaplain with the 13th Infantry Battalion, had made himself conspicuous for going out in broad daylight despite the danger from enemy fire to help carry back the wounded, as well as to succour the injured or dying, no matter how deep in No-Man's Land. During the attack on the Drocourt-Quéant Switch Line he was constantly in the most forward areas, exposing himself to the risk of enemy machine-gun fire and shelling. It was largely due to his efforts that so many of the wounded were successfully evacuated.

DSO   Capt
RefScs: DHist JP   DSOb 39

HUTCHESON Bellenden Seymour

"Tended the Wounded on the Battlefield"

Bellenden Hutcheson was an American doctor who joined the Canadian Medical Corps when WW1 started. He had already been decorated with the Military Cross for his services under fire before winning the Victoria Cross on September 2, 1916, during the attack on the Drocourt-Quéant Switch Line. Attached to the 75th Canadian Infantry Battalion, during the attack and while under the most intense fire from artillery, machine guns and mortars, Hutcheson coolly stayed on the battlefield to dress the wounded until they had all been attended to. Then, after bandaging a seriously wounded officer, with the help of some German prisoners he evacuated the officer to safety running the gamut of enemy bullets. Immediately afterwards he rushed back under a hail of rifle and shell-fire, and in full view of the Germans, to tend to an NCO who had been badly hit.

A native of Mount Carmel, Illinois, Hutcheson was a graduate of the Northwestern Medical School. Following the war he joined the staff of St. Mary's Hospital in Cairo, Illinois. He died in 1954 at age 70.

VC MC Capt   Born Dec 16 1883   Died April 9 1954
RefScs: CVC 142–3   VM 138–9

DURY-ARRAS

YOUNG John Francis

"Stretcher-Bearer Risked His Neck to Save Wounded"

During an attack on an enemy-held ridge in the Dury-Arras sector, D Company of the 87th Canadian Infantry Battalion (Canadian Grenadier Guards) sustained heavy casualties. Despite a complete absence of cover and in open fire-swept ground, stretcher-bearer John Young disregarded the danger to tend to the wounded. When he ran out of bandages and dressings, he risked intense German gun fire to race back to headquarters to replenish his supplies. It took him an hour to perform his ministrations but in spite of the exposure he stayed with the wounded. Later, when the Canadians had reached their objective and the fire had abated, Young organized rescue parties to bring in the men he had tended. For his valour Young received the Victoria Cross.

Born in Kiddermaster, England, he moved to Canada where he worked for a tobacco company in Montreal before the outbreak of the war. After the war he returned to his job but some years later developed tuberculosis. After a lengthy period in hospital in St. Agathe, P.Q., he died in 1929.

VC   Pte   Born Jan 14 1893   Died Nov 7 1929
RefScs: CVC 146–7   VM 140–1

DURY
September 2-4

BLAIR Harold John

"Quick-Thinking under Fire Won Him a Decoration"

In command of the right flank support company, Harold Blair was responsible for the capture and consolidation of the town of Dury, all the while under heavy enemy shelling. When the Germans counter-attacked, Blair successfully led a mopping-up operation of those enemy who were able to infiltrate the village. In the skirmish that followed, 20 Germans were killed and the remainder taken prisoner. Blair was officially praised for his decisiveness and quick thinking under fire.

MC   Capt
RefScs: DHist JP   MCb 31

Canal du Nord

BLACKSTOCK George Grant

"Personally Led Reconnaissance Patrols"

During the attack on the canal, George Blackstock, in command of the 4th Infantry Battalion, was constantly in the forefront of the battle directing as well as leading his men on reconnaissance patrols. By his example he was an inspiration to all those about him. And due to those efforts Blackstock was able take suitable actions throughout the advance.

DSO   Maj
RefScs: DHist JP   DSOb 9

September 4

TORRANCE Harvie James

"Took Out Patrols under Heavy Fire to Determine Enemy's Position"

Harvie Torrance had already been wounded twice, once in 1915 and again in 1917. But between times he'd also managed to win the MM. Now, as a lieutenant with the Western Ontario Regiment, he was about to receive the MC for his part in the fighting along the canal. At one point during the battle the situation on his flank had become obscure. But despite heavy artillery shelling and vicious machine-gun fire all around, Torrance took out a patrol to ascertain the position of the German advance troops. While doing so he sent back invaluable reports allowing suitable action be taken and his regiment's advance to continue. His conduct under fire was described as nothing short of "conspicuous."

MC MM   Lt
RefScs: DHist JP

EAST OF ARRAS
September 4/5

RAYFIELD Walter Leigh

"Cited for Gallantry on Three Occasions in Same Battle"

During the fighting east of Arras on these two days, Walter Rayfield, a corporal serving with the Canadian 7th Infantry Battalion, earned the Victoria Cross for myriad acts of bravery. In the first instance, ad-

Walter Rayfield (PA 60586)

vancing ahead of his company, he rushed a heavily occupied German trench, bayoneting two of the enemy and taking 10 prisoners. On another occasion Rayfield, under constant rifle fire, located an enemy sniper who was causing heavy casualties to his company. Rushing the section of the trench from which the German sniper had been shooting, he so demoralized the Germans with his coolness and daring that he added 30 more prisoners to his collection. Later he left his cover and under heavy enemy machine-gun fire rescued a badly wounded comrade from No-Man's Land.

Born in Richmond-on-Thames in England, Rayfield attended school in London before coming to Canada where he went into the real estate business in Vancouver. When WW1 started he joined the 7th Battalion (British Columbia Regiment). Besides winning the VC he was also awarded the Royal Order of the Crown of Belgium. On his return from overseas Rayfield spent some time in hospital before turning to farming as a means of improving his health. He eventually moved to Toronto and for some time he was sergeant-at-arms in the Provincial Legislature. He later joined the staff of the Toronto Jail of which he became governor. He also served as an officer in the Queen's York Rangers. Rayfield died in 1949 and, at his own request, was buried in the Soldier's Plot of Prospect Cemetery in Toronto,

VC ROCB Cpl   Born Oct 7 1881   Died Feb 19 1949
RefScs: CVC 144–5   VM 142–3

COLLAPSE AT CAMBRAI
September 27 - October 9, 1918

*P*ositioned along the Canal du Nord, the Canadians' job was to protect the left flank of the British 3rd Army with the initial objective of seizing the high ground dominating the Sensée Valley, and capturing the Bourlon Wood. Preceded by a thunderous artillery barrage and supported by British tanks, the First and Fourth Divisions attacked at 5:20 a.m. September 27. The Canadians' rapid advance stunned the Germans. By 9:00 a.m. they had reached the outskirts of the wood and by 1 p.m. were in full possession of it.

Five days later they had reached the heights overlooking Cambrai from the west. The attack on the textile town began at 4:30 a.m. on October 8, and before dawn the next morning the Canadians were pushing into the outskirts. By noon Cambrai was in their hands. That was the last major engagement of WW1 for the Canadians; the Germans were collapsing in all sectors and retreating. Since the start of the final offensive on August 28, the Dominion forces had taken 18,585 German prisoners and had captured 371 heavy guns along with 1,923 machine guns and trench mortars. More than 116 square miles of French soil had been overrun and 54 towns and villages liberated. But the sacrifice had not been cheap. Canadian casualties for the period totalled 31,806 killed, missing and wounded.

MARQUION
September 27

APPLEBY Edgar

"Led Heroic Charge across the Canal"

During the assault across the Canal du Nord, the job of Edgar Appleby's company of the 13th Infantry Battalion was to capture the town of Marquion. All his other officers and many other ranks had become casualties almost from the outset. Appleby himself was wounded, though only slightly, and certainly not enough to prevent him from leading his men in attack that so effectively broke the German resistance he was able to stabilize a line several hundred yards beyond the village. For the feat Appleby was awarded the MC, a fine complement to the MM he had won earlier in the year when in the ranks.

MC MM Lt
RefScs: DHist JP MCb 11

BOURLON WOOD

KERR George Fraser

"Lone Escapade Netted Four Machine Guns, 31 Prisoners"

By all rights "Bobbie" Kerr should have been in sick bay. With a badly injured arm, the cheery lieutenant with the 3rd Canadian Infantry Battalion was really in no condition to take part in the attack across the Canal du Nord against the Bourlon Wood. But Kerr, who had earlier been awarded the Military Cross and Bar, was not one to let a mere bullet wound stand in the way of battle. Well ahead of the left support company he commanded, Kerr suddenly encountered a German redoubt on the outskirts of the small village of Raillencourt. Close to the Arras-Cambrai Road, it threatened to impede the advance. With total disregard for his own safety, Kerr rushed the position capturing four machine guns and taking 31 enemy soldiers prisoner. Kerr won the Victoria Cross for his exploit.

Born in Deseronto, Ont., following the war Kerr went into business in Toronto. He lost his life in a freak accident when he was overcome by carbon-dioxide fumes while starting his car. His funeral at Mount Pleasant Cemetery was attended by six other VC holders: Barron, Geary, Holmes, Robson, Rutherford and Shankin.

VC MC & Bar   Lt   Born June 8 1894   KA Dec 8 1929
RefScs: CVC 150-1   TS May 25/91   VM 144-5

LYALL Graham Thomson

"Captured 183 Prisoners, 26 Machine Guns, One Field Gun in Two Days"

During the Battle of Bourlon Wood and its aftermath, Thomson Lyall set an all-time Canadian record for numbers of enemy soldiers and equipment captured. On the first day of the assault, while leading his platoon, they overran a German strongpoint with a flanking movement, taking 13 German prisoners and capturing a field gun along with four machine guns. Later, though his unit was weakened by heavy casualties, Lyall led what remained of the platoon up to an enemy redoubt, then springing forward alone, killed the officer in charge, took another 45 German prisoners and netted five more machine guns. On October 1, in the neighbourhood of Blécourt, he captured another German defence position which yielded 80 prisoners and 17 machine guns. For this exploit and his earlier feat at Bourlon Wood, Lyall received the Victoria Cross.

A native of Manchester, England, Lyall emigrated to Canada before the start of WW1. When hostilities started he joined the army. Following the war Lyall returned to Great Britain, and when WW2 broke out, he joined the British army. He was killed at Mersa Matruh in Egypt in 1941.

VC   Lt   Born March 8 1892   KIA Nov 28 1941
RefScs: CVC 152-3   VM 146-7

BUISSY AND HAYNECOURT

ANDERSON Sedley Cantrell

"Brought Up Ammo under Heavy Fire"

During the Canal du Nord crossing, artilleryman Sedley Anderson of the 3rd Battery, 3rd Brigade, Canadian Field Artillery, brought up ammunition to the guns under heavy enemy fire, and by his efforts prevented many casualties. Later, near Haynecourt, he conducted a highly dangerous and difficult reconnaissance for his forward section. Anderson was praised for his "Marked . . . conduct and ability."

MC Lt
RefScs: DHist JP MCb 4

HONEY Samuel Lewis

"Former School Teacher Distinguished Himself in Bourlon Wood Battle"

One of the heroes of the Bourlon Wood battle was a former school teacher. Samuel Honey, an officer with the 78th Canadian Infantry Battalion, so distinguished himself during the fighting that he was awarded the Victoria Cross. That was for his bravery in battle, but his teaching qualities were not overlooked either. Shortly after joining the Canadian army he was made an instructor of physical training and bayonet fighting in England. In August, 1916, he was sent to France where, in January, 1917, he won the Military Medal. Then at Vimy Ridge in April he was decorated again, this time with the Distinguished Conduct Medal. Following a stint at the Officers' Training School back in Britain, Honey rejoined his unit as a lieutenant on the Western Front. At the outset of the attack on Bourlon Wood, his company commander and all other officers in the unit quickly became casualties. Honey unhesitatingly took command and continued the advance. Then, when machine-gun fire began cutting down many of his men, he charged the German nest single-handedly, captured the guns and took 10 prisoners. Later he repelled four enemy counterattacks. After dark he went out alone and located a German outpost. He led an attack to capture it and seized three guns.

Samuel Honey (C 33052)

Two days later, while again leading his company against a German strongpoint, he was severely wounded. Next day he died from his injuries. He was buried at the Quéant Cemetery in France.

VC DCM MM   Lt Born Feb 9 1894   DoW Sept 30 1918
RefScs: CVC 148-9   VM 148-9

CANAL DU NORD

AITCHISON John Miller

"Overcame Potential Annihilation from the Rear"

After the canal had been crossed, John Aitchison of the 4th Infantry Battalion noticed that a large German dugout near the waterway had been completely overlooked. About 20 of the enemy began pouring out of the redoubt and were preparing to set up their machine guns into position to fire on the Canadian attackers from the rear. Aitchison shouted to his men to about-face and even though badly wounded led a charge and continued to give orders until all German resistance was overcome.

MC Lt
RefScs: DHist JP   MCb 3

NEAR BOURLON
September 27/28

LIVINGSTONE Andrew

"Worked All Night despite German Shells, Got the Ammo Through"

During the night, the 36th Battalion of the 9th Brigade, Canadian Field Artillery, came under heavy German shelling. Andrew Livingstone was in charge of a supply column delivering ammunition to the battery. This was essential for artillery support for an all-out attack the next morning. Despite the ever-present danger from shrapnel, Livingstone got his cargo through.

MC Lt
RefScs: DHist JP MCb 185

EAST OF CANAL DU NORD
September 27-29

APPERSON James McKee

"Platoon Commander Exhibited Daring in Three-Day Attack"

For three days during the attack east of the canal, James Apperson of the 8th Infantry Battalion led his platoon with such "great skill and gallantry" that he was awarded the MC. On the night of the 27th he ventured out on a reconnaissance bringing back information of inestimable value in launching the forthcoming assault. Later, when the attacking battalion became severely handicapped by German machine-gun fire, he led his unit forward to provide support in spite of the intense enemy resistance.

MC Lt
RefScs: DHist JP MCb 11

INCHY-EN-ARTOIS

BAKER Edwin Godfrey Phipps

"Commended for Leadership Skills"

During the battle at Inchy-en-Artois, Edwin Baker commanded the 47th Infantry Battalion and during particular heavy fighting demonstrated his capacity as a born leader. In particular, on the night of the 28th, when the situation appeared to be getting out of hand, he maneuvered his unit so competently that not only was the position restored to order, but following an attack on the German defences this portion of the Canadian line was consolidated well in advance of the area previously held. For his stewardship skills displayed during this period, Baker received the DSO.

DSO Maj
RefScs: DHist JP DSOb 15

BOURLON WOOD AND BLÉCOURT
September 27/28 and October 1

DUNLOP William Waugh

"Personal Reconnaissance Allowed for Tactical Troop Dispositions"

On the 27th, upon learning that the commanding officer and adjutant had both been wounded, William Dunlop rushed forward to assist the officer placed in charge. That night he also engaged in a reconnaissance which greatly assisted in establishing the tactical disposition of troops the following day. On the morning of October 1, near Blécourt, Dunlop again made a personal reconnaissance of German positions. And again it was due to his efforts that the Canadian companies were able to take up strong defensive posts after attaining their objectives.

MC Lt
RefScs: DHist JP MCb 93

BEFORE CAMBRAI
September 27-October 1

CARMICHAEL Dougall

"Bemedalled Commander Added to His Laurels"

To the men under his command, not to mention his superiors, Dougall Carmichael appeared impervious to danger and fear. Already wearing the DSO as well as the MC and Bar, the period from September 27 to October 1 was no exception. On the 28th he was in command of the 58th Infantry Battalion when it captured the western portion of the village of St. Olle. Next day he led the unit in an attack that cleared the rest of the hamlet. Some days afterwards, while commanding his battalion he was badly wounded in the face, but he stayed to continue leading his men to press on to capture Ramilies, the final objective. For these exploits and his exhibition of bravery, to Carmichael's string of decorations was added a Bar to the DSO.

DSO & Bar, MC & Bar   Maj
RefScs: DHist JP

NEAR CAMBRAI
September 28

GREGG Milton Fowler

"VC Winner Wounded Five Times under Fire"

Milt Gregg won the VC while wounded on three different occasions. Prior to September 28, he had also been previously wounded in battle twice and had already earned two medals for bravery. Born in Mountain Dale, N.B., Gregg was one of Canada's most distinguished educational, political and diplomatic figures as well as an outstanding soldier. A graduate of Acadia and Dalhousie universities, he taught school before joining the Black Watch in September 1914. As a stretcher-bearer on the Western Front, Gregg was wounded twice before receiving his officer's commission and transferring to The Royal Canadian Regiment. He won his first decoration in battle, the Military Cross, at Lens in 1917. Then, in August 1918, during the Second Battle of Arras, he was awarded a Bar to the medal. On September 28, near Cambrai, the advance of Gregg's brigade was held up by the pounding of a German artillery barrage, and by thick, uncut barbed-war defences. Gregg crawled forward and found a small gap in the entanglement through which he led his men in a charge on the Marcoing Line. With the use of Mills hand grenades he made a deadly attack on the German strongpoint, overcame the enemy machine-gun crews, took 48 prisoners, and captured half of the line. However, by this time the Canadians had run out of bombs and now the Germans began counterattacking in force. Though wounded at this point, Gregg returned to his lines alone to acquire a fresh supply of bombs then, through heavy gun fire and despite being wounded a second time, rejoined the unit. Two days later, despite his wounds, he led his men in another attack until he was so severely wounded again

Milton Gregg (PA 4877)

he had to be evacuated from the field. It was for these feats that Gregg received the VC.

Following WW1 he worked for the Soldiers Settlement Board and the *Halifax Herald*. From 1934–39 he was sergeant-at-arms of the House of Commons in Ottawa. During WW2 he served overseas as second-in-command of the RCRs and later as CO of the West Nova Scotia Regiment. He then became commandant of officers' training schools at Vernon, B.C., Brockville, Ont., and Sussex, N.B. After the war he was made president of the University of New Brunswick. In 1947 Gregg was elected MP and served as Minister of Fisheries (1947–48), Veterans Affairs (1948–50) and Labour (1950–57). In 1958 he was made the Canadian United Nations representative in Iraq and in 1960 of UNICEF in Indonesia. In 1963 and 1964 he served as the Canadian representative to the UN, then as Canadian Commissioner and High Commissioner to British Guiana and Guyana. In 1968 he was made president of the Canadian Council for International Co-operation. He received the Order of Canada. Gregg died in 1978 at Fredericton, N.B. at age 85.

VC MC & Bar   Lt   Br/G(WW2)   Born April 10 1892   Died March 13 1978
RefScs: CF 938   CVC 154-5   VM 150-1

Raillencourt

Sharpe Henry Arthur

"Killed 80 Germans in Defensive Action"

When the 50th Infantry Battalion was held up by German resistance in front of the Marcoing Line due to heavy machine-gun fire and barbed-wire entanglements, Henry Sharpe led his platoon to a position where he could direct his fire along the entire length of the enemy trench. In this way he killed 80 of the defending Germans and forced the rest to retreat. This allowed two battalions, including his own, to proceed forward. For his prompt action which turned a grim stalemate into a successful advance, Sharpe was awarded the MC to add to the MM he had won earlier while in the ranks.

MC MM   Lt
RefScs: DHist JP   MCb 304

BOURLON WOOD

September 29

McNEIL Hector

"Took Charge of Entire Line, Held It Intact"

In the course of a daylight attack by two companies to establish an outpost around a small village, four out of the five officers, including two company commanders, engaged in the operation had become casualties. Hector McNeil of the 85th Infantry Battalion took charge of the entire line, held it intact and also succeeded in overcoming several German gun posts. For his "excellent work throughout," McNeil received the MC.

MC   Lt
RefScs: DSHist JP   MCb 229

NEAR THE DOUAI-CAMBRAI ROAD

September 29/30

ANDERSON William

"Wounded while in Constant Liaison with Front-Line Troops"

On this night William Anderson of the Canadian Light Horse was in charge of a patrol to keep in touch with the front-line troops. This called for him to make several trips in the open through the German shelling to the advancing infantry, locating cavalry routes as well as keeping his commanding officer posted on enemy movements. In the process he was wounded by machine-gun fire but refused to leave the field and continued on with his duties.

MC   Lt   Died May 16 1948
RefScs: DHist JP   MCb 9

CAMBRAI
September 29-October 3

MacGREGOR John

"Flushed Out Enemy Machine-Gun Nest Single-Handedly"

A captain with the 2nd Canadian Mounted Rifles during the attack of Cambrai, John MacGregor led his company under intense fire. When the advance was stemmed by German machine guns, although wounded, he pushed on and located the enemy gun nest. Then, in the face of heavy fire from all directions, and in broad daylight, he ran forward with rifle and bayonet single-handedly putting the enemy crews out of action, killing four Germans and taking eight prisoners. After reorganizing his command, he took charge of the advance and established his unit at Neuville-St. Remy which greatly assisted in the capture of Tilloy. For these deeds MacGregor, one of Canada's most decorated soldiers, won the Victoria Cross. Previous to the award of the VC, MacGregor had earlier been decorated with the Distinguished Conduct Medal as well as the Military Cross and Bar.

Born in Nairn, Scotland, he came to Canada in 1909 and went into the contracting business in British Columbia before joining the army when WW1 broke out. When WW2 started he enlisted as a private in the Canadian Scottish Regiment and later became a lieutenant-colonel commanding a training camp at Wainwright, Alta. Following the war he returned to his home at Powell River, B.C., and established a concrete plant at Cranberry Lake. He died in June 1952 in Powell River Hospital following a lengthy illness.

VC MC & Bar DCM ED   Capt   Lt/Col (WW2)   Born Feb 11 1888
Died June 9 1952
RefScs: CVC 156-7   VM 152-3

ABANCOURT
October 1

MERRIFIELD William

"Daring Assault on Machine-Gun Emplacements"

During the Battle of Passchendaele in November 1917, William Merrifield of Sault Ste. Marie, Ont., was awarded the Military Medal for bravery under fire. This was but a warm-up for the action that won him the Victoria Cross at Cambrai. In an attack by the 4th Canadian Infantry Battalion near Abancourt, Merrifield's men were held down by two German machine-gun emplacements. Merrifield attacked them both. Dashing from shell-hole to shell-hole he killed the occupants of the first post. Then, although wounded, he attacked the second position by throwing a Mills bomb into it which killed the crew. Though bleeding profusely he refused to be evacuated and continued to lead his men until he was again wounded so severely that he had to be taken from the field.

Born in Brentwood, England, Merrifield moved to Canada prior to the war. He died in Toronto in 1943.

VC MM Sgt Born Oct 9 1890 Died Aug 8 1943
RefScs: CVC 158–9 VM 154–5

CAMBRAI
October 8/9

MITCHELL Coulson Norman

"In Face of Enemy Attack Prevented Demolition of Bridge"

In the attack on Cambrai on the night of October 8/9, 1918, Norman Mitchell, an explosives expert with the 4th Battalion, Canadian Engineers, led a small party ahead of the the first wave of infantry. His assignment was to prevent the Germans from blowing up the Pont d'Aire which spanned the Canal de l'Escaut. When they reached the bridge Mitchell posted a sentry, then he and a sergeant dashed across to find it heavily charged with explosives. Mitchell and a sergeant cut the electrical circuit and then began working on the leads and charges when they were suddenly interrupted by shouting and rifle fire. An enemy guard at the bridge had heard them and charged. The Canadian sentry killed two of the Germans and Mitchell shot a third. Then more infantrymen attacked but Mitchell and his men repelled them. Mitchell then removed six charges consisting of some 500 pounds of explosives. At dawn the German demolition team surrendered to Mitchell's party who maintained the bridgehead until reinforcements arrived. For this action Mitchell received the Victoria Cross. This was his second decoration. At Ypres in 1916 he had been awarded the Military Cross.

Born in Winnipeg, Mitchell graduated from the University of Manitoba as an engineer and joined the army when the war started. During WW2 he served with the Royal Canadian Engineers in England and finally became commandant of the Royal School of Military Engineers at Chilliwack, B.C. After the war he joined a major Canadian corporation as a senior executive making his home in Beaurepaire, P.Q. He was also active with the Norman Mitchell VC Branch of the Royal Canadian Legion.

VC MC Capt Lt/Col(WW2) Born Dec 11 1889
RefScs: CVC 162-3 VM 156-7

A portrait of Mitchell hangs in the Canadian War Museum in Ottawa.

BOIS DE GATTIGNY
October 9

DUNWOODY James Moore

"Bold Attack Turned Enemy's Flank"

In 1916 James Dunwoody won the DCM for a particularly daring reconnaissance of the German trenches. On this final day of the Cambrai fighting he was assigned with his troop to "ride down" the enemy machine guns to the right of his company's position. The objective was to draw their fire and if possible capture them, enabling the battalion to turn the enemy's flank. Dunwoody led his troops over 2,000 yards through intense machine-gun fire and, although he and a number of his men became casualties, he succeeded in driving the Germans from their guns, 15 of which were captured. His gallantry and determination prevented much heavier casualties, and by silencing the machine guns the advance was able to continue.

DSO DCM Lt
RefScs: DSOb 95

James Dunwoody (Private Collection)

FINAL PURSUIT
October 11 - November 11, 1918

During the remaining days of WW1, the Canadian Corps continued to spearhead the Allied attack in an uninterrupted advance through Valenciennes and Mount Huoy, reaching historic Mons on the day the Armistice was signed. It was all over — for 20 years at least.

NORTHEAST OF CAMBRAI
October 11

MARR George

"Help Reform Troops despite Wounds"

During a particularly heavy German artillery barrage, the forward companies of the attacking force became badly disoriented. George Marr of the 20th Battalion moved forward to assist in reorganizing the dissassembled troops. While performing this self-appointed task he was severely wounded. He nevertheless continued in the face of heavy German shelling until the companies were reformed and the advance continued.

    MC Capt (Temp)
    RefScs: DHist JP

IWUY

ALGIE Wallace Lloyd

"Spirited Leadership Led to Capture of Village"

Northeast of Cambrai, German machine-gun fire from the village of Iwuy was causing heavy casualties among the ranks of the 20th Canadian Infantry Battalion. Moreover, the enemy was observed to be bringing up additional machine guns toward positions that would threaten the entire 4th Brigade. Wallace Algie took a small party of men, moved around the battalion's left flank, and charged. In its first onrush the group captured two enemy machine guns and killed the crews. Using the German guns, as well as a Lewis gun of their own, Algie's party opened fire on advancing squads of Germans and, after a brief struggle, the survivors were taken prisoner. The result was that the east end of the village was cleared making its capture possible. Algie now went back to his battalion for reinforcements but was killed while leading them forward. For his leadership and valour he received a posthumous Victoria Cross.

Algie was born in Alton, Ont., and before joining the army he entered the banking business in Toronto and Vancouver. He is buried in Niagara Cemetery, five miles north of Cambrai.

    VC   Lt   Born June 10 1891   KIA Oct 11 1918
    RefScs: CVC 164-5   VM 158-9

HORDAIN
October 12/13

DENMAN Edward Percival

"Risked His Neck Establishing Forward Posts"

On October 12 during operations at Hordain, Edward Percival Denman of the 24th Infantry battalion established a line of outposts 700 yards in advance of the troops on his flank, performing the feat all the while under murderous German crossfire. Then, on the following day, he again exhibited his daring when he made a dangerous reconnaissance to keep battalion headquarters posted on forward enemy conditions.

    MC   Capt
    RefScs: DHist JP   MCb 82

LEDEGHAM
October 14

RICKETTS Thomas

"Youngest Canadian VC"

Having joined the army before his 16th birthday, at 18 Thomas Ricketts became the youngest Canadian ever to win the Victoria Cross. He received the award for bravery he displayed during an attack by the Royal

Newfoundland Regiment. Held down by fierce German fire, Ricketts' platoon suffered severe casualties. Ricketts immediately volunteered to go forward with his section commander, armed with a Lewis gun, in an attempt to outflank the enemy. Advancing in stages under heavy fire, by the time they reached the German post they were out of ammunition. Seeing this, the Germans began bringing up extra guns in teams. Ricketts dashed back to his own lines to get ammunition for the Lewis gun and rushed forward again. He and his platoon leader then, by accurate fire, drove the German gun teams into the refuge of farm buildings. Ricketts' platoon was then able to advance without further casualties capturing four enemy field guns, four machine guns and eight prisoners. Later they also captured a fifth field gun.

Born in Middle Arm, Nfld., by lying about his age Ricketts was accepted in the army in 1916. In 1917 he was posted to France where he was wounded that same year; however he was sufficiently recovered from his injuries to return to combat in April 1918. Ricketts died in St. Johns in 1967.

VC   Sgt   Born Oct 14 1900   Died Feb 10 1967
RefScs: CVC 160-1   VM 160-1

At Ricketts' investiture at Buckingham Palace, King George V, after pinning the coveted medal to his tunic, turned to Princess Mary and others in attendance and announced proudly: "This is the youngest VC in my army."

VALENCIENNES
October 22

WORTHINGTON Frederick Frank

"Soldier of Fortune Fathered Canadian Armoured Corps"

During an advance, Frederick Worthington of the 1st Motor Machine Gun Brigade, along with a battery of machine guns and a selection of armoured cars, pushed forward to the Canal de l'Escaut in front of the infantry. Here he found the Germans trying to blow up a bridge. After a skirmish that lasted half an hour, during which the enemy tried three times to rush his guns, Worthington established his position and drove the Germans from the bridgehead allowing the infantry to advance. For that feat Worthington won the Military Cross, but it was only one

Frederick Worthington (Private Collection)

incident in a long and adventurous career that began when "Worthy," still in his teens, became involved in revolutions in Mexico and Central America. During WW1 he enlisted in the Black Watch, and in Europe was decorated with the MM and Bar and MC and Bar. In 1936 he became the first commandant of the Canadian Tank School. In 1940 a document he had submitted was accepted thus creating the Canadian Armoured Corps which he took overseas in 1942. After the war he was appointed Commander of Pacific Command retiring in 1947 to become Canada's Civil Defence Co-ordinator.

CB MC & Bar MM & Bar CD   Capt (Maj-Gen)   Born 1890   Died Dec 8 1967
RefScs: DHist JP   MCb 362-3   TS Fall 1947   W (biog)

October 27

DEACON Arthur Weymss

"Led Successful Foray against Enemy Pillboxes with Shattered Arm"

Arthur Deacon of the Canadian Mounted Rifles was leading an attack on two German pillboxes when his right arm was shattered by enemy fire. He continued to press home the assault and direct his company's operations until the positions had been won and secured. For his "fortitude" he was credited with largely being responsible for the success of the venture and was awarded the MC.

MC   Lt   Died Oct 31 1934
RefScs: DHist JP   MCb 81

CANAL DE L'ESCAUT
End of October - Beginning of November

ALLEN Ralph Fleton

"Kept Communications Lines Open"

As brigade signalling officer of the 4th Divisional Signal Company, during the attack on the canal Ralph Allen organized a chain system of communications that never once failed. As a result of his efforts the brigade headquarters was able to maintain constant touch with all battalions throughout the operations. Most of the time Allen was under heavy enemy fire, too. The citation said that "Without his diligent devotion to the job at hand it would not have been possible to cross the Grand Honnelle River."

MC   Lt
RefScs: DHist JP   MCb 6

VALENCIENNES
November 1

BERNER Adolph

"Rushed Two Machine-Gun Nests at Short Range to Win Bar to MC"

Late in September, Adolph Berner was awarded the MC for bravery. Now, little more than a month later, his gallantry earned him a Bar to the medal. When several companies around him became confused and demoralized due to the high casualties of officers and NCOs, Berner stepped into the breech to take command. He then personally rushed two German machine-gun nests even though they were at close range. The Bar to his MC was awarded for "His determination and great courage . . . a powerful factor in maintaining the morale of the whole unit under very heavy fire and trying circumstances."

MC & Bar   Capt (Act)
RefScs: DHist JP   MCb 27

CAIRNS Hugh

"Last Canadian to Win VC in WW1"

Ten days before the armistice, in the fighting around Valenciennes, a German machine gun suddenly opened up on the 46th Canadian Infantry Battalion. Hugh Cairns, a sergeant in this Saskatchewan regiment, wasted no time springing into action. Grabbing a Lewis machine gun, in the face of direct enemy fire he charged the position, killing 12 of the gunners and capturing 18 of them along with their guns. Later, when the Canadian attack was bogged down by machine and field guns,

Hugh Cairns (PA 6735)

Cairns led a party to outflank them, killing several more Germans, forcing 50 others to surrender and seizing all their guns. After consolidating his position, he joined a patrol advancing on Marly. Breaking down a barnyard door, he found himself face-to-face with another 60 Germans who threw up their hands in surrender. But it was a treacherous gesture; as they filed past, the officer in charge pulled out his revolver and shot Cairns in the stomach. His knees buckling from pain, Cairns nevertheless responded with a rapid burst of fire with his Lewis gun before collapsing from loss of blood. He died next day of his wounds. Cairns' gallantry and determination earned him the Victoria Cross, the third time he had been decorated. At Vimy Ridge in April 1917, Cairns was awarded the Distinguished Conduct Medal and the French Legion of Honour.

Born in Ashington, England, Cairns came to Canada in 1911 and became an apprentice plumber in Saskatoon. He is buried in Auberchicourt British Cemetery, east of Doaui in France. In the City Park at Saskatoon a monument stands to his memory erected by his comrades and the citizens of the community.

VC DCM Ld'H(Fr) Born Dec 4 1896 DoW Nov 2 1918
RefScs: CVC 166-7 VM 164-5

In March 1936 at Valenciennes, where Cairns won his VC, the town renamed one of its streets in his memory: "Avenue Serjeant Hugh Cairns." It is believed to be the first time a French town paid such a tribute to anyone under officer rank in the Allied services.

KNIGHT James Archibald

"Repaired Vital Road Link under Heavy Fire"

During the attack on Valenciennes it became necessary to repair a main road extending along an exposed ridge to bring up guns and ammunition. The trouble was the area was under direct German observation and heavy enemy fire. James Knight disregarded this danger, personally reconnoitered the road, led a working party forward and supervised the needed repairs despite constant shelling and machine-gun fire. His disregard of the risk meant that the road was quickly put into working condition allowing the ammunition to get through.

MC Lt
RefScs: DHist JP MCb 174

VALENCIENNES-MONS
November 5-11

BLAIR John Freeman

"Ensured Evacuation of Wounded"

During this final but still hard-fought stage of WW1, John Blair acted as liaison officer between the regimental aid posts and the forward collecting stations. Keeping in close touch with the rapidly advancing infantry, he was almost continuously under German fire. But he ensured the rapid evacuation of the wounded, remaining forward in the open supervising the carrying of the wounded by stretcher-bearers.

    DSO Maj
    RefScs: DHist JP DSOb 31

SOUTHEAST OF MONS
November 10

ALLEN Norman Burke

"Captured Key Post"

On the day before WW1 ended, Norman Allen, serving with the 20th Infantry Battalion, led his company in the capture of the key post of Saint Symphorien. He then established several outposts beyond the town. Later in an attack on a German patrol of 25 men, his unit killed five of them and captured four. Allen himself personally took the enemy NCO in charge as his prisoner.

    MC Lt
    RefScs: DHist JP MCb 6

MONS
November 10/11

GRAFFTEY William Arthur

"First to Penetrate Mons"

William Grafftey, of the 42nd Infantry Battalion, led his company in one of the final acts of the war to win a decoration: the penetration of Mons, the scene of one of the first major battles in which the British engaged the Germans. Grafftey maneuvered his unit with great skill and daring, surrounding two enemy machine-gun nests. Later, when working his way through the city, he cut off three other posts which were holding up the advance on his right. Then by eleven o'clock on the 11th the guns were silenced at long last.

MC & Bar Capt
RefScs: DHist JP MCb 124

RUSSIA
TUGLAS
November 11

ARNOLDI Frank Fauquier

"Canadians' Gallant Battle against the Bolsheviks"

While a truce was being signed as the Germans laid down their arms along the Western Front after more than four long years, and the thunder of guns was at last absent, nearly 1,000 miles to the east, in the province of Archangel, a battle raged in which Canadians were playing the major part. In October, Frank Arnoldi had reverted from lieutenant-colonel to major's rank to command the 67th Battery, Canadian Field Artillery in northern Russia. Its purpose was to assist the White Russians in their struggle against the Red Bolsheviks with the objective of keeping Russia in the war against Germany. On the date the war in Europe ended, the 67th was locked in mortal combat in the defence of the town of

Tuglas against the Red infantry. Firing over their sights in sub-zero temperatures, Arnoldi's gunners prevented the village from being overrun. For his part in the battle, during which he personally made difficult and dangerous reconnaissances, Arnoldi was awarded the DSO. The White Russians awarded him the Imperial Russian Order of St. Stanislaus for his services as commander in the campaign which lasted until May 1919. During World War 2 Arnoldi served as an artillery colonel in Canada.

DSO OSS(Rus) Lt-Col (Col)
RefScs: DSOb RCMIC

Arnoldi's decorations are on display at the Royal Canadian Military Institute in Toronto.

GERMANY
BONN
December 4

CURRIE Sir Arthur William

"The Canadian Army of Occupation"

The Canadians remained in Europe to share in the Allied occupation. Marching to the tune of "The Maple Leaf Forever," they crossed the Rhine into Germany at Bonn on December 4. Taking the salute was the man who was known as the "general who cared for his men," generally regarded as a rare breed in WW1. To boot, this field officer was also acknowledged as an authentic military genius.

Sir Arthur Currie, the first to reach the rank of full general in the Canadian army, was born in Napperton, Ont. Educated in Strathroy, he moved to British Columbia where he taught school for a brief period before entering into the insurance and real estate business. Between 1897 and 1913 he served with the B.C. Brigade, Canadian Artillery, rising from the ranks to command the regiment. In 1914 he was given command of the 50th Regiment Gordon Highlanders; in August that year he became commander of the 2nd Brigade which he took overseas. In 1915, in recognition of his services at the Second Battle of Ypres and at St. Julien, he was knighted and placed in command of the First Canadian Division.

The Canadians finally came home in 1919 where they were greeted

Sir Arthur Currie (PA 1564)

by enthusiastic crowds across the country. Currie became inspector general of the Canadian militia. From 1920 until his death in 1933 he served as principal and vice-chancellor of McGill University in Montreal.

GCMG KCB Gen Born Dec 5 1875 Died Nov 30 1933
RefScs: CBH 55 CE 184 CS&GB 447 451-2

WORLD WAR II

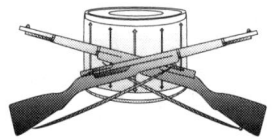

WORLD WAR 2
September 1, 1939 - August 14, 1945

During the Second World War, of the 1,000,000 Canadian men and women who served from 1939-45 (quite remarkable for a country with a population of just over 12,000,000), 730,629 wore khaki, making the Canadian army the third-largest allied army in the world.

Within four months of the declaration of war, the first of five divisions and auxiliary troops that the army maintained in the European theatre embarked at Halifax. In June, 1940, a contingent landed at Brest after the Dunkirk evacuation but was soon withdrawn. Canada's troops first saw action in WW2 in the Pacific when the Japanese overran the British garrison of Hong Kong in 17 days. The first major action in Europe for the Canadians came with the ill-fated raid at Dieppe in August 1942.

In 1943 Canadian troops went ashore in the invasions of Sicily and Italy, and served in the Italian campaign. Canadian troops landed on the Normandy beaches on D-Day, 1944, and fought across France, the Lowlands and Germany taking part in such actions as Falaise, the Scheldt, the liberation of the Netherlands and the Rhineland invasion.

(Overleaf) Dave Currie on his tank. (PA 140875)

THE HAPLESS HORROR OF HONG KONG
December 8 - 25, 1941

The first unit of the Canadian army to fight in WW2 was D Company of the Winnipeg Grenadiers. Part of a force of two battalions sent to bolster the Hong Kong garrison defences, on the night of December 9/10 one company was dispatched to the mainland to join the British and Indians in trying to help stem the Japanese attack that began the day before. Though it had been conceded that any defence of the 32-square-mile island was hopeless (it had no naval support and no air cover), the addition of the Canadian force was intended to deter Japan from making war on the British and Americans in the Pacific. Also, because the sister battalion of the Grenadiers was the Royal Rifles of Canada from Quebec City, it was hoped to foster and display national unity. It may have achieved the latter to some degree, but anything else was wishful thinking. Japanese plans for the conquest of Southwest Asia were not about to be upset by the addition of fewer than 2,000 troops to a remote outpost. And any support those troops could render against a Japanese invasion was questionable to say the least. Both battalions were classified in the least-trained category of any of the 26 infantry battalions in Canada at the time. In fact, some of the men had only been in the army for 16 weeks. Neither unit had had proper battle or weapons training and, through misadministration, their 212 vehicles never reached them. Yet C Force fought gallantly against a battle-hardened, well-

Canadian Contingent in Hong Kong (C 49744)

equipped, numerically superior enemy. Well supported by aerial and artillery bombardment, the Japanese crushed the garrison in just over two weeks. At 3:15 p.m. on Christmas Day, Hong Kong surrendered to the invader. Canadian losses were 290 killed and 493 wounded. But the ordeal did not end there. Those who were captured were imprisoned in Hong Kong and Japan under the foulest conditions. Forced into slave labour, and subjected to brutal treatment and near starvation, many died. Four soldiers were shot trying to escape; a diphtheria epidemic killed another 50 who were denied proper medical care. Two hundred and sixty-seven died in captivity. In all, more than 550 Canadians who had sailed from Vancouver in October 1941 never returned. After the war several Japanese commanders who were responsible were given life sentences for barbarism.

Sano Force

*B*ecause the garrison commander erroneously feared an invasion from the sea, the Canadian battalions were assigned the defence of Hong Kong's south shore while two British battalions manned the mainland defences. On the morning of December 8, the Japanese began their attack on the colony by bombing Kai Tak airfield on the mainland and by strafing the barracks there and on the island. At the same time three infantry regiments of the 38th Division of the Japanese 23rd Army — named "Sano Force" after the division commander General Sano Tadayoshi — crossed the frontier. Next day they reached the British mainland Gin Drinkers' Line defences. By December 13 the mainland was completely abandoned.

Between 8:30 and 9:00 p.m., December 18, the Japanese began landing on the northeast shore of the island. Rain coupled with smoke from burning oil tanks made the darkness that night impenetrable. The fighting was bitter and continued for a week but the outcome was never in doubt. The Allies were simply overwhelmed and by December 25 it was all over.

Lye Mun
December 18

Bishop Wells Arnold

"Skillful Maneuvering Saved Situation from Disaster"

At seven-thirty in the evening, the Japanese tried with considerable force to penetrate the gap at Lye Mun towards the Royal Rifles of Canada battalion headquarters at Tai Tam Gap. Wells Bishop maneuvered his outnumbered force with such skill that he saved the situation from total disaster. During the action he personally covered the retirement force so adeptly that his men were able to cope with superior enemy numbers until reinforcements arrived.

DSO   Maj
RefScs: DHist 713 065 (D2)   NRW 142-3 151-4 169 180 198 254-5

WONG NEI CHONG
December 18/19

PHILIP Robert William
BLACKWOOD Thomas Alexander

"Pair Led Gallant Holding Action"

Both Robert Philip and Thomas Blackwood were attached to D Company headquarters of the Winnipeg Grenadiers. Because their position controlled the main road across Hong Kong, the post had to be held at all costs. In the subsequent assault by the Japanese the company commander was killed and Philip took over. Then Philip was wounded by a hand grenade, losing his right eye and suffering chest and leg wounds from shrapnel. He was so badly injured he had to rely on Blackwood to carry out his orders. Under their leadership and brave example their small band of 40 men held out for three days until they were overwhelmed and forced to surrender. But their gallant action had denied the enemy access to the main road and bought precious time for the rest of the garrison to reorganize.

Philip
MC   Capt
RefScs: DHist 713 065 (D2)   NRW 256-7

Blackwood
MC   Lt
RefScs: DHist 713 065 (D2)   NRW 257-8

Major-General Charles Maltby, the Hong Kong commander-in-chief, said later: "A Company of Winnipeg Grenadiers fought so magnificently that the Japs believed the sector was held by two battalions. When it was over, the Nips would not believe they had been opposed for three days by only one company. They were incredulous and indignant and they showed it by slapping the faces of the Canadian officers of the company when they interrogated them."

Lye Mun Gap

STANDISH Colin Alden

"Kept His Company Supplied while under Fire"

Despite sniper fire, mortars and machine guns, Colin Standish of the Royal Rifles travelled back and forth to keep his company supplied with ammunition. On one occasion his vehicle received a direct hit. Undeterred, he made the necessary repairs and then was on his way. At times when transport was not available, he carried the supplies on his back taking time to hunt snipers as he went.

DCM   CQMS
RefScs: DHist 713 065 (D1)   259

Mount Parker

BLAVER Collinson Alexander

"Fought Gallant Action against Overpowering Odds"

With a force of 40, during the night Collinson Blaver of the Royal Rifles of Canada was ordered to clear the Japanese off Mount Parker. As they neared the top of the 1,500-foot slope, the enemy suddenly opened up with mortars, machine guns and hand grenades at close range. As the attack developed it became clear that the Japanese greatly outnumbered the Canadians and were firmly entrenched. When the order was given to withdraw, Blaver and two noncommissioned officers remained behind to cover it. Both the NCOs were killed and Blaver was wounded, but he managed to hold the enemy off long enough to allow his men to reach a new position.

MC   Lt
RefScs: DeHist 713 065 (D2)   NRW 258

BLUE POOL VALLEY
December 19

RIX Derek Everard

"Though Wounded Stayed to Fight On"

At dawn, when Derek Rix and his section of Winnipeg Grenadiers were cut off, they worked their way above Blue Pool Valley to join a section of the Hong Kong Volunteer Defense Corps who were holding a pillbox. Around noon the Japanese captured another pillbox and began engaging the crew of the first one. Under Rix's leadership the enemy position was overcome, and although he was wounded he refused treatment and stayed to see the fight to the finish.

DCM   Cpl
RefScs: DHist 713 065 (D1)   NRW 259-10

MOUNT BUTLER

OSBORN John Warren

"First Canadian VC of WW2"

That morning, during an attack on the steeply rising Mount Butler, a company of the Winnipeg Grenadiers became divided. Part of the unit, led by John Osborn, captured the heights from the Japanese at bayonet point and held on for three hours. But due to superior enemy numbers and an exposed flank that attracted intense fire, the position became untenable. Forced to move to a more defensible site, Osborn and a small party covered the withdrawal. When their own turn came to fall back, Osborn single-handedly engaged the enemy, all the while dodging heavy machine-gun and rifle fire to allow the remainder to get away. That afternoon the company became separated from the rest of the battalion. Completely surrounded they now found themselves within grenade-throwing reach of the enemy. When the Japanese began lobbing the projectiles into the depression in which they had quartered themselves, Osborn picked up the missiles and hurled them back. But one landed in a place where it was impossible for him to pick it up before it went off. Shouting a warning to the rest he fell on the grenade to muffle the effects of the explosion. This action, for which he received the Victoria Cross, killed him instantly.

John Osborn (PA 37403)

Born in Norfolk, England, Osborn served in WW1 as a seaman in the Royal Navy and saw action in the Battle of Jutland. At the end of the war he emigrated to Canada where he farmed for several years at Wapella, Sask. He also worked with the maintenance division of a railroad in Manitoba. In 1933 he joined the Winnipeg Grenadiers and went on active service at the outbreak of WW2 in 1939. Osborn has no known grave but his name appears on the Hong Kong Memorial. Though he was the first Canadian to win the VC in WW2, the award was not made until after the war. Osborn Barracks in Hong Kong is named in his honour.

VC CSM   Born Jan 2 1899   KIA Dec 19 1941
RefScs: CVC 200-1   DHist 713 065 (D1)   GM Dec 7/91   NRW 159 254   TS Dec 8/91   VM 168-9p

WAN HILL

ATKINSON Frederick Temple

"Made Valuable and Dangerous Reconnaissances"

In the early hours of the day Fred Atkinson, the Royal Rifles of Canada adjutant, went forward to select a position for one of the companies despite the danger of heavy enemy fire. This was vital work; only in this way could important information for the disposition of the battalion be brought back to headquarters. But the incessant Japanese shelling, mortar and machine-gun fire also made it extremely dangerous.

MC   Capt
RefScs: DHist 713 065 (D2)   NRW 255-6

WONG NEI CHONG

HODKINSON Ernest

"Intrepid Onslaught Demoralized Enemy"

Ernest Hodkinson, commander of the Headquarters Company of the Winnipeg Grenadiers, was ordered to take three platoons to relieve D Company at Wong Nei Chong, clear the area of Japanese, and attack the police station there, an enemy strongpoint. After overcoming all resistance and reaching D Company, Hodkinson proceeded to lead a patrol through the Japanese lines to reconnoitre the police station. While enroute his patrol successfully annihilated a Japanese section. However, the assault on the station failed due to superior enemy forces. But it did succeed in drawing Japanese attention away from D Company enabling it to advance to a pre-set limit line. During the fighting Hodkinson was wounded and all members of his patrol became casualties. But they had inflicted heavy losses and demoralized the enemy.

DSO   Maj
RefScs: DHist 713 065 (D2)   NRW 255

LAITE Uriah

"Chaplain Impressed Captors with His Insistence that the Wounded Be Spared"

Early on the morning of December 19, Uriah Laite, Chaplain of the Winnipeg Grenadiers, and a small group were attacked by the Japanese and cut off. Practically all of the company became casualties. Water, food and ammunition were rationed and no medical personnel were present. But the party held the position for three days until, with all ammunition and supplies gone, no further resistance was possible. During this period Laite tended the wounded day and night. Due to his intervention with the Japanese many of the wounded were taken prisoner instead of being shot since the enemy intended to murder all those who were unable to walk. They were so impressed with Laite's efforts that they released him and instructed him to return to his battalion headquarters.

MC   Hon Capt
RefScs: DHist 713 065 (D2)   NRW 256

BRIDGE HILL
December 21

POWER Francis Gavan

"Kept on Fighting to the Last"

As leader of a platoon of the Royal Rifles, Francis Power led an attack on Bridge Hill in which many Japanese were killed, making an advance possible that temporarily relieved the situation. Four days later, on the date the garrison surrendered, Power again led an assault, this time on Stanley Village in the face of heavy fire without artillery or mortar support. In this latter engagement Power was wounded before being taken into captivity.

> MC Lt
> RefScs: DHist 713 065 (D2)   NRW 258-9

Lieutenant Power was the son of Charles Gavan "Chubby" Power, then Associate Minister of National Defence and later Canada's first Minister of National Defence for Air.

BENNET'S HILL
December 24

NUGENT William Francis

"Fended Off Enemy Attack in Spite of Crippling Leg Wound"

At seven o'clock in the evening, Bill Nugent's platoon of Winnipeg Grenadiers was in a defensive position on the hill when the Japanese began shelling it with mortar fire. This lasted for an hour, then the enemy attacked in force, hoping to secure the heights which commanded the only cross-island road still held by the garrison. His platoon sergeant was badly injured, and Nugent received a crippling leg wound. But despite his wounds, he and his platoon managed to drive off the main force of the enemy attack as well as inflict heavy casualties on the attackers. Nugent held onto the position until relieved the next day at which time he was hospitalized.

MC Lt
RefScs: DHist 713 065 (D2)   NRW 258

CHRISTIE Kathleen Georgia

"Brave Nursing Sister of 'Incalculable Worth' Survived Captivity"

Kay Christie of Toronto was one of two Nursing Sisters who sailed with the Canadian troops for Hong Kong, both of whom (see PA) survived nearly two years of captivity in a Japanese prisoner-of-war camp. On arrival at the British colony, however, their services could not be used in the Canadian camp so they were assigned to the British military hospital on Bowen Road. The irony was that the British had requested male medical orderlies from the Canadian authorities, but the nurses, who were recognized for their "incalculable worth," were sent instead. When the Japanese began shelling the island, Christie and the other nurses were ordered to shelters located under the hospital: "Like sleeping at a main intersection," Christie later described it. On Boxing Day the Japanese took charge and officially designated the hospital a prisoner-of-war camp. In August 1942, for a reason never explained, all the female nursing personnel were transferred to another camp at Stanley on the other side of the city, leaving the patients without nursing care. There the nurses lived in appalling conditions: limited rations, bed-bugs, flying cockroaches, huge centipedes, not to mention idleness and boredom. In September 1943, under the auspices of the International Red Cross, the nurses were repatriated.

Lt N/S
RefScs: DHist 593 (D2)   NRW 121-2   RCMI 1979 Yr Bk 11-13

The other N/S was May Waters of Winnipeg.

THE DEBACLE AT DIEPPE
August 19, 1942

*E*arl Mountbatten said it gave the Allies the "priceless secret of victory." But the Canadian raid on the highly fortified coastal port of Dieppe, some 100 miles across the English Channel from Portsmouth, will forever raise doubts as to its feasibility, its necessity and whether the price was worth what it achieved. And what did it achieve? Even its objectives are still blurry and obscure. Was it to satisfy Stalin that the British and Americans were just as prepared and willing to sacrifice men on the field of battle as was the case with the Red Armies locked in mortal combat in the east? Or was it to show the Soviet premier and the Americans that a frontal assault on Hitler's Festung Europa was an impossibility at this time? There is another theory: that it was designed to alleviate pressure on the Russian Front by luring the Luftwaffe to the west.

In more practical terms it could possibly have been an opportunity to test new weapons and invasion techniques. To Bernard Montgomery, originally slated to lead the incursion, none of these or any of the other arguments added up or made any practical sense: he advised calling the whole thing off.

The bare facts of the matter were that at 4:50 a.m., 5,000 men from six infantry battalions of the Second Canadian Division, along with the 14th Calgary Tank Regiment, 1,075 British commandos and 50 American

Abandoned Canadian scout car. (C 29861)

Rangers, made five landings on a front 10 miles wide upon the pebble beaches and surrounding flanks of the French coastal resort. The odds were against their success in capturing the town and holding it. The landings were made without preliminary bombing or bombardment. (The entire force was supported by only four British naval destroyers.) Because the attack fell behind schedule, the element of surprise that darkness might have provided was never realized. The well trained, highly equipped German 571st Infantry Regiment, superbly positioned on the heights, was in complete control of the beaches which were swept with gun fire. Canadians were slaughtered as they came ashore, though some managed to escape by reaching the sea wall. Their tanks, which bogged down on the beach, were of no avail. In most areas evacuation was impossible. The raid, which was to have lasted at least a day, was over at 1:00 p.m. Undoubtedly some lessons were learned but the price proved frightful. Of the 4,963 Canadians that embarked on the venture, only 2,210 returned to England, many of them wounded. Among the 3,367 casualties, 1,946 were taken prisoner and 907 lost their lives.

South Saskatchewan Regiment

*A*t five minutes past five o'clock in the morning, the advance party of the South Saskatchewan Regiment landed near Pourville — "Green Beach" — and blew holes in the barbed-wire defences with Bangalore torpedoes. The objectives were for two companies east of the Scie River to advance along the high ground to a radar station on the cliff edge and another to attack Quâtre Vents Farm. Another two companies were to seize Pourville, a village on the high ground to the west. Through an error in navigation the bulk of the regiment was landed west of the river where they were met with heavy mortar and machine-gun fire. Temporarily held up, they finally crossed the bridge and overran two antitank guns. But with no artillery support the situation soon became untenable. All they could do was hang on and wait for the order to withdraw. That signal did not come until nine-thirty.

SCIE RIVER

MERRITT Charles Cecil Ingersoll

"Bare-Headed, Led Four Charges across Bridge"

Before the South Saskatchewans could achieve their objectives, they first had to get across a bridge spanning the Scie River. Wide and exposed, it was 200 yards long and the Germans began sweeping it with

Cecil Merritt (PA 161935)

mortar, machine-gun and artillery fire. The first groups to try and get across were mowed down; the bridge became littered with Canadian dead. Cec Merritt, CO of the regiment, took his helmet off and wiped his forehead. "What's the holdup?" he asked. He was told "It's a hotspot. We can't get over." Merritt ran forward and, waving his helmet, shouted "Follow me. We're going across. There's nothing to stop us here." Four times the bare-headed Merritt led his men across. (See PA below.) Once over the bridge, the opposition stiffened but not before Merritt had led his regiment through a group of pillboxes, personally destroying one of them by throwing hand grenades into it. When it came time to withdraw, Merritt, though twice wounded, continued to direct operations. While organizing them he killed a sniper with his Bren gun. After giving orders to retire to the landing area, he then marched forward announcing his intention to "get even" with the enemy. He was last seen by his regiment collecting Bren and Tommy guns in readiness to cover his regiment's withdrawal from the beach. He was subsequently captured and made a prisoner of war. For his gallantry and leadership during the raid Merritt was awarded the Victoria Cross.

A native of Vancouver, Merritt was a graduate of Royal Military College at Kingston, Ont. In private life he became a barrister and soliciter. During that time he was also an officer of the Seaforth Highlanders of Canada. In 1942 he was transferred to the South Saskatchewans. Following the war he became MP for Vancouver-Burrard and served in that capacity until losing his seat in 1949. He then returned to his law practice in Vancouver. In 1951 he was appointed commander of his old reserve unit, the Seaforth Highlanders, which post he held for three years.

VC Lt Col Born Nov 10 1908
RefScs: CVC 172-3 DHist 713 065 (D2) DI 82 88 VM 170-1

Canadian war correspondent Wally Rayburn was on the scene. Later he said, "[Merritt's] helmet hung from his wrist as he walked. As I watched him lead his men through that thundering barrage, I felt a quiver run up and down my spine. I'd never seen anything like it."

O'HARE Howard Adolf

"Coolly Shot Away Enemy Machine-Gun Nest"

When Howard O'Hare's section became pinned down by German crossfire, he unhesitatingly stood up in the open, and in the face of bullets flying all around him, shot one of the nests out of action. This action by the Weyburn native enabled his unit to advance without further casualties.

MiD Pte
RefScs: DHist 713 065 (D1)

DICKEN Leonard Lloyd

"Took Over Company, Personally Led Attacks"

Leonard Dicken of Saskatoon had to take command of a company when no other officers were available, personally leading attacks on German machine-gun posts allowing the unit to advance. During the withdrawal he organized the defence lines enabling his men to reach the beaches.

MiD Lt
RefScs: DHist 713 065 (D2)

A Churchill tank of the Calgary Regiment. (C 29878)

BERTHELOT Guy Bernard

"Daring Lone Attack Overcame Weapons Pits"

At the height of the Dieppe raid, Guy Berthelot's platoon commander was wounded and the unit became temporarily disorganized. Berthelot, a native of Regina, with the help of another soldier, took over. With the Germans fully entrenched in weapons pits, Berthelot covered his platoon's advance with his Bren gun from the corner of a house. When this failed, he charged up a hill alone, firing his gun right into the pits putting them out of action. Following close behind, his platoon, attacking with hand grenades and mortars, helped to account for 27 enemy dead and 30 taken prisoner.

DCM L/Cpl
RefScs: DHist 713 065 (D1)

SMITH Basil Henry

"Leadership Kept Casualties to a Minimum"

While advancing with his platoon, Basil Smith of Weyburn and his men were held up by German machine-gun and mortar fire. They suddenly found themselves in danger of being surrounded and cut off. In the face of superior numbers Smith successfully extricated his unit with comparatively few casualties and, when the evacuation order came, brought his men back to the beaches despite enemy machine-gun fire and dive-bombing attacks, again with relatively light losses.

MiD Sgt
RefScs: DHist 713 065 (D1)

Queen's Own Cameron Highlanders of Canada

*L*anded astride the Scie River near Pourville, the Queen's Own Cameron Highlanders of Canada came under German fire as their landing craft approached the beach. The commanding officer was killed at the moment of touch down. On top of that they found themselves on the east side of the river when they should have been on the west. With the bridge under murderous fire, the regiment detoured along the west bank of the river to Petit Appeville to rendezvous with the tanks. But when one company neared the bridge there, it was under heavy fire. Another company secured high ground on the right, but the tanks were nowhere to be seen.

Time was running out and the objective of capturing the airfield in the vicinity had to be abandoned. At 9:30 a.m. the order came to begin retreating back to Pourville for evacuation at 11:00 a.m. Of the 500 Camerons who had landed, only 270 got away and many of those in retreat were wounded.

LAW Andrew Thompson

"Demonstrated Leadership Quality"

When the CO of the regiment was killed as his landing craft touched down, Andrew Law of Winnipeg immediately took command. Throughout the forthcoming action he proved worthy of the responsibility, directing the regiment's attack in the face of relentless opposition. The regiment inflicted heavy casualties on the enemy. When the order came to withdraw he fought a rearguard action and, despite heavy losses to his battalion, kept the unit intact throughout the evacuation.

DSO   Maj
RefScs: DHist 713 065 (D2)

RYNE Stanley Edward

"Single-Handedly Wiped Out Snipers' Nest"

A former miner from Winnipeg, Stan Ryne displayed the type of grit and guts for which Canadian soldiers became so respected by the Germans at Dieppe. When his section was held down by enemy sniper fire, Ryne imperturbably crawled forward alone, then within yards of the nest, rushed the position and forced the enemy riflemen to surrender.

MiD   Pte
RefScs: DHist 713 065 (D1)

ROSS Norman Hugh

"Set Example to His Company"

By his own example, company commander Norman Ross inspired his men to follow him no matter what the odds against them in any situation. Throughout the operation he exhibited a tactical and organizational ability that was responsible for beating off all enemy opposition during the advance and for successfully evacuating his men throughout the withdrawal.

MiD   Maj
RefScs: DHist 713 065 (D2)

The Royal Regiment of Canada

Shortly before five o'clock in the morning, landing craft carrying the Royal Regiment of Canada crept along the narrow entrance to the village of Puys on the inner left flank of the Dieppe attack. Its objective was to capture the East Headland from the rear. While still some yards offshore, the regiment came under German rifle and machine-gun fire. Some men in the leading boat were hit. As the craft touched down on the 200-yard-wide beach, the men were met with more fire from both flanking cliffs and the top of the 10-foot-high sea wall. The first to disembark were cut to pieces but some others who landed right after them managed to reach the wall. With Bangalore torpedoes they blew holes in the barbed-wire on top of the wall and then struggled through the gaps. Their bodies were later found tangled in the wire on the cliff top.

At the western end of the beach a small band cut through the wire and scaled the cliff. The men then attacked two houses to silence heavy German fire. But when they tried to return to the beach, they were cut off and later taken prisoner.

Two more waves that landed on the beach could only huddle against the sea wall and wait to be rescued. But when the ships arrived they came under such heavy German shelling that only a handful of Royals were taken off. This few hours of brutal action cost the regiment 227 dead, while 264 men were taken prisoner, 103 of them wounded.

JONES Ralph Gordon

"Weaponless, Aided Evacuation of Wounded under Fire"

On Blue Beach, one mortar crew was unable to land its equipment and had to cope as best it could. Ralph Jones of Toronto made himself useful by assisting the wounded into the boats time and time again despite merciless withering machine-gun and rifle fire.

MiD   Pte
RefScs: 713 065 (D1)

MURPHY James

"During and after Raid Engaged Enemy Guns, Aircraft"

For Torontonian Jim Murphy, Dieppe was a day he remembered for a long time. During the disembarkation he provided covering fire often in the face of constant fusillades from commanding and inaccessible — to the Royals — German posts. Repeatedly exposing himself to danger, he kept engaging these enemy positions. One of the lucky ones to get back in the boats, throughout the return voyage Murphy was again in action, this time firing at attacking enemy aircraft.

MM Pte
RefScs: DHist 713 065 (D1)

ELLIS Leslie George

"Display of Initiative, Skill and Daring"

Landing with the first wave on the Puys beach, Leslie Ellis of Toronto was one of those who got through the barbed-wire on the sea wall and climbed the hill to the right. Dismantling booby-traps along the way, he stumbled into an abandoned German gun post and upon arriving at the top engaged an enemy gun nest east of the beach. Disposing of it, he found himself alone and, seeing the second wave of Royals coming in, climbed down towards the beach to guide them forward. Enroute he found a comrade who was badly injured and paralyzed in both legs. He dragged him almost to the wall before the man was killed by enemy gun fire, and Ellis himself was wounded. But he managed to pull himself over to the wall and down to the beach where he was evacuated as a casualty.

DCM L/Cpl
RefScs: DHist 713 065 (D1)

Royal Hamilton Light Infantry

The Royal Hamilton Light Infantry was one of two battalions that carried out the main assault on the beaches of Dieppe, the other being the Essex Scottish. As the regiment touched down at 5:20 a.m. on White Beach, the centre left flank, one company was all but wiped out by German machine-gun fire. Men dropped, killed or wounded, as they raced for the sea wall. Even there fire rained down close by from the East Headland. But some broke through into the town and after fierce fighting captured the casino which was infested with German machine gunners. But the victory was short-lived as most of those who broke out were captured.

WHITAKER Denis

"Only Officer in His Battalion to Survive; Dash and Daring Earned DSO"

For his whirling-dirvish performances from the time he landed on the beach shortly after 5:30 until he was evacuated at 11:00 a.m., it was no wonder that Denis Whitaker was awarded the DSO. A rare honour seldom bestowed on an officer of captain rank, the real wonder was that he had lived to wear it. During those five-and-a-half hours, the former football star survived against all odds.

As the ramp in the landing craft dropped, Whitaker led 30 men along the stony beach just short of a barbed-wire obstacle. Having blown a hole in the defence with a Bangalore torpedo, they were then pinned down by the sea wall. However, Whitaker spotted the Dieppe casino about 50 yards from the edge of the beach and, laying down canisters of smoke, led his men forward to the building which they found full of Germans. In the hand-to-hand combat that followed many of the enemy were killed. At the side of the building lay a row of slit trenches filled with enemy gunners. Using a Bren gun, and with the help of one of his men wielding a PIAT antitank gun, Whitaker soon cleared the position. The Canadian infantrymen then jumped out of a window and made their way to a low shelter. However, the Germans soon found their range from the surrounding headlands and mortars rained down on them. As soon as the Germans let up, they made a dash across the esplanade. By ten o'clock Whitaker realized that they could never gain any deeper entrance into the town. In fact any movement brought instant death from a sniper bullet. They had no alternative but to dash back to the casino. By then word arrived that an attempt to evacuate them would be made at eleven o'clock. Whitaker organized an all-round defence, arranged to lay a smokescreen and settled down to wait. The worst part of the entire morning was the terrifying dash to the boats through a hail of bullets, mortar and shell-fire. Whitaker was the only officer in the brigade who advanced to the perimeter of the town and returned to the beach. But his war was far from over. Later, during the campaign in Europe, as commander of the RHLI, he was again decorated for bravery — with a Bar to the DSO.

A graduate of RMC, Whitaker was born in Calgary. Following WW2, after retiring from the army in 1952, he held senior positions with a leading brewery and a major broadcast company before joining a Toronto brokerage firm as a consultant. A former quarterback with the Hamilton Tigers, Whitaker became chairman of the Canadian Equestrian Team and a director of Olympic Trust. In 1990 he was inducted into Canada's Sports Hall of Fame.

Denis Whitaker (Courtesy Denis and Shelagh Whitaker)

DSO & Bar Capt Lt-Col Brig-Gen Co-Author (with his wife Shelagh) *Tug of War; Rhineland: The Battle to End The War; Dieppe: Tragedy to Triumph*

RefScs: DHist 713 065 (D2) DTT 242-4 252-3 263-4 268 TS&TG 2-3 315 338-9 340 341-2 345 347 375 380 403

The morning after the Dieppe raid Whitaker was summoned to a debriefing conducted by Admiral Louis Mountbatten. At the session General Hamilton Roberts, the Canadian Dieppe military commander, reported that he did not believe tactical surprise had been achieved. Whitaker asked to be heard and told of interrogating a prisoner on the beach who boasted that "We have been waiting for you for a week." Mountbatten summarily dismissed both reports. What, thought Whitaker, is going on? To find out his startling conclusions, read *Dieppe* which he co-authored with his wife Shelagh. It is one of the most enlightening Canadian military histories ever written.

FOOTE John Weir

"The Gallant Padre"

Born in Madoc, Ont., John Foote was the only member of the Canadian Chaplain Services to win the Victoria Cross. A graduate of Western, Queen's and McGill universities, Foote entered the Presbyterian ministry, serving congregations in Fort Colougne, P.Q., and Port Hope, Ont. Enlisting in the Chaplain Services when WW2 started, Foote was attached to the Royal Hamilton Light Infantry as that regiment's chaplain. When the battalion landed on White Beach, Foote attached himself to the Regimental Aid Post. For the next desperate hours while the battle raged, he assisted the regimental medical officer in ministering to the wounded. Time and again he left the post to inject morphine, give first aid to others wounded on the battlefield, and carry the more badly injured back to the post. Exposing himself to the inferno of fire on the beach, his efforts saved many lives. When the time came to evacuate, Foote helped load the wounded into the landing craft. By the time the last boat was about to leave Foote climbed out of it and marched towards the German positions to surrender himself. He had decided he could best serve his regiment as a prisoner-of-war. As such he was able to console and minister to his comrades who, for the next few years, were confined behind in prisoner-of-war camps, a good deal of that time in chains. After the war Foote remained with the Chaplain Service of the army until 1948. He later became MPP for the County of Durham, Ont., making his home in Cobourg. Later he was given the Post of Minister of Reform Institutions of Ontario.

VC CD   Maj(Chap)
RefScs: CWC 198-9   DHist 713 065 (D2)   VM 172-3

John Foote (r.) (PA 113251)

Canadian prisoners marching down Rue de Sygogne behind the casino. Left front is RHLI Padre H/Captain John Foote, who was awarded the VC. (Bundes archiv, Koblenz)

As a reporter I interviewed John Foote on his return to Canada. He struck me as a more assured, forceful type than any member of the clergy I had ever met. Strong and burly despite his years in confinement, he was at that time concerned about how Canadian combat veterans would adjust to civilian life.

Les Fusiliers Mont Royal

*A*t seven o'clock in the morning, 27 personnel landing craft deposited Les Fusiliers Mont Royal — the floating reserve — on Red Beach, the left centre flank at Dieppe, whose objective was to attack the East Headland. But a strong current caused by the ebbing tide swept the flotilla to the west, and with the beach obscured by smoke dropped by Royal Air Force planes, many of the boats had no idea of their position until it was too late to turn away. As a result much of the battalion was strung out along White Beach to the right. Nearly half the unit was landed on a narrow strip to the west of the headland off the main beach altogether.

The men on White Beach were met with intense fire from the headland and from houses on the beach. Faced with unscalable cliffs, they were *trapped. There was no way out except by sea, so 300 Mont Royals, many of them wounded, had to remain until the end of the day and be taken prisoner. Those who were not killed or wounded sought shelter while others pressed on to the sea wall where they joined the RHLI in clearing the casino. They then fought their way along the esplanade and many of them were captured before they were able to withdraw.*

CLOUTIER Gerard

"Batman Died Saving His CO"

When communications broke down between battalion headquarters and the company commander, his batman, Gerard Cloutier, volunteered to run messages between the BHQ and his CO. Under incessant enemy fire he not only carried out this mission a number of times, but also found time to attend to the wounded enroute. At the end of his final sortie his group was subjected to an intense German machine-gun barrage. Seeing that his CO, who was wounded, was in extreme danger he threw himself across his body saving his life but in the process lost his own. His last words were: "It's all right, Sir; they've got me, but you can do more for the company than I could."

    MiD   Pte   KIA Aug 19 1942
    RefScs: DHist 713 065 (D1)

BERUBE Robert

"Dodging Bullets, Carried Wounded Back to the Boats"

Montrealer Robert Berube was so keyed up to do battle that even before landing on the beach he let go at enemy positions with his machine gun while still in the boat. Once ashore he engaged the Germans with his fire until it came time to withdraw. Then, with bullets whizzing all about him, he carried several men on his shoulders back to the landing craft. On one occasion when a boat became bogged down in the sand he assisted in pushing it free despite the danger of harassing enemy fire.

    MM   Cpl
    RefScs: DHist 713 065 (D1)

The Essex Scottish

*O*f all the regimental losses suffered at Dieppe, the Essex Scottish's were the most horrific. An hour after the battalion hit Red Beach — with the objective of capturing the harbour then looping eastward along the headlands to meet up with the Royals — their casualties already numbered 75 percent. The main force only made it through two wire obstacles as far as the sea wall that formed the near perimeter to the town. There they huddled, falling prey to guns on the East Headland that denied them access to the main beach. However, a small squad of 15 men did penetrate into town to meet the Germans head on before returning to the wall. A garbled signal led the force commander, General Hamilton Roberts, to believe the entire regiment had captured the city. The result was more confusion. The Essex Scottish had been decimated. Of the 583 officers and men who landed at Dieppe, 530 were casualties, 382 of them taken as prisoners of war. Only 51 returned to England and half of these were wounded.

JASPERSON Frederick

"Gave Encouragement to His Men in Trapped Situation"

Despite the predicament facing his regiment, Fred Jasperson, the commanding officer, was a rallying force encouraging his men to fight on. When the landing craft touched down, Jasperson was first ashore, pistol in hand, urging on those next to him, alive one minute, dead the next. Men stumbled, pitched forward on their faces, and lay still on either side. Jasperson reached the sea wall, four feet high, threw himself behind it, and cursed aloud at the large flat expanse of wire-filled space separating the wall from the buildings on the other side of the esplanade. But he immediately made successive attempts to organize assaults through the wire. He soon realized, though, that his unit was caught in a death trap because of the immense concentration of German fire. He was shocked by the fury in which the enemy cut down his wiring parties, yet persisted in establishing loose contact with his companies spread along the wall. Within minutes this was lost. His wireless sets were destroyed; his headquarters signaller was killed. Now Jasperson could no longer establish even sparse control of his regiment. Yet, as best he could, he organized the wall defences and moved along it, giving morphine to the wounded, and even in a beleagured situation tried to offer encouragement. In reality it now became simply a matter of waiting to be annihilated or taken prisoner. "We were all afraid. Mortar and shell splinters were whistling all around me," he wrote in his diary. "The experience was quite harrowing and how I was missed God only knows." That afternoon the Windsor lawyer surrendered along with 382 of his officers and men to spend the rest of the war in captivity.

DSO   Lt/Col
RefScs: DHist 713 065 (D2)   DTT 71   TS&TG 41 110 310-12 314 326-7 335 365-6 380 410 413 418

Offshore

GARNEAU Marie-Edmond Paul

"Bravery Aboard LCT #8"

During the Dieppe expedition, Paul Garneau, a member of the Royal 22nd Regiment from Quebec City, held down the job of acting staff captain of the 4th Canadian Infantry Brigade aboard Landing Craft Tank #8. Under heavy shell and machine-gun fire, he steadily maintained radio contact with the units ashore and communicated all developments to the headquarters ship. When all the engine room staff were put out of action and the boat was drifting helplessly, Garneau got the engines running

Dieppe survivors boarding a destroyer from an LCA (NAC)

and the craft under way again. In addition, he not only reorganized the anti-aircraft battery after the crew had suffered heavy casualties, but also acted for a time as the number two gunner of one of the ship's Pom-Pom guns. He was credited with being responsible for preventing the loss or possible destruction of the LCT.

DSO Maj
RefScs: DHist 713 065 (D2)

THE CONQUEST OF SICILY
July 10 - August 18, 1943

Shortly after dawn on July 10, the First Canadian Division, under the command of Major-General Guy Simonds, formed the left flank of the British landings on Sicily. The British-Canadian invasion spread across 40 miles of shoreline, near Pachino at the southeastern tip of the island, the largest (180 miles wide by 120 miles deep) in the Mediterranean. To the west the 7th United States Army established three more bridgeheads. Operation Husky, employing 180,000 men, 15,000 vehicles, 1,800 guns, 3,000 vessels of all types, and covered by 2,500 aircraft, in terms of troops was the biggest amphibious assault ever. Its initial aim was to trap the German and Italian armies and prevent their retreat across the Strait of Messina.

At first the Canadians encountered little resistance from Italian troops. But as they advanced inland through choking dust, over tortuous mine-filled roads, in intense heat, the resistance stiffened when they came up against the battle-hardened German troops of the tough Hermann Goering Division. Though the Germans fought a delaying action the outcome was never in doubt. Through twisting mountainous terrain the Canadians saw bitter fighting in the towns of Valguarnera, Assoro, Leonforte, Agira and Regalbuto. While the Canadians and British advanced northward, the Americans pushed in from the west towards Messina across from the Italian mainland. The final Canadian task was to capture Adrano. When it fell, the way was prepared for the closing of the Sicilian campaign which ended on August 18. The conquest had taken 38 days during which Canadian casualties totalled 562 killed, 1,644 wounded and 84 taken prisoner.

SIMONDS Guy Granville

"The Man Who Led the Canadians in Sicily"

The soldier who commanded the Canadians in Sicily was a thorough professional who was engaged in almost every major operation in Europe. Bernard Montgomery called Guy Simonds the "most brilliant Canadian field general." Born in Bury St. Edmonds in England, he emigrated to Canada with his parents when he was nine years old and attended a private school in Ottawa. On graduation he was accepted in the Royal Military College. Commissioned into the Royal Canadian Horse Artillery in 1925, he attended the gunnery staff course in England in 1932, returning to Canada to become gunnery instructor at the School of Artillery in Kingston.

Guy Simonds with James Ralston, Minister of Defence. (PA 136762)

After attending the Staff College at Camberley in England, Simonds became instructor in tactics at RMC in 1938. By the time the Second World War broke out, few serving in the Canadian army had as much experience and know-how in gunnery and field tactics. When the First Canadian Division was mobilized in 1939, Simonds was appointed a general staff officer. In 1940 in England he was given command of the 1st Field Regiment of the Royal Canadian Horse Artillery. During the winter of 1941 he conducted the first Canadian War Staff course.

In 1941 Simonds was appointed senior staff officer of the First Canadian Corps and headed a special staff planning an operation against the Norwegian coast in 1942 which was cancelled in favour of the raid on Dieppe. After commanding the 1st Canadian Infantry Brigade from 1942-43, he was made a staff officer of the First Canadian Army. Then, in 1943 as commander of the First Canadian Infantry Division, he was one of the first ashore when the Canadians, British and Americans invaded Sicily and, later, southern Italy. In November Simonds took command of the Fifth Canadian Armoured Division as its commander. At the end of January, 1944, he was promoted to Lieutenant-General and given command of the Second Canadian Corps and served temporarily as commander of the First Canadian Army during the Battle of the Scheldt.

Following VE-Day, Simonds was appointed commander of the Canadian forces in the Netherlands. In 1948 he attended the Imperial Defence College and then became an instructor there. He returned to Canada in 1949 to head the National Defence College and the Army Staff College at Kingston. He served as chief of the Canadian General Staff from February 1951 to August 1955, at which time he retired from the army after 30 years of service.

CB CBE DSO   Gen   Born Apr 23 1903   Died 1974
RefScs: DHist Bio

Simonds had a knack of getting what he wanted out of people and having them appreciate it at the same time. I served on the board of the National Ballet of Canada when Guy was chairman. At one meeting he asked for everybody's views on a matter, thanked each person, sifted the ideas then presented them as he thought they should be executed. That done he turned to each person in turn and said: "What can I do to help you?"

D-Day

COSTA DELL'AMBRA
July 10

GARDNER John "Jack"
GRIGAS Joseph

"First Canadians to Win Decorations in Sicily"

By mid-morning as all three battalions of the 1st Canadian Infantry Brigade reached their prime objective, Pachino airfield, which they found deserted but extensively damaged by aerial bombing, A Company of the Royal Canadian Regiment encountered a powerful enemy battery a few hundred yards to the north. Protected by machine guns, its occupants put up a stiff fight and the RCR suffered their first casualties. However, launching a savage attack, six privates, the most eager among them, Joseph Grigas and Jack Gardner, turned the tide. Cutting through barbed-wire entanglements, and by using rifles, Tommy guns and hand grenades, the Canadians knocked out three of the enemy machine guns. The Italians soon lost their ardour and surrendered en masse. For their part in the action Grigas was awarded the DCM, and Gardner the MM.

    Grigas
    DCM Pte
    RefScs: TDD 36

    Gardner
    MM Pte
    RefScs: TDD 36

ISPICA
July 11

MITCHELL George

"Forced Enemy Roadblock into Surrendering"

On his way north by carrier from Ispica to direct fire from a British warship onto the town of Modica, six members of the Royal Canadian Artillery No 1 Bombardment Unit led by "Duff" Mitchell encountered an Italian roadblock. Mitchell dismounted and with the support of two Bren guns forced the enemy detachment of about 20 Italians to surrender and at gunpoint ordered them to dismantle the wire, mines and two antitank guns.

MC Capt
RefScs: JZ 1

North from Piazza Amerina

Having captured the first two objectives of Grammichele and Piazza Armerina where they encountered the Germans for the first time, at noon on July 17, the Canadians now advanced northward to the town of Valguarnera. It was here after two days of fighting that, because of the skill they displayed in the mountainous terrain, that the Germans labelled them the "Mountain Boys."

VALGUARNERA
July 17

SUTCLIFFE Bruce Albert

"Led Attack at Close Quarters"

Having led the Hastings and Prince Edward Regiment to an advantageous point above the town, Bruce Sutcliffe, who had already distinguished himself a few days earlier in the skirmish at Grammichele, personally took a small party into the town to capture it. In the centre of Valguarnera his section ran into a group of German vehicles and tractors. With small-arms fire and antitank guns, he led an attack at close quarters knocking out six large enemy transports and one field gun, and killed upwards of 40 Germans. For the rest of the day he and his men hunted down enemy snipers and machine-gun nests. When one of his men was wounded he personally dressed his wound and under heavy fire shepherded him to safety. Sutcliffe was killed three days later by an artillery shell.

DSO (Immediate) Lt/Col KIA July 20 1943
RefScs: DHist 713 065 (D2) TDD 62

July 18

KAY William

"Charged Heavily Defended Ridge with Only Five Men"

When the 48th Highlanders of Canada attacked Valguarnera from a ridge two miles to the south and became pinned down by German snipers and machine gunners, William Kay rushed to the rescue. Leading a five-man charge to dead ground where they were immune to enemy fire, he followed it to the top of a ridge manned by 17 German soldiers and three machine guns. Although hit in the arm, Kay threw 32 hand grenades at the Germans. Three of his men were cut down, but every German was killed or wounded. That skirmish proved to be the key to the Highlanders' eventually securing the ridge.

DCM   Cpl
RefScs: TDD 59

Two-Day Battle Earned 21 Medals for Bravery

By July 19 the First Canadian Division faced two new objectives, Assoro and Leonforte, both heavily-manned, high-perched, aerie-like fortifications. And both turned out to be heavily contested battles. But although no decorations were awarded to the 1st Brigade for the capture of the former, the taking of Leonforte earned the 2nd Brigade, under Christopher Vokes, 21 medals, including one for its aggressive commander himself.

On the night of July 21, with strong artillery support, the Loyal Edmonton Regiment took possession of the town. Then the Germans counterattacked. The Eddies were on their own. Canadian artillery could not risk shelling the town for fear of hitting their own men, and until the engineers built a bridge across a 50-foot ravine on the south side, the tanks and antitank guns couldn't get through. The battalion commander ordered a retreat but his own headquarters and most of one company were soon cut off and, at this critical moment, their radio failed.

Meanwhile, the engineers were assembling a portable Bailey bridge across the ravine, the first time one of these bridges had been installed under fire on a battlefield. But the trapped men inside Leonforte were still cut off with no means of communication. They had almost been given up for lost when a 10-year-old Sicilian boy made his way to the brigade headquarters with a message that the Eddies were holding on. With the Bailey bridge completed at 4:30 a.m. on July 22, at 9:45 a.m. tanks entered the town to rescue the beleagured Alberta infantrymen.

SOUTH OF LEONFORTE
Night of July 20/21

SOUTHERN Kenneth
WALSH Geoffery
WELSH George Arthur

"Triple Defence Action Earned Three DSOs"

While Ken Southern's 3rd Field Company, under the supervision of Geoff Walsh, the divisional engineer chief, struggled to put a portable Bailey bridge across the ravine south of Leonforte, they were constantly harassed by German machine-gun and mortar fire. Seeing two tanks and a small party of enemy infantry moving down the road from the town towards them, Southern collected a handful of Loyal Edmonton Regiment infantrymen and attacked. Although only equipped with small arms, the action discouraged the Germans from coming any closer.

Soon afterwards, with the bridge completed in darkness thanks to Walsh's determination to ignore the enemy fire, "Tiger" Welsh of the 90th Canadian Anti-Tank Battery maneuvered two 6-pound antitank guns across the ravine and knocked out a German machine-gun post and one of the tanks. Then, hearing a group of German soldiers talking, he snuck up on them taking all 20 prisoner. In Italy that December Welsh received a Bar to his DSO during the Battle of Ortona.

Southern
DSO   Maj
RefScs: TDD 70

Walsh
DSO   Maj
RefScs: TDD 69-70

Welsh
DSO   Lt-Col
RefScs: DHist 713 065 (D2)   TDD 70

LEONFORTE
July 21

VOKES Christopher

"Victor of Leonforte a Soldier's Soldier"

Chris Vokes received the DSO, his first decoration, at Leonforte, his initial baptism of fire as commander of a battle. Brave and ebullient, the commendation for his award, signed by the commander of the British

Eighth Army, Bernard Montgomery, characterized his spirit and style — "remarkable coolness and leadership" — "complete disregard for his own safety" — "forceful and aggressive" — "a tremendous inspiration to his men." Vokes was a soldier's soldier who believed his duty was simply to "seek out and destroy the enemy." This credo he proceeded to prosecute with the utmost dedication and determination throughout the Sicilian campaign as commander of the 2nd Canadian Brigade, in Italy where he first took charge of the First Canadian Division and then the First Canadian Corps, and in Europe where he commanded the Fourth Canadian Armoured Division.

Born in Ireland, he migrated to Canada with his parents as a boy. After leaving school he attended RMC where he graduated in 1926. He then joined the Royal Canadian Engineers. In 1927 he attended the School of Military Engineering in England. Before WW2 he held a variety of

Chris Vokes (PA 140573)

posts and by September 1940 was assistant quarter-master general of the First Canadian Division, which he was to command three years later.

With the German surrender in 1945 he was appointed Canadian Army Occupation Force commander. He returned to Canada to take over Central Command in Oakville, Ont. Subsequently appointed commander of Western Command with headquarters in Edmonton, Vokes retired in 1958 to live in Oakville where he died in 1985 at age 80.

CB CBE DSO   Maj-Gen   Born April 13 1904   Died March 28 1985
RefScs: DHist 713 065 (D2)   TDD 69-70 VHMS(biog)

For all his military bluster, Chris was a humanitarian at heart. Case in point: Kurt Meyer, the German general sentenced to death by an Allied war crimes tribunal for having ordered seven Canadian soldiers to be shot. "That order was never proved to my satisfaction," Chris told me, "and I was not going to have his unwarranted death on my conscience." Chris had the sentence commuted to life imprisonment.

Agira
July 23-28

*E*nroute along the main highway to Agira, a collection of stone hovels surrounded by low hills and ridges, the Canadians encountered some of the stiffest resistance of the Sicilian campaign. Three successive attacks were beaten back until finally, in an assault heavily supported by massive artillery and air strikes, the town fell.

July 27/28

HOFFMEISTER Bertram Meryl

"Bravery an Inspiration to All Ranks"

During these two days the Seaforth Highlanders of Canada bore the brunt of the fighting. The battalion's objective was to capture some high ground that completely dominated the town. Throughout the final stages communications became difficult. Bert Hoffmeister, the commanding officer, with disregard for his own safety, made his way from company to company under heavy German fire and personally directed the attack on the enemy position. For this action he was commended for his "coolness, determination and personal bravery . . . an inspiration to all ranks . . . " and was awarded the DSO.

But that was only the beginning of an incredible combat record. Between December 9 and 12, as commander of the 2nd Canadian Infantry Brigade, he was awarded a Bar to his DSO for his leadership in forcing the Moro bridgehead in Italy. Then the following year, from May 24 to 30, during the battle for the Hitler Line, Hoffmeister, as head of the Fifth Canadian Armoured Division, won a second Bar to the decoration for his part in breaching the fortification and directing the crossing of the Melfa and Liri rivers. During the engagements his division captured three German villages, countless tanks and self-propelled guns, as well as killing many of the enemy and taking prisoners while advancing more than 20 miles.

Later under his leadership the division was responsible for breaking through the Gothic Line and Hoffmeister was given the OBE for his efforts. In April 1945, he led the unit in breaking out of the Arnhem bridgehead in Holland and thrusting to the Zuider Zee, an action that earned him the Netherlands Award.

OBE DSO and two Bars ED NA Maj/Gen Col
RefScs: 713 065 (D2)

Bert Hoffmeister's bravery in battle became so legendary — not to mention contagious — that an apochryphal story went the rounds that his batman had been recommended for the VC just for following him around. In the view of Dr. Bill McAndrew of the Directorate of History, he was "the army's outstanding fighting commander."

July 28

MATTHEWS Albert Bruce

"Reconnaissance under Fire Assured Effective Artillery Positions"

The hilly nature of the countryside around Agira seriously limited suitable gun emplacements, making necessary a close view of the ground held by the enemy into which artillery could be effectively placed as the attack progressed. In order to reconnoitre these areas and secure

Troops of Princess Patricia's Canadian Light Infantry entering Agira. (PA 138269)

suitable gun observation posts, Bruce Matthews, the First Canadian Division's artillery chief, made a personal survey under heavy enemy fire at the height of the five-day battle. As a result of his daring reconnaissance very suitable gun positions were charted enabling the artillery to lay down an extremely effective barrage support contributing largely to the successful capture of the town. Matthews later commanded the Second Canadian Division in Europe in 1944-45.

CBE DSO (Immediate-Sicily)   LdeH CdeG OOS   Maj-Gen   Born Aug 1909
RefScs: DHist 713 065 (D2)   TDD 21 69   WWIC M49(1984-85)

BELL-IRVING Henry Pybus

"In Forefront of His Company's Assault"

As commander of A Company of the Seaforth Highlanders of Canada, Henry Bell-Irving was ordered to gain and hold a sharp ridge which the Germans were holding in strength. This entailed a precipitous climb up the side of a hill under direct enemy machine-gun fire from two hidden tanks. Despite the gun fire and resulting casualties, Bell-Irving attacked and routed the tanks. He then continued to advance positioning himself in the forefront as his company stormed the hill, gained a foothold and, in spite of repeated German counterattacks, held their ground.

DSO   Maj
RefScs: DHist 713 065 (D2)

Final Phase

CATENANUOVA
July 30

DRAPEAU Rene

"Attacked Enemy Gun Position under Withering Fire"

On a hill near the town, platoon leader Rene Drapeau of the Royal 22nd Regiment, with the head of the leading section, rushed a German antitank gun post that had been firing at the regiment's troops. Throwing hand grenades as they attacked, they killed the gun crew. But now they faced an even more formidable obstacle; a 105mm gun 100 yards directly in front of them. Despite relentless enemy fire Drapeau led a fresh charge that quickly put the weapon out of action.

DCM (Immediate)   Sgt
RefScs: DHist   713 065 (D1)

BETWEEN AGIRA AND REGABULTO
August 1

LOW John

"Treated Wounded under Murderous Fire"

Near the Salso River, the Germans had inflicted such heavy casualties on the Loyal Edmonton Regiment that the call went out for volunteers to treat the wounded. John Low and another soldier proceeded forward, dodging behind boulders to avoid enemy fire. Then Low's companion was hit. In full view of the Germans, Low dressed the man's wounds, pulled him behind a rock for safety then crawled 30 yards further to reach the wounded in the field. All along his path bullets from enemy riflemen whizzed around him kicking up a trail of dust. In the open and under murderous fire Low dressed the wounds of each man, then pulled them to cover.

DCM   Pte
RefScs: JZ 1   DHist 713 065 (D1)

REGALBUTO
August 1

Detachment of RCE clearing a road at Regalbuto while Sherman tanks of the 1st Canadian Tank Army go through. (PA 116849)

DONALD Archibald Scott

"Valiant Assault on High Peak"

Objective of C Company of the Loyal Edmonton Regiment, led by Archie Donald, was the 500-yard-high rocky and precipitous hill four miles north of the town. In three days of fighting the peak had been captured and lost four times. This afternoon the Eddies faced German mortar and machine-gun fire that dominated the 1,500 yards of open ground approaching the hill.

Under supporting fire from his own company and artillery shelling, and by taking what little cover was available, Donald led a charge so successfully across and around the enemy position that the height was captured with a minimum of losses to his company. Not a single German escaped netting Donald four prisoners.

DSO (Immediate)   Maj
RefScs: DHist 713 065 (D2)   TDD 93-4

REGALBUTO
August 5

DOUGAN John Alpine

"Wounded in Both Hands and Arms; Led Capture of Enemy Hill"

The objective of D Company of the Loyal Edmonton Regiment was a hill north of the town that was devoid of cover and securely protected by strong mortar and machine-gun posts. Leading the forward platoon, John Dougan led his men to within 300 yards of the objective where they were met wicked enemy machine-gun fire. Dougan was wounded in both arms and could only hold his revolver by gripping it with both hands which were also mutilated. Nevertheless, despite the intense pain and while under continous fire, he directed the capture of the objective before he had to be carried from the field.

MC   Lt
RefScs: DHist 713 065 (D2)   TDD 93-4

This was one of the last Canadian actions in Sicily. Two days later the Division was pulled out of the field for a rest.

THE CANADIAN CAMPAIGN IN ITALY (1)
September 3 - December 28, 1943

As a result of the Allied landings in Sicily, Benito Mussolini was overthrown, but the Germans seized control of Italy and it was German troops the Canadians faced in their advance up the Italian peninsula. As part of the British Eighth Army, the First Canadian Division and 1st Canadian Army Tank Brigade invaded the Italian mainland across the Straits of Messina of Reggio on September 3, 1941, and began moving northward. On September 9, the United States 5th Army landed at Salerno and a Canadian brigade was diverted to seize Potenza and assist the Americans to break out of the bridgehead. The Canadian force now moved forward fighting its first real battle with the Germans in Italy on October 1 at Motta.

Meanwhile, the Canadian forces in the Mediterranean had been strengthened with the arrival of the Fifth Canadian Armoured Division which was placed under the command of General Guy Simonds, Major-General Christopher Vokes taking over command of the First Division. Both came under the First Canadian Corps headed by Lieutenant-General Harry Crerar.

By the end of November a stalemate had developed along the Italian Front. The Eighth Army struck hard at the Germans along the Sangro River on the Adriatic Coast to relieve pressure on the U.S. 5th Army driving towards Rome in the west. Now it fell to the Canadians to take Ortona on the Adriatic in three weeks of the bitterest fighting they encountered during the entire Italian campaign. The town finally fell on December 28 by which time total casualties for the Corps had reached 9,934, of which 2,119 were fatalities.

POTENZA
September 20

PELLY Howard William

"Repulsed German Onslaught Single-Handedly"

With the objective of seizing this town to allow the U.S. 5th Army to break out from the Salerno bridgehead, an improved unit known as "Boforce," made up of tanks, artillery, machine guns and engineers, was diverted from the main Canadian force. During an attack on a railway embankment south of the village, Howard Pelly of the West Nova Scotia Regiment was detailed to stay with an officer who had been temporarily blinded and guard a captured German tank. As his platoon advanced the enemy attacked. Using his Thompson machine gun along with hand grenades, Pelly repulsed the German assault, an action that prevented the tank from being recovered and the platoon from being cut off. As a result artillery fire was then brought to bear on the enemy allowing the advance to continue.

MM (Immediate)   Pte
RefScs: DHist 713 065 (D1)

MOTTA MONTECORVINO
October 1

CHARBONNEAU Arnold James

"Used Tank as Pillbox to Fend Off German Assaults"

Under the command of Arnold Charbonneau, a troop of the 14th Canadian Armed Regiment led an armoured advance towards the centre of the town supported only by fire from its other tanks. As Charbonneau approached, both of his other tanks were knocked out. Ignoring the fact that he was alone in the face of fierce German 88mm antitank fire, he continued to move forward until his own vehicle was finally immobilized. However, Charbonneau remained in his tank using it as a pillbox despite relentless fire from a 50mm gun and the German infantry that surrounded him and tried to destroy the vehicle. When the tank was set on fire, Charbonneau evacuated his entire crew and got them safely back to their own lines. This action had forced the bulk of the Germans to withdraw from the town eventually permitting the regiment to occupy it.

MC (Immediate) Lt
RefScs: DHist 713 065 (D2)

SAN MARCO
October 4

URUSKI Angus Alvin

"Deliberately Drew Enemy Fire to Expose Their Position"

While attacking the village, a platoon of The Royal Regiment of Canada ran into enemy machine-gun fire. Angus Uruski deliberately exposed himself to one position after another, sometimes as close as 600 yards away, to allow the Bren guns from his carrier platoon to take out the German nests. In each case he engaged the German gunners in running fire-fights despite the danger to himself.

MM (Immediate) Pte
RefScs: DHist 713 065 (D1)

MONTE INGOTTO
October 4

EBY Blair Stewart

"Captured Key Position"

Capture of this position east of St. Marco was vital to the Canadian advance on the Fortiore River. With a raiding party of 14 men and the help of tanks, Blair Eby of the 48th Highlanders of Canada led a charge up the slope against machine-gun fire with no cover whatsoever. In the face of the Highlanders' determined assault, however, the Germans abandoned their gun pits and fled in confusion. Though Eby lost five of his men, his inspired attack caused heavy casualties to the enemy and resulted in taking the position which dominated the whole right flank of the area.

MC (Immediate) Lt
RefScs: DHist 713 065 (D2)

FORTIORE RIVER
October 6

BERNATCHEZ Joseph Paul Emile

"Braved Artillery Barrage to Ensure River Crossing"

By the time the Royal 22nd Regiment arrived in place to cross the Leopold Bridge spanning the Fortiore River, its fire had given away its position. The result was an intense German artillery barrage along with machine-gun and rifle fire directed at the Van Doos. But despite it, Paul Bernatchez, the battalion commander, went from one company to the other to ensure control over the river crossing was maintained. By skillful tactical maneuver the enemy was pinned down and eventually dislodged from its positions.

Several months later, Bernatchez was given command of the Canadian 3rd Brigade.

DSO (Immediate) Lt-Col
RefScs: DHist 713 065 (D2) TDD 221

The Bitter Battle for Ortona

As winter fell, the British Eighth Army struck at the German line along the Sangro River on the Adriatic coast while the U.S. 5th Army pushed north along the Sangro River on the Adriatic coast while the U.S. 5th Army pushed north from Naples in the west towards Rome. At the beginning of December the Canadians had drawn up along the south shore of the Moro River, and their objective now became the port of Ortona perched high on a ledge of the Adriatic coast. The battle began on the night of December 5/6 when the Canadians crossed the Moro

River at three points: the coast road leading directly to the city, San Leonardo on a road linking up with the east-west highway into Ortona, and Villa Rogatti to the west. Along the two-mile advance through the Vino ridge "gully," at a three-storey farmhouse called Casa Berardi, and past the Cider crossroads, they were repeatedly engaged in bitter hand-to-hand combat with the stubborn German defenders. When they finally reached Ortona on December 20, its steep, narrow, rubble-filled streets meant neither tanks nor artillery could be brought to bear. This reduced the conflict to an infantryman's struggle. During a week of vicious house-to-house fighting, with the use of explosives and portable PIAT antitank guns, the attackers smashed gaping holes in the walls through which they charged with machine guns blazing. "Mouseholing" they called it. By the time Ortona fell, since the start of the battle three weeks earlier, the Canadians had sustained 4,000 casualties. Major-General Christopher Vokes, commander of the First Division, reported that every one of his nine battalions had been reduced to half-strength.

VILLA ROGATTI
December 6

DEMMY William
ROBERTSON Robert Frank

"Staved Off Two Powerful Counterattacks"

The regiment having consolidated the town the night before, at seven-thirty the next morning two companies of the Princess Patricia's Canadian Light Infantry came under heavy German infantry counterattack. A Company was completely overrun leaving B Company's right flank exposed. The enemy also succeeded in penetrating both flanks of the right platoon firing from as close as 75 yards' range. Robert Robertson, the company commander, made his way down a bullet-swept street to reorganize the platoon's defences. Meanwhile, the platoon commander, William Demmy, rallied the unit from a house where he not only succeeded in holding the position but in killing 30 Germans as well.

At one forty-five that afternoon, the enemy attacked again, this time with tanks. The house now came under fire from the tanks supported by antitank gun, machine-gun and rifle fire from the German infantry which almost totally destroyed the building. When the platoon could survive no longer in the house, Demmy ordered an evacuation. All this time, Robertson ran from section to section reconnoitering positions and encouraging his men. Finally, when all danger of further counterattacks had passed, Demmy reported that he had been wounded.

During the battle 40 Germans were taken prisoner and the PPCLI had lost eight men killed, 52 wounded and eight captured.

Demmy
DCM Sgt
RefScs: DHist 713 065 (D1)

Robertson
MC Capt
RefScs: DHist 713 065 (D2)

SAN LEONARDO
December 6

McLean John

"Show of Fearlessness Won DSO — a Rarity for Subalterns"

It was as brief as it was gallant. On this date John McLean of the Seaforth Highhlanders of Canada fought courageously in the streets of San Leonardo. Ignoring enemy machine-gun fire, he began flushing out the German defenders in door-to-door combat. Before he was through McLean and his men had accounted for at least eight enemy dead and another 18 captured, along with 10 machine guns.

DSO (Immediate)   Lt
RefScs: TDD 161

MOUTH OF THE MORO RIVER
December 6-9

KENNEDY Albert Arnott

"Commanded Four Days of Relentless Fighting"

On the evening of December 6, Bert Kennedy, commander of the Hastings and Prince Edward Regiment, led a feint attack at the mouth of the Moro River to enable another brigade to cross the river on his left. Next day he established a bridgehead astride the coast road to Ortona. On December 8, Kennedy maintained his battalion's position despite sporadic German attacks while subjected to heavy mortar and artillery fire. Again on the following day the regiment came under a determined counterassault to dislodge the regiment from its position. During the fighting Kennedy was everywhere, exhorting his troops and so inspiring them that large numbers of Germans were killed, and 50 were captured while not one inch of ground had been yielded. During the four days it was Kennedy's leadership and aggressiveness that allowed the regiment to establish its foothold and hang onto it.

DSO Maj
RefScs: DHist 713 065 (D2)   TDD 157-8 182

SOUTH OF THE ORSOGNA-ORTONA HIGHWAY
December 13

JONES James Harvey

"Though Wounded Stayed to Fight On"

James Jones and his platoon of the West Nova Scotia Regiment rode on three tanks in a surprise combined infantry and tank attack that resulted in three German tanks and an antitank gun being knocked out. During the swift fracas only one enemy shot was fired, but a shrapnel splinter struck Jones in the arm. However, he continued to lead his men in securing their position until the balance of his company arrived three and a half hours later. Although he asked to be allowed to continue the fight, the company commander ordered him to the rear for medical treatment.

MC (Immediate) Lt/Capt(Act)
RefScs: DHist 713 065 (D2)

CASA BERARDI
December 14

TRIQUET Paul

"Fearlessness at the Farmhouse"

Capture of the key "Cider" road junction of the Orsogna-Ortona Highway depended on securing a position at a three-storey farmhouse named Casa Berardi. No easy task. With the German 90th Panzer Grenadier Division, made up of infantry and tanks, holding it, and a gully in front of it, it presented a formidable redoubt. Paul Triquet's company of the Royal 22nd Regiment, with the support of the Canadian Armoured Regiment, was ordered to cross the gully and secure the position. As the Canadians attacked they were met with heavy mortar and machine-gun fire. Except for Triquet, all of the company officers and 50 percent of the men were killed or wounded. Triquet urged on the remainder encouraging the men by shouting: "Don't mind the Germans, they can't shoot straight." (See PA "B" below.) By this time the attackers were virtually surrounded by the Germans. But Triquet chose to ignore the predicament. "The safest place is dead ahead," he cried out over the noise of the shell-fire. Charging forward with his men, they broke the enemy resistance, putting four tanks out of action and silencing a nest of machine guns. Then, in close cooperation with their own tanks, they forced their way into the position. By this time Triquet's company was reduced to two sergeants and 15 men. Expecting a counterattack, Triquet organized his unit into a defensive perimetre around the remaining tanks and passed the word: "Iles ne passeront pas" borrowed from Petain's famous order at Verdun in 1916 — "They shall not pass." Nor did they. At the head of his troops Triquet personally accounted for several of the attacking enemy himself. This assault and subsequent attacks were beaten off with heavy losses to the Germans, while Triquet rallied his men to hold their ground. This they did against overwhelming odds until the remainder of the battalion relieved his unit the following day. It was a truly magnificent performance in which Triquet displayed not only courage and leadership, but his cheerfulness in the face of fierce and determined resistance served as an inspiration. The capture of Casa Berardi opened the way to the attack on the vital road junction. For the action, Triquet received the Victoria Cross, the only French Canadian to be so decorated.

Born in Cabano, P.Q., Triquet attended the academy there and later took six years of night school in Quebec City. While at school he was a member Cabano Cadet Corps which his father organized and trained. In 1937 he enlisted as a private in the Van Doos (Royal 22nd). Triquet

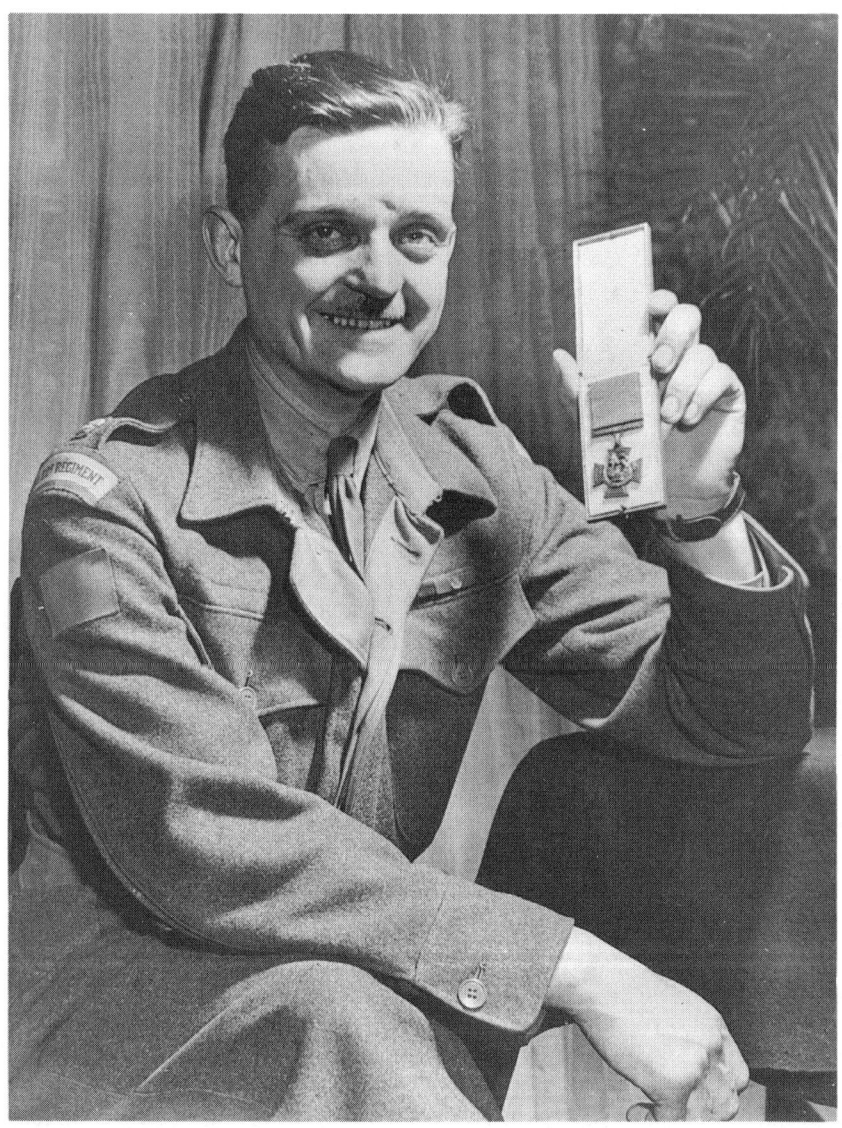

Paul Triquet (PA 157376)

retired from the army in 1947 and engaged in sales work until 1951 when he joined the reserve as CO of the Régiment de Levis. In 1954 he was given command of the 8th Militia Group. He lived in Quebec City before retiring to Florida. In addition to the VC, Triquet was also awarded the French Legion of Honour.

VC Ld'H(Fr)   Capt Maj(R) Col(R)   Born April 2 1910
RefScs: CAW 95   CVC 176-7   DHist 713 065 (D2)   VM 176-7

"A": Appended to the commendation for the VC is a hand-written comment from Chris Vokes, commander of the First Canadian Division. It reads: "I have seen the ground on which Major Triquet fought this action. In view of the difficult conditions then prevailing and the strength of the enemy position I consider it an outstanding deed of heroism."

"B": Some sources, i.e., the *London Gazette*, have reported these quotations differently. I have told them the way Paul related them to me at a dinner in honour of living Canadian VC winners at the Canadian Military Institute in Toronto.

December 18

AMERO Alfred John

"Led Rescue Party in Hail of Enemy Fire"

When both his platoon commander and sergeant were killed in an attack on a position near the stone farmhouse, Alfred Amero, as second-in-command of the rifle section, immediately took charge. A short time later two members of his unit were badly wounded and lay on open ground dangerously exposed to German artillery and machine-gun fire. In the face of it Amero led a small party across the bullet-swept area to rescue the wounded men and drag them back to safety. But for his bold action, observers later stated, the two men would have been killed without a doubt.

MM Pte
RefScs: DHist 713 065 (D1)

Ortona
December 20 - 28, 1943

December 20

HARLEY Donald Stuart

"Led Bayonet Charge to Rescue Situation"

At noon the Seaforth Highlanders of Canada began attacking this coastal town to create a diversion for the main thrust by the Loyal Edmonton Regiment from the south. As they reached the outskirts, C

Loyal Edmonton Regiment troops advance down a street in Ortona. (PA 116852)

Company of the Highlanders, led by Donald Harley, encountered stiff opposition. Avoiding a frontal attack, he guided his men up a precipitous cliff-like slope on the enemy's flank and so surprised the Germans that 14 machine-gun nests were silenced immediately.

The next objective was a church that formed an enemy stronghold. In the attack Harley's left flank ran into tough resistance resulting in such heavy losses that he had to commit his reserves. Though they beat off a counterattack, Harley realized that without a reserve platoon a second assault on his right flank, already weakened by casualties, might penetrate and endanger not only his own company but the right flank of the Eddies' main thrust. In the face of it he reorganized his own right flank and personally led a bayonet charge inflicting casualties upon the enemy and securing the situation.

MC (Immediate) Lt
RefScs: DHist 713 065 (D2)

December 21

GALBRAITH John MacNeill

"Crossed Minefield to Set Up Communications Link"

By this date the Loyal Edmonton Regiment had secured a foothold in the town and had moved its battalion headquarters to the outskirts. John Galbraith of the Seaforth Highlanders was charged with running a communications cable line into the town to provide first-hand information for the command post. That night, with two linesmen, carrying two miles of cable and a telephone, Galbraith set off for his destination. By the time they reached it a sign reading *Achtung Minen!* warned them not to enter a minefield they had just walked through! All the while, and again on the return journey, they came under heavy shell-fire. But within two hours they had set up the much-needed communications centre.

MC Capt
RefScs: DHist 713 065 (D2)

December 23

RATTRAY Charles Gordon

"Single-Handed Action Netted Bag of Enemy Soldiers and Weaponry"

During bitter street fighting — door-to-door and house-to-house — D Company of the Loyal Edmonton Regiment struggled down the main street to the square in the centre of the town. At the entrance to a building on the left they faced three German machine-gun posts supported by two others on the right. Charles Rattray with two others crawled over a pile of rubble to the building, all the while exposed to machine-gun fire from 30 yards' range and harassment from snipers and grenades. As they entered the house Rattray left his two comrades to mop up the ground floor while he charged up to the top storey and single-handedly captured five German paratroopers, three machine guns, four rifles, three pistols and quantities of ammunition and hand grenades. This enabled the rest of the company to knock out the machine-gun nests and continue its advance.

MM Pte
RefScs: DHist 713 065 (D1)

December 24

THOMSON Sydney Wilfred

"Repelled Fierce Counterattack"

As a company commander with the Seaforth Highlanders of Canada, Syd Thomson had already won the MC back in October at Decorata. By this time, when the CO was wounded some days earlier, he had assumed command of the regiment. At noon on December 23, the Highlanders were ordered to stage an attack to protect left flank of the Loyal Edmonton Regiment which had captured the southeast part of the town. By dusk they had reached their position by beating the enemy back but next morning the Germans launched an assault that jeopardized control of the coast road and the salient exits from the town. Although constantly exposed to sniping, machine-gun, mortar and shell-fire, Thomson remained forward with his men directing their defence, consolidating gains and encouraging them. The result was that by late afternoon the enemy attack had been beaten off and the advance allowed to continue to take possession of Ortona. For his leadership under sustained fire a DSO was added to Thomson's previously won MC.

DSO MC   Maj
RefScs: DHist 713 065 (D2)

O'NEIL George Edward

"Gallant Action Allowed Rescue of 'Buried' Comrades"

While attempting to rescue their comrades buried in debris from a house the enemy had blown up, a party of the Loyal Edmonton Regiment was subjected to harassment from Germans throwing hand grenades from a nearby building. George O'Neil worked his way under fire into the house forcing the enemy to withdraw. By thus engaging the Germans and distracting their attention, four men were extricated from the rubble who might otherwise have died from lack of medical attention.

MM   Cpl
RefScs: DHist 713 065 (D1)

December 26

CRANE Robert Basil

"Daring Charge Decimated Enemy Machine Gunners"

In the final stages of the bitter fighting for Ortona, Robert Crane's platoon of the 48th Highlanders was pinned down by German machine-gun fire from two directions. Crane and another member of the unit worked their way forward with a light machine gun of their own and drew the enemy fire onto themselves. This enabled the platoon to occupy improved positions from which they were able to silence one of the German guns. However, the other one continued to inflict heavy casualties. Then at this point Crane's own weapon jammed. With no regard for his own safety, he jumped up out of cover and charged the enemy post, killing the two Germans manning it with his bayonet. This single action manifested itself in the regiment being able to maintain its position to threaten the enemy as they withdrew from the town.

MM Pte
RefScs: 713 065 (D1)

Anzio
January 22 - May 23, 1944

On the Western Front, to break the deadlock created by the strong German defences against the U.S. 9th Army along the Gustav Line, simultaneously with a northward attack, on January 22, 1944, the U.S. 6th Corps made an amphibious landing on the Anzio beaches on the Mediterranean coast south of Rome. The Americans had hoped the maneuver would draw away German strength allowing a breakthrough on the Gustav Line. But the Germans held and by shuffling units and bringing in reinforcements the invasion forces at Anzio were held in check. Not until May, when Monte Casino finally fell, did the Americans in the south join up with the six Allied divisions at Anzio.

Canadians participated in operation "Shingle," as the invasion was called, as members of the First Special Service Force, a combined American-Canadian elite shock unit trained to tackle objectives otherwise considered impregnable. Known to the Germans as the "Black Devils" due to their ability to fight at night, the force numbered some 1,250 hand-picked men of which nearly 800 were Canadians. At Anzio 117 of these troops were lost.

Saskatoon Light Infantry in the advance beyond Ortona. (PA 116845)

February 8

PRINCE Thomas

"Canada's Most Decorated Native Soldier"

After dark, Tommy Prince, a member of the First Special Service Force, went enemy tank hunting with a field telephone. Creeping across a canal and playing out the phone line as he walked, Prince slipped into a farmhouse 200 yards from the German lines. There he waited until daylight at which time he could clearly spot German tanks as they rumbled back and forth, constantly shifting position to avoid American shells. During the morning he called down accurate artillery fire on a pair of the vehicles, destroying them both.

Though the enemy was unaware that Prince was in the house, around noon some mortar bombs fell behind it severing his telephone line. Prince donned a black hat and jacket he found lying in the house and, imitating an excitable Italian, rushed outside, darting about, waving his arms, all the while searching for the break in the telephone cable. When he found it, he made the necessary repairs. Then, making out his way to the front, he put on another performance for any Germans who might be watching and went back inside. He then called down more shell-fire which destroyed another two enemy tanks.

A former lumberjack, Manitoba-born Prince was a great-great-grandson of the legendary Indian chief Peguis. He survived WW2 to fight in Korea. His memory is honoured by a barracks named after him at Camp Petawawa, Ont., and by a statue unveiled in 1989 at Winnipeg Park.

MC SS(Am)   Sgt   Born 1916
RefScs: DHist 713 065 (D1)   TDD 225-6

Prince, who with the award of the Military Medal and the United States Silver Star became Canada's most decorated Native soldier, often complained that had he not been an Indian he would have won the VC instead. Though it is doubtful whether he meant it seriously, it is nevertheless a point well taken. After the battle of Ortona when his company commander congratulated him, Joseph St. Germain, a Native from northern Alberta, replied: "I hope I'll be killed in this war. Here I lead a platoon and the boys call me 'Saint,' but back in Canada I'm just a poor goddamn Indian with no right to vote and unable to even go in a bar." The sergeant got his death wish some months later when he was cut down by enemy fire during the fight for the Canale Naviglio in northern Italy.

BURMA
February 1944

Since November 1943, the Japanese had increased their strength in Burma from five divisions to eight. By February of the new year the British advance had come to an abrupt halt. The Nipponese objective was to invade East India and create a general rebellion against the British. The initial attack came in the Arakaran Hills to capture the port of

Chittagong and draw the British forces to that area. Holding the 5th Division down on the coast, the Japanese forces swung around the 7th Division inland. Within a few days the 7th was surrounded and the Japanese had cut the coastal road behind the 5th Division. They had expected the two divisions to withdraw, but they had reckoned without British aerial support. For two weeks supplies were delivered to the troops allowing them to stand firm and fight it out. The Japanese had no such support and their own supplies were soon exhausted. This, coupled with the pressure applied from the north by the British 26th Division, forced the Japanese to withdraw leaving behind 5,000 dead.

Charles Hoey (PA 112657)

HOEY Charles Ferguson

"Stormed Japanese Stronghold by Himself"

On the night of February 16, 1944, Charles Hoey's company of the Lincolnshire Regiment was ordered to capture a Japanese outpost near Maungdaw at all costs. After a night march through the Burmese jungle, the unit reached the foot of the position to be met by intense machine-gun fire. Hoey led his company right up to the objective. Wounded in the leg and head, he seized a Bren gun from one of his men and, firing from the hip, charged right into the enemy stronghold. Despite his wounds, the rest of his company had difficulty keeping up with him. This resulted in his storming the outpost alone. He succeeded in killing all its occupants but in the process was mortally wounded. For his bravery in this action Hoey, who had earlier been awarded the Military Cross, received a posthumous Victoria Cross.

Born in Duncan, on Vancouver Island, B.C., Hoey went to England in April 1933 where he enlisted in the British army. After graduating from Sandhurst Royal Military College, he joined the Lincolnshires. Posted to Burma in 1942, he served in that theatre until his death. Hoey is buried in Taukkyan Cemetery at Rangoon in Burma.

VC MC   Maj   Born March 26 1914   KIA Feb 16 1944
RefScs: CVC 178-9   VM 178-9

THE CANADIAN CAMPAIGN IN ITALY (2)
Liri Valley
May 11 - 31, 1944

*I*n April and early May, as part of the British Eighth Army, the First Canadian Corps was moved from the Adriatic coast in eastern Italy to the west to join in the U.S. 5th Army's struggle for Rome. Because, as in WW1, the Germans had come to associate the presence of Canadians with impending offensives, the transfer had to be made in secret. Half a million Allied soldiers took part in the offensive which began on May 11. After four days of heavy fighting they had cracked the Gustav Line. By May 18 the German defences were broken from Casino to the Tyrrhenian Sea and the Germans moved back to a second line of defence, the Adolf Hitler Line. On May 23 the Canadians attacked this fortification. Under heavy mortar and machine-gun fire, they breached the defences and the tanks of the Fifth Armoured Division poured through towards the next obstacle, the Melfa River. Although bitter fighting ensued forming a bridgehead, once across the waterway the major assault for the Liri Valley was over. Now the operation developed into a pursuit as the Germans retreated north. By May 31 the Canadians had occupied Frosinone, and their campaign in this area came to an end as they were withdrawn for a rest.

Crossing the Gari River May 11 - 13, 1944

At eleven-thirty on the night of May 11, as 1,700 Allied guns heralded the start of Operation Diadem, the First Canadian Armoured Division was spearheading the attack in support of the 8th Indian Division. Once the Indians had gained a foothold across the Gari River, it was the Canadians' task to span the 65-foot waterway with bridges to allow tanks to pour across into the bridgehead. This they achieved in three instances, one of them highly unique.

May 12

KINGSMILL Hugh Anthony Gault

"Guided Own Bridge Innovation into Place under Fire — Then Beat Off Enemy Attack to Dislodge It"

Tony Kingsmill of the 14th Canadian Armoured Regiment had devised a method of launching a mobile Bailey bridge across a river by mounting it on the back of two tanks, fore and aft. During the crossing of the Gari River, under intense machine-gun and mortar fire, he coolly directed the operation walking backwards over open ground, guiding the tank-bourne bridge into place. Wounded by an exploding shell he remained at the scene until the bridge was firmly secured. When a German attack developed to dislodge the Bailey, Kingsmill climbed inside one of the piggyback tanks and raked the enemy attackers with machine-gun fire while he called for artillery support. Only after the Germans were beaten off did Kingsmill finally leave to have his wounds attended to.

MC (Immediate)   Capt
RefScs: DHist 713 065 (D2)   TDD 239

CARSON Frederick Lyall

"Supervised Freeing of 23 Bogged-Down Tanks while under Sniper Fire"

Near San Angelo, 23 tanks of the 14th Canadian Armoured Regiment became bogged down in the soft, marshy flats of the Gari River. Frederick Carson, despite murderous sniper fire from the opposite riverbank, personally supervised the recovery and evacuation of the vehicles.

When one of the tanks was hit by a shell and caught fire, after all attempts to put out the blaze had failed, Carson lashed a cable to the burning vehicle and pulled it into the river thereby preventing its total destruction. His efforts resulted in the tanks finally being able to be put into action at a crucial time for the regiment.

MM Sgt
RefScs: DHist 713 065 (D1)   TDD 240

May 12 and 13

TAYLOR Donald Clarke

"Dashing Tank Charges Allowed Consolidation of Bridgehead"

Commanding a squadron of tanks of the 14th Canadian Armoured Regiment in support of the 3/8 Punjab Regiment, Donald Taylor successfully crossed the Gari River and smashed into the Gustav Line penetrating 1,500 yards into German-held territory. In the process his unit destroyed one enemy tank, three self-propelled guns and a strong antitank post. This position he held without any infantry support until dusk when he was ordered to withdraw. Next morning he returned, recapturing the position and repelling countless enemy counterattacks. His determination to hold on at any cost enabled the 19th Indian Infantry Brigade to consolidate the bridgehead.

MC (Immediate) Capt
RefScs: DHist 713 065 (D2)

Advance to the Hitler Line

With the Gustav Line behind them, the Canadians now advanced to the secondary German defences six miles farther up the Liri Valley — the Adolf Hitler Line. The date for an assault on the Line itself had been set for May 23, giving the Canadians several days to prepare for the most difficult battle of the entire Italian campaign.

OVERLOOKING FORME D'AQUINO
May 17

BALLARD Norman Alexander

"Captured German Bare-Handed"

In leading his platoon against enemy 75mm gun posts, Alexander Ballard of the 48th Highlanders used up all his hand grenades attacking enemy gun crews. Suddenly he found himself unarmed, looking down the barrel of a pistol held by a German *Oberleutnant*. With a roar Ballard leapt at the German officer, overpowered him with his bare hands and forced him to surrender. All told that day, Ballard's actions resulted in killing nine Germans, taking 12 prisoners, and capturing three 75mm machine guns and a half-track vehicle. In the process, despite heavy losses to his unit, he had managed to consolidate his company's position.

DSO Lt
RefScs: DHist 713 065 (D2)

BETWEEN PIGANATARO AND PORTECORVO
May 17

SHAW Robert James

"Halted Self-Propelled Gun Attack"

That night as the 48th Highlanders advanced up the valley, suddenly out of the darkness they heard the rumble of tracked vehicles. Robert Shaw promptly ordered mortar flares which revealed three German self-propelled guns and infantry moving into attack only 40 yards away. Shaw calmly fired his 6-pound antitank gun in the face of enemy 75mm and machine-gun fire, destroying two of the SPs and forcing the third out of range. As his own Bren gunners sprayed the German infantry, Shaw knocked out an enemy vehicle trapped on the side of a gulley. This marked the last attempt by the Germans to stop the Canadians from closing in on the Hitler Line.

MM (Immediate) Sgt
RefScs: DHist 713 065 (D1)   TDD 243

Assault on the Hitler Line

*B*acked by 810 guns throwing down the heaviest barrage up to this stage of the war, at six o'clock on the morning of May 23, the First Canadian Division attacked the vaunted Adolf Hitler Line between Aquino in the east and Pontecorvo to the west. This was the strongest German fortification the Allies had run into to date. Fortified with Panzerturm *concrete heavy gun and rocket emplacements, the enemy threw up a stiff shield of fire from the start. The 2nd Brigade on the right flank was stopped in its tracks, one of its regiments cut off. But on the left flank a regiment of the 3rd Brigade that had done a proper job of reconnaissance the day before broke through the line with comparative ease. By eight o'clock it had penetrated the German defences. Heavy fighting continued all day but by evening the battle of the Hitler Line, which the division commander Chris Vokes said was "the best battle I ever fought," was all over.*

May 23

ZIEGLER William Smith

"Artillery Architect Went Three Days without Sleep"

If there was a single individual most responsible for the Hitler Line victory it was Bill Ziegler, the First Canadian Division's chief gunner. Previous to the assault, the Calgarian and his staff worked for 72 hours without a break to organize every detail of the artillery support, one of the most complex fire plans ever devised and the heaviest in WW2 up to that time. It involved a series of concentrations on selected targets with a creeping barrage of high explosives that moved three hundred yards every three minutes. Added to this was a steady harassing fire of a thousand shells per hour.

During the battle, when the Canadians became halted in the Aquino sector, Zeigler drew up a contingency plan within 30 minutes that saw 668 guns open up. In less than a minute, 3,509 shells, totalling 92 tons of high explosives, fell on Aquino and its airfield. Throughout the day Ziegler spent much time forward ignoring the danger of enemy fire, checking artillery results, ordering changes on the spot.

Ziegler went on to distinguish himself further in the Italian campaign and also in Europe, but he never again planned another barrage which he concluded was "one hell of a waste of time — a lazy man's way of doing the job." He later maintained that since present-day gunners to do not employ barrages, he was truly "the author of the death of the barrage."

CBE DSO ED NA   Brig
RefScs: DHist 713 065 (D2)   TDD 256 248 257-8 261 263

After the battle of the Hitler Line ended, Chris Vokes summoned Ziegler, who expected a dressing down because the two had never hit it off, to his command dugout. He was surprised therefore when the division commander handed him a bottle of rye and told him to pour himself a drink. Ziegler emptied a few ounces into a tumbler and took a sip whereupon Vokes growled "Goddamnit. Pour yourself a drink!"

Ziegler added a little more but not enough to satisfy Vokes who shouted "Goddamnit, Ziegler, don't you understand English? *Pour yourself a drink!*"

This time Zeigler filled the glass and Vokes, satisfied, told him "Now drink it." Zigeler gulped it down then promptly passed out as a result of alcohol on top of three days on his feet. Exactly what Vokes had intended. When Ziegler awoke some hours later he felt "like a new man" and he and Vokes became life-long friends.

AQUINO
0600 Hours

EDKINS Roy Douglas

"Wounded, Refused Aid, Captured Enemy Sniper"

Leading his platoon against the deadly enemy 88mm and 75mm fire from the *Panzerturm* concrete pillboxes, Roy Edkins of the Princess Patricia's Canadian Light Infantry sustained multiple shrapnel wounds.

But he continued to lead his men until he was wounded a second time. Even then he refused to allow stretcher-bearers to carry him to the rear. After his platoon had moved forward he spotted a sniper holding up the advance of another of the regiment's companies. In spite of his wounds Edkins stalked the German rifleman and took him prisoner.

MM (Immediate) Cpl (A/Sgt)
RefScs: DHist 713 065 (D1)

SNELL Frederick William

"Machine Gunned Snipers from a Tree"

When his platoon commander was killed, Fred Snell of the PPCLI took command and reorganized the unit which had run into a minefield. Noticing movement in a tree ahead of him, he closed in on what turned out to be a pair of German snipers. Snell coolly felled them both with his Thompson machine gun.

DCM (Immediate) Cpl (A/Sgt)
RefScs: DHist 713 065 (D1)

0740 Hours

CARR-HARRIS Peter Raymond Victor
IRVINE Alfred

"Injured Clearing Minefield, Carried On"

Alfred Irvine of Royal Canadian Engineers was one of a mine-clearing party led by Peter Carr-Harris. The objective was to ensure that the tanks in support of the Princess Patricia's Canadian Light Infantry could get through the German defences. At close to eight o'clock that morning, the tanks were held up. Despite heavy artillery, mortar and machine-gun fire, the party swept a line through the minefield allowing the advance to continue. In this operation both Carr-Harris and Irvine were severely wounded but refused to leave the field until they had completed the job.

Carr-Harris
MC Lt
RefScs: DHist 713 065 (D2)

Irvine
MM Cpl (A/Sgt)
RefScs: DHist 713 065 (D1)

0900 Hours

KIDD Edmund Andrew

"Tended Wounded despite Being Struck by Shrapnel"

Casualties to the Loyal Edmonton Regiment during the attack were so numerous that Edmund Kidd was the only stretcher-bearer left in his company. Then while attending a casualty he was himself injured by mortar fire. However, he dressed two more casualties before crawling forward. With bullets and shrapnel bursting all around him, Kidd despite the pain from his own wounds, nevertheless tended to six more casualties and then hauled them to safety. He remained with the wounded men until ordered to report to the regimental aid post to have his own injuries tended to.

MM Pte
RefScs: DHist 713 065 (D1)

1000 Hours

DUDDLE Joseph McPhee

"Busy Day Fighting and Caring for Casualties"

Few people were as busy as Joe Duddle of the Seaforth Highlanders of Canada once the attack got under way. Early in the day, when all the officers in his company had either been killed or wounded, Duddle took charge. With two others armed with PIAT antitank gun he disabled an enemy tank in the face of severe machine-gun fire. Then advancing further he led an attack on three German posts knocking them out and taking prisoners.

At four o'clock that afternoon he was advised that there were several wounded ahead of his position. He improvised stretchers from pieces of railing and webbing and, despite heavy mortar fire, organized the evacuation of the wounded. In fact he continued this operation until relieved at one o'clock the following morning.

DCM (Immediate) CSM
RefScs: DHist 713 065 (D1)

CONWAY John Joseph

"Lost a Hand Saving His Men"

When one of the forward platoons his company became pinned down by German gun fire and its commander was killed, John Conway of the Seaforth Highlanders of Canada organized a detachment of four men from his headquarters and led them against the enemy machine-gun position. In the act of throwing a hand grenade, one of his group dropped the explosive on the ground. Unhesitatingly, Conway picked it up and was about to throw it clear when it burst and blew off his right hand. The audacious act saved his party, and despite his serious injury he continued to lead his men on the attack.

MC   Capt
RefScs: DHist 713 065 (D1)

PONTECORVO

SMITH Lloyd Russell

"Paralyzed from Waist Down, Continued to Direct Battle"

Due to uneven terrain and the German foxhole defences, the German line was difficult to penetrate. Lloyd Smith of the 4th Canadian Reconnaissance Regiment consolidated his position before advancing some distance into enemy territory by himself. He took a stand on a flat mount where he could observe his platoon's fire. Exposed as he was, he immediately became the target for a sniper. A bullet that struck him paralyzed him from the waist down, and at that moment his section came under severe shell, mortar and small-arms fire. Although in excruciating pain, Smith refused to allow his men to move to safety, and seeing several of his unit cut off by enemy machine-gun fire, he continued to direct his platoon's fire until the German gun was silenced.

Mc   Lt
RefScs: DHist 713 065 (D2)

PASFIELD William

"Injured, Rescued Wounded Comrades, Provided Covering Fire Allowing Lead Armoured Car to Escape"

Bill Pasfield of the 4th Canadian Reconnaissance Regiment was gunner in a light armoured car when it was struck by a land mine. Shaken up and groggy from a head injury he managed to get other more seriously wounded crew members free of the vehicle and drag them to safety. He then returned to the car and manned the machine gun in the turret to provide covering fire for the lead vehicle in the formation. His accuracy inflicted heavy casualties on the Germans and allowed the lead car to escape from the enemy minefield.

MM   Tpr
RefScs: DHist 713 065 (D1)

The Melfa River Crossing May 24 - 29, 1944

Coincidentally with the collapse of the Hitler Line, the Americans broke out of the Anzio bridgehead to the northwest, threatening to cut off the German 10th Army. Its salvation depended on how long it could hold out along the shallow Melfa River six miles to the north of collapsed German fortifications. At three minutes to eight on the morning of Wednesday, May 24, tanks of the Fifth Canadian Armoured Division began their assault. Desperate fighting took place as the Allies tried to advance across the narrow 50-yard-wide river. But once the Canadians were over in force, the fighting for the Liri Valley was over. The operation quickly developed into a pursuit as the Germans hastily pulled back to avoid being trapped. On May 29 the Canadians entered Ceprano and, with the fall of Frosinone two days later, the road to Rome was open. The Americans entered the ancient capital on June 4. But by then the Canadians had been withdrawn for a well-earned rest and reorganization except for the 1st Canadian Armoured Brigade which accompanied the British in the push northward to the final line of German defence.

The battle for the Liri Valley had cost the First Canadian Corps 789 men killed, 2,463 wounded and 116 taken prisoner. But during the 41-mile advance the Corps had captured 1,400 Germans and killed and wounded a great many others.

MELFA RIVER
May 24

FUNK Jacob Kippenstain

"Knocked Out Self-Propelled Gun at Close Range"

Armed with a PIAT antitank gun, Jacob Funk of the 2nd Armoured Regiment and two Bren gunners went stalking a German self-propelled gun that was firing on Sherman tanks of his regiment, the Lord Strathcona's Horse, from the other side of the river. Crawling along the bank he waited until he came within 150 yards' range, then fired. His shot, however, went awry into overhanging foliage. Funk edged still closer — to within 100 yards — but his next shot fell short. Funk fired again but this time he was too high. But his fourth try found the mark; it struck the target and the crew bailed out of the position, two of them dropped in their tracks by the two covering Bren gunners. Three others fled taking what remained of the SP gun with them.

MM Tpr
RefScs: DHist 713 065 (D1)   TDD 267-8

BONNEVILLE Hector

"Led Daring Assault on Machine-Gun Nests, Directed Fire against Pillbox"

Hector Bonneville led a patrol of four to take out two German machine guns holding up the advance of the Irish Regiment of Canada. In the subsequent action they killed and wounded nine of the enemy but two of Bonneville's men were also injured. Bonneville covered them until they were safely evacuated, then proceeded to direct tank fire against an enemy pillbox. The fortification was eventually destroyed and one German was taken prisoner.

MM Pte
RefScs: DHist 713 065 (D1)

PERKINS Edward James

"Undeterred by Carriers, Tanks, Strongholds, Guns, Mortars"

"Perky" Perkins had been given the assignment of taking a small reconnaissance force of the 2nd Canadian Armoured Regiment — three Honey Tanks (one other had broken down) and 13 men across the river to seize and hold a position in advance of the main Regimental Group. Early in the afternoon, while enroute, they encountered a German half-track carrier and killed the entire crew. Next they faced a defended house. Taking it by surprise they captured 11 prisoners. A short while later a Panther tank appeared in their path. Perkins quickly immobilized it with a sharp burst from his five-point Browning gun which killed the crew commander. To get tanks across the river it became necessary to widen a path up the far bank. Under Perkins' direction this was quickly accomplished even though the group all the while came under heavy German mortar and machine-gun fire. Later in the day Perkins stood on the top of two of his own tanks in succession to direct fire against a German 88mm self-propelled gun that was harassing Canadian tanks of A Company of the Westminster Regiment to the rear (see Mahony).

DSO Lt
RefScs: DHist 703 065 (D2)

MACEY Clifford Norman

"Perkins' Right-Hand Man during the Crossing"

Riding shotgun in "Perky" Perkins Honey tank was "Chum" Macey, acting as troop sergeant for the small advance 2nd Canadian Armoured Regiment force. Macey took part in all the action that afternoon and was of inestimable assistance in helping expand the tank path while under vicious German fire. That night he insisted that slit trenches be dug and thus prevented casualties from enemy bombardment.

DCM Sgt
RefScs: DHist 703 065 (D1)

MAHONY John Keefer

"Ignored Injuries, Consolidated Bridgehead"

Commanding A Company of the Westminster Regiment, John Mahony was ordered to establish the initial bridgehead across the Melfa. Although he led the crossing in full view of the enemy under heavy machine-gun fire, he did succeed in gaining a small foothold. But due to the terrain, it was only possible to dig shallow weapons pits. That was the least of the company's concerns. The Germans had ringed the area on three sides with one 88mm self-propelled gun 450 yards to the right, and four anti-aircraft guns 100 yards to the left of that. On their left flank the Canadians faced a heavy Spandau gun, a second 88mm weapon, and an infantry company armed with an arsenal of mortars and machine guns. Shortly after the bridgehead had been consolidated, the inevitable counterattack took place. But the Westminsters managed to beat it off with PIAT antitank guns, mortars and hand grenades. Mahony became wounded, once in the head and twice in the leg, but refused medical aid. Though every movement was agony, he continued to direct the defences. By this time company strength had been reduced to 60 men and all but one of the platoon officers had been wounded. Then, an hour later, German tanks formed up some 500 yards in front of the bridgehead along with a company of infantry for a second counterassault. At one stage a section of the Westminsters was pinned down by intense machine-gun fire. But by using smoke grenades, Mahony was able to rescue the unit for a loss of only one man. The counterattack was finally beaten and, in the process, the Canadians had destroyed three self-propelled guns, a Panther tank, and had decimated the enemy infantry.

By the time reinforcements arrived, made up of the regiment's remaining companies and supporting weapons. Mahony's company had held off the enemy for five hours. Only then did Mahony agree to have his wounds dressed though he refused to be evacuated. His defence of the small perimeter against overwhelming odds and under the severest conditions was crucial to the outcome of the Liri Valley battle. During the time that his company had come under siege, the Germans realized that Mahony was the moving spirit behind the stubborn resistance. As a result they took constant aim on him. But in the same manner in which he disregarded his injuries he also ignored the enemy fire. For his stoicism during the fighting, which proved to be an inspiration to all those around him, Mahony was awarded the Victoria Cross.

Mahony was born in New Westminster, B.C., and after leaving school became a newspaper reporter. Prior to WW2 he served in the Westminster Regiment of the militia and was among the first to enlist for active service when war broke out. After the cessation of hostilities he remained in the army and served successively as Command Cadet Officer, Western

John Mahony (PA 167002)

Command, Director of Publications, and Assistant Adjutant and Quarter-Master General of the Western Ontario Area. In 1954 he was posted to Washington D.C. as Canadian Army Liaison Officer.

VC Maj   Born June 30 1911
RefSCs: CVC 180-1   TDD 267-9 270 298   VM 180-1

On July 31, 1943, Mahony was invested with the VC in the field by George VI. The King was travelling incognito as "General Collingwood" when he reviewed Canadian troops near Raviscanina in the Volturno Valley.

MELFA RIVER
May 25

BURTON Alan

"Led Tank Advance that Netted 100 Prisoners"

Before starting across the river on May 24, intelligence advised Alan Burton that his squadron of the Governor-General's Horse Guards would face upwards of 48 German tanks. To the GeeGees' surprise as they advanced with their dozen Sherman tanks and assorted armoured vehicles, the enemy forces retreated without firing a shot. "They thought we were part of a much larger group and didn't realize we were out in left field," Burton later explained. By the end the second day they had taken a hundred Germans prisoner, one of them an officer carrying enemy codes.

DSO Maj
RefScs: DHist 713 065 (D2)   TDD 271

SOUTH OF CEPRANO
May 27

MUNRO Hamish Coull

"Directed Gun-Ferrying Operation while under Fire"

When a troop of the 4th Canadian Anti-Tank Regiment Royal Canadian Artillery began moving seven antitank guns to the Liri River to be ferried across by raft, they came under heavy German artillery and mortar fire. Then, as they neared the raft site, an enemy machine gun and two snipers opened up on them. Nevertheless, under Hamish Munro's direction they began loading the guns aboard. As the fourth one was being moved Munro spotted the location of the German machine-gun nest and immediately put a 6-pounder into action to wipe it out. That unnerved the enemy and the troop was able to finish loading the raft and get the guns across to the bridgehead and into position. This now allowed the infantry to cross.

MM Bds (A/Sgt)
RefScs: DHist 713 065 (D1)

FROSINONE
May 29

PEDEN Donald Campbell

"Determination and Action Got Convoy Moving Again"

While pushing towards the town, nine Royal Canadian Army Service Corps trucks suddenly came under heavy enemy shell-fire bringing the convoy to a halt. All of the drivers except one ran from their vehicles and took cover. This left the line of trucks a highly vulnerable target. Don Peden and another soldier climbed down from their trucks and marched to the front of the convoy where they found the driver and spare driver of the lead truck dead from a shell burst. They proceeded on to the crossroads where they persuaded the drivers to return to their trucks. By taking charge they got the convoy moving again and out of danger. This action not only saved the vehicles and resulted in fewer casualties, it also succeeded in getting much-needed material and supplies to the forward area.

MM   Cpl
RefScs: DHist 713 065 (D1)

EUROPE
June 6, 1944 - May 7, 1945

From D-Day, when the Allies landed on the beaches of Normandy, to VE-Day, the day of the German surrender at a school house in Reims, the First Canadian Army under General Harry Crerar fought in seven major battle campaigns. These included the invasion itself, the capture of Caen, the Falaise Gap, clearing the coastal ports, the Scheldt, the Rhineland and the liberation of Holland. In 11 months of steady fighting the Canadians had advanced some 450 miles to help bring about victory in Europe.

The Battle of Normandy
June 6 - August 20, 1944

*B*efore he became Supreme Allied Commander of Southeast Asia, over the vigorous objections of almost everyone, including Winston Churchill, Lord Louis Mountbatten as head of Combined Operations selected the Baie de le Seine area in France as the most feasible venue for the Allied invasion of Europe. Despite the manifold initial protestations, his choice was later ratified by the Combined Chiefs of Staff. It was a logical decision. For although Festung Europa was a propoganda fortification, an attack in the Pas de Calasis was still out of the question. The Atlantic Wall may have been nothing more than a series of widely spaced concrete gun emplacements; it was impossible to effectively protect 3,000 miles of coastline. Nevertheless, because the Germans expected that any major assault would come in the Pas de Calais (the exceptions being Field Marshal Erwin Rommel and Adolf Hitler who believed the Allies would strike at Normandy), strong defences were concentrated in that area and, despite all the advantages of a short Channel crossing, an invasion there would have been suicidal. Also, Dieppe had demonstrated the folly of attacking a well-fortified port. To succeed the landing had to be on an open beach or beaches.

On the night of June 5/6, one British and two U.S. airborne divisions, consisting of 20,000 paratroopers (of which the 1st Canadian Parachute Battalion was a part) were dropped into Normandy on Le Contentin Peninsula and at the mouth of the Orne River. At dawn the next morning — D-Day — supported by a pulverizing bombardment from the air and at sea, two divisions of the 1st United States Army and two Second British Army divisions, one of them the Third Canadian Infantry Division supported by the 3rd Canadian Armoured Brigade, landed on five different beaches: "Omaha," "Utah," "Sword," "Juno," and "Gold." Juno, between Courseulles and St. Aubin-sur-Mer, was assigned to the Canadians. The invasion fleet numbering 7,000 ships also towed two pre-fabricated "Mulberry" harbours and an underwater pipeline across the Channel into the bay. By day's end 50,000 men had been landed on the beaches and the Allies had penetrated inland in some areas as far as 11 miles. That night Rommel's crack 12th S.S. Panzer Division reached the battleground with orders to "throw the enemy back into the sea." They never succeeded, but their determined counterattacks did manage to blunt the British-Canadian advance.

Initial objectives were the capture of the Cherbourg Peninsula and the ancient Norman capital of Caen, former seat of William the Conqueror. By July 1, on the western flank the Americans had cleared the upper part of the Contentin Peninsula including Cherbourg. Farther south their forces were within striking distance of St. Lô. To the east

German counterattacks kept the Anglo-Canadian forces out of Caen until July 10. By this time the second Canadian Corps had arrived in France, and on July 23 the First Canadian Army under General Harry Crerar became operational. The Allies now had a million men in Normandy, and with the Anglo-Canadian advance across the Orne and south toward Falaise the stage was set for the breakout.

Two days later the Americans stabbed their way through the enemy positions at St. Lô and the Germans pulled their forces from the Caen front to meet this new threat. But it was too late. They were caught in a trap. The Americans swept around from the south enveloping the Germans in a pocket as the Canadians advanced on Falaise which fell on August 16. That was the end of the fighting in Normandy and the end of the German hold on France. On August 25 the Americans entered Paris. By mid-September the Canadians had overrun the V-1 corridor and were rapidly putting an end to the flying bomb menace to London. The job now was to clear the Channel ports, but although some of them offered stiff resistance, by the end of September the only Germans left in France were KIA, or taken prisoner.

D-Day

On the morning of June 5, Canadian troops of the 3rd Division under the command of Major-General Rod Keller, known as "Force J," set sail with the invasion fleet from the Isle of Wight to begin the 100-mile cross-Channel voyage due south to Normandy. At ten-thirty that night a company of the 1st Canadian Parachute took off from Harwell Field as part of the pathfinder force of the 6th Airborne Division to mark drop-zone positions around the Caen area. An hour later the main force took off from Down Ampney to arrive over the D-Z by 1:30 a.m. on June 6. Their objective was to destroy bridges and other installations at the mouth of the Orne River.

Juno was split into two beaches. "Mike" beach included the villages of Courseulles-sur-Mer, Bernières-sur-Mer and the western outskirts of St. Aubin-sur-Mer. "Nan" beach to the west was much more open, half a mile wide at low water, with only the hamlet of Vaux and the village of Graye-sur-Mer a quarter of a mile inland.

At seven-thirty in the morning, delayed by bad weather and rough seas, the 7th Brigade stormed ashore in the face of strong enemy strongholds which had survived the bombardment, and mined beach obstacles hidden by the rising tide. Opposition was intense — one battalion lost 65 men in a few minutes — in the fight to capture Courseulles and the inland villages of St. Croix-sur-Mer and Banville. By evening the brigade was consolidated near Cruelly.

Once established on the beachhead, the 8th Brigade moved inland to seize Bernières. Beyond that progress was slow but by nightfall Beny-sur-Mer had been taken.

The 9th Brigade landed shortly before noon at Bernieres, then advanced to Buissons, less than four miles from Caen. But there machine-gun fire held up the advance and the brigade was forced to halt just short of the divisional objective of Carpiquet airfield.

By the end of D-Day some 14,000 Canadians had landed in Normandy. Casualties numbered 1,074 of which 359 were fatal, but this represented a fraction of the losses suffered at Dieppe. And, this time, the foothold was permanent.

1st Hussars, Royal Winnipeg Rifles, Regina Rifles and Canadian Scottish Regiment land at Normandy. (PA 132468)

VARAVILLE

HANSON John Philip

"Paratrooper Took Charge when Company Commander was Killed"

When his company commander was killed during an attack on a German position near this Norman hamlet, John Hanson of the 1st Canadian Parachute Battalion immediately took charge. Though wounded during the subsequent action, showing exceptional leadership and audacity, Hanson enabled his company to consolidate the position inflicting heavy casualties on the enemy and taking 40 prisoners. Despite heavy mortar fire Hanson remained at his post until relieved.

MC Capt
RefScs: DHist 713 065 (D1)   OTC 63 72-3

NAN BEACH
The Dynamic Daltons

At time of the invasion both Charlie Dalton and his brother Elliot were company commanders in the Queen's Own Rifles of Canada.

Charles and Elliott Dalton at Aldershot, May 1943. (Private Collection)

On D-day both distinguished themselves in battle, Charlie suffering a wound to his head. Six days later in Normandy, Elliot was also wounded and ended up in hospital beside his brother. Both Daltons recovered from their injuries and were soon back into combat continuing to fight until the war ended in Europe. A unique pair of Canadian soldiers, both of whom received the DSO.

DALTON Charles Osborne

"Despite Head Wound Led His Men in Charge on Enemy Gun Post"

On Nan, the Queen's Own Rifles of Canada landed directly in front of a strongpoint at Bernières. Before it disembarked, Charles Dalton's company had already suffered casualties in the landing craft from mines and other obstacles. Upon reaching the beach the unit came under heavy German fire; 65 men were wiped out in minutes and Dalton himself was severely wounded in the head. To make matters worse the supporting tanks had not yet shown up. Nevertheless, Dalton led his men across the sand to the assault position and was instrumental in knocking out one of the enemy pillboxes. In spite of stiff opposition, due to Dalton's dauntlessness and leadership, the German fortified post was quickly overrun. As a result the company following Dalton's was able to land on the beach without a single casualty.

DSO Maj
RefScs: DHist 713 625 (D2)

DALTON Hume Elliot

"Dashing Assault Ensured Safety of Supporting Troops"

During the initial assault on the beach by the QOR, Elliot Dalton led his men in such a fierce attack that German resistance was instantly overcome. He then advanced with his unit through the town of Bernières-sur-Mer driving the enemy into the fields beyond. This operation was completed so quickly and efficiently, and with such dash, that the reserve companies of the battalion coming in behind were able to land on the beach without a shot being fired at them.

DSO MiD Maj
RefScs: DHist 713 065 (D2)

BUCHANAN Norman Bruce

"Won MC Three Times"

In Italy, "Ike" Buchanan was twice decorated with the MC before landing with the reserve company of the Queen's Own Rifles at Bernières where he continued to exhibit the same kind of dash, daring and coolness under fire he had shown in the Mediterranean campaign, earning him a second Bar to the MC. Shortly after embarking on the Normandy beach, when a fellow officer was hit by enemy machine-gun fire, he collected a stretcher and, with the help of one of the men in his regiment, carried the wounded man to safety. The following day at an advanced observation post he repelled a German counterattack. For the next three days he was constantly moving from OP to OP rallying his men and directing artillery fire against attacks by German tanks. At the same time he also organized evacuation of OPs when they came under overwhelming assault by the enemy.

MC & 2 Bars Capt
RefScs: DHist 713 065 (D2)

BOND Thomas

"Bravery under Fire Made Advance Possible"

Tom Bond, attached a forward observation officer to Le Régiment de la Chaudière, the reserve battalion following in behind the QORs, was responsible for detailing the unit's advance to Beny-sur-Mer and the hamlets beyond. Bond stood forward with the leading company, and on two occasions, although under heavy German artillery and mortar fire, remained at his observation post until the objective had been reached.

Near Le Hamel he was shelled out of his OP and while directing fire on an enemy position went forward to another post to continue giving support to the infantry.

MC Capt
RefScs: DHist 713 065 (D2)

ADAIR Robert William

"Ignored Danger to Tend to Wounded"

During the attack on the beachhead at St. Aubin-sur-Mer, when three other stretcher-bearers were killed, Bob Adair of the North Shore Regiment found himself to be the only one left in his entire company. Although the battalion was under heavy German fire, with total disregard for his own safety the Maritimer rendered first aid to the injured. When he had finished treating the wounded on the beach, although he had been warned that the enemy had placed booby-traps all over the grounds, throughout the day and that night he searched around the buildings for those in need of care until his medical supplies ran out.

DCM   Pte
RefScs: DHist 713 065 (D1)

GRAYSON William David

"Led Three Daring Raids, Netted 40 German Prisoners"

D-Day was a field day for Bill Grayson of the Regina Rifle Regiment. While entering a block of houses at Courseulles-sur-Mer, a German machine-gun crew made a dash with their weapons for their slit trenches from a house beyond the seawall. Grayson ran over and, armed only with a Colt automatic pistol, forced the enemy gunners to surrender.

Later in the morning he led three others from the safety of a group of houses into an enemy pillbox, and took 10 more prisoners. That same day, with five of his men he cleared out a large tunnel along a river bank during which a number of Germans were killed and 25 others taken prisoner.

MC   Lt
RefScs: DHist 713 065 (D1)

ARIS James Edwin

"Efficient Ammo Dump Operation"

Jim Aris of the Royal Canadian Army Service Corps had a uniquely risky job on invasion day. At Bernières he was put in charge of the ammunition dump. Organizing the off-loading from the landing craft he carried out the chore so efficiently that not one of his men was lost.

That night, the dump came under heavy bombing starting a number of fires that illuminated the area. Despite the danger from sniper fire, Aris continued to direct the action.

His skills did not end there. Throughout the advance through France, Belgium, Holland and the Rhineland, he continued to render valuable service often under the most difficult and dangerous conditions.

MM Sgt
RefScs: DHist 713 065 (D1)

BUELL Donald Bowie

"Won DSO for Direction of Widespread Operation"

As the left-flank battalion during the assault on St. Aubin-sur-Mer and the advance beyond south to Tailleville and east to Langrune-sur-Mer, the North Shore Regiment was badly exposed on that side and German opposition was tougher than expected. But although progress was slow the unit managed to reach all of its objectives until halted by an enemy position near a radar station. The regiment was ordered to by-pass it. Due to a frequent breakdown in communications with brigade headquarters, the battalion commander Donald Buell had to make most tactical decisions on the spot, a task not made any easier by the fact that the operation branched out in several different directions. Thanks to the leadership of Buell, who was at all times well forward with his troops to keep in constant touch with the situation, by day's end all of the battalion's objectives had been attained.

DSO Lt Col
RefScs: DHist 713 065 (D2)

MOOREHEAD Charles Hamilton

"Wounded Stretcher-Bearer Saved Others"

Throughout the landing at Courseulles-sur-Mer, though wounded twice during the 45 minutes his company was on the beach, stretcher-bearer Charlie Moorehead of the Regina Rifle Regiment carried the dead and wounded onto the beach and began treating the injured. As the tide rolled in he pulled them to dry land, all the while subjected to German machine-gun and mortar fire. After dragging a wounded comrade from the three feet of water, struggling and faltering with every step, Moorehead was evacuated and taken to hospital to have his own injuries attended to.

MM   Rfn
RefScs: DHist 713 065 (D1)

LE MESNIL
June 8

GRIFFIN Peter Ryerse

"Paratrooper Led Attack, Directed Orderly Withdrawal"

At nine o'clock in the morning, with 75 other men, Peter Griffin of the 1st Canadian Parachute Battalion assaulted a group of farm buildings occupied by soldiers from the German 857 and 858 Grenadier Regiments and well defended by machine guns. The attack was made through an orchard; the paratroopers captured a farmhouse. When their position came under a strong counterattack, Griffin ordered an orderly withdrawal. Due to his skillful leadership, the retreat and subsequent holding of a new position were accomplished with a minimum of casualties.

MC   Capt
RefScs: DHist 713 065 (D2)   OTC 78-9

PUTOT-EN-BESSIN
June 10/11

FROST Alfred Leo

"Took Charge of Platoon, Dispersed Enemy with Bren Gun"

At night Alfred Frost of the 1st Canadian Scottish Regiment took charge of a platoon reconnoitering German positions at the bridge to the town when his commander had become a casualty. Frost personally accounted for three of the enemy killed and by skillful use of his Bren gun he dispersed the Germans when the unit was pinned down by machine-gun fire. On returning to his own lines he carried a wounded comrade to safety.

MM Cpl (A/Sgt)
RefScs: DHist 713 065 (D1)

NORREY-EN-BESSIN
June 17

TUBB Charles Stuart Thorne

"Repulsed Eight Consecutive Enemy Attacks"

Holding down a defence post in the village, Charles Tubb's company of the Regina Rifles Regiment was attacked eight times and also subjected to artillery and mortar fire. But although casualties were high, due to Tubb's leadership all attacks were repulsed and heavy losses were in turn inflicted on the Germans.

DSO Maj
RefScs: DHist 713 065 (D2)

CHÂTEAU DE LA LONDE
June 28

FETTERLEY James

"Captured Tank Intact, Overcame Mortar Nests"

While leading his company for an attack on the château through severe machine-gun and mortar fire, John Fetterley of the British East Yorkshire Regiment captured a German tank intact. He then led his men with such dash that all German mortar positions were overcome and their crews killed. Later the platoon was attacked by five enemy tanks, but although the unit had been reduced to 12 men, the Germans failed to dislodge them and they were able to hang on until relief arrived.

MC Lt
RefScs: DHist 713 065 (D2)

Rauray

James James Alan

"Wounded Twice, Returned to Fight"

Serving with the British Durham Light Infantry, Jim James was wounded twice — once in the head — when his platoon attacked the village. After his second injury he had his wounds dressed but he insisted on returning to battle to lead his unit against a German counterattack.

    MC Lt
    RefScs: DHist 713 065 (D2)

Le Petit Seminaire
July 13

Snodgrass Henry James

"Injured by Shelling, Asked to Have Comrade Treated First"

When Henry Snodgrass, a member of the headquarters staff of the 9th Canadian Infantry Brigade, was hit by shrapnel, he remained at his post, even though his wound was painful. Then, as his comrades began to dress his injuries, he insisted that another guard who had taken shelter in a man-hole should be treated first because his injuries were more severe.

    CdeGwb (Fr) Pte
    RefScs: DHist 713 065 (D1)

Build-Up to the Breakout

During the period prior to the breakout, the Canadians, alongside the British, experienced some of the toughest fighting of the entire European campaign. Powerful German Panzer divisions did their best to prevent the capture of Caen. Progress was slow and losses were heavy.

It took a month before Carpiquet airfield finally fell to the Canadians who then took Caen on July 10. The task of the Canadian Corps was now to break out of the city across the Orne River with the double objective of expanding the bridgehead as well as holding down the German troops to assist in an American breakout in the west. The fighting, especially around the Verrières Ridge area, was bitter and bloody. However, the strategic gains were rewarding. With some of Germany's best armoured formations engaged on the Anglo-Canadian front, the Americans were able to break out of Le Contentin Peninsula to begin the encircling movement around the German forces. In the final stage of this strategy, on July 25 the Canadians attacked on either side of the road from Caen to Falaise. Casualties were heavy and the Germans held their ground, but on that same day the U.S. 1st Army broke out of St. Lo forcing the Germans to begin moving their troops from the Caen sector to stem the American advance on Avranches.

CARPIQUET VILLAGE
July 4

DUCHNICKI Frank Albert

"Directed Artillery Fire to Secure Observation Post"

In the morning the North Shore Regiment, supported by the 12th Field Regiment Royal Canadian Artillery, was ordered to establish an observation post on the northeastern corner of the village overlooking the approaches to Caen. Immediately the area came under intense German artillery fire, and the observation officer was seriously wounded. Gunner Frank Duchnicki evacuated the man to the nearest medical aid post, then returned to the position. All through the day he directed the RCA's fire during enemy tank and infantry counterattacks and while under heavy and continuous mortar fire, thereby consolidating the post.

CdeGwb (Fr)   Gnr
RefScs: DHist 713 065 (D1)

Carpiquet Airfield

Sinclair Carnet William

"Enemy Infantry Surrendered to Unarmed Stretcher-Bearer"

During the day's fighting Carnet Sinclair of the Royal Winnipeg Rifles took over as the sole stretcher-bearer for three of the battalion's companies when all of the other bearers had themselves become stretcher-cases. Working under the most hazardous conditions through heavy enemy shell and mortar fire, Sinclair made five trips bandaging and evacuating the wounded. On one trek four Germans surrendered to him, even though he was unarmed.

MM (Immediate) Rfn
RefScs: DHist 713 065 (D1)

Grant Donald Ian

"Photographer Impervious to Danger to Get the Job Done"

On D-Day Don Grant, a photographer with the Canadian Film and Photo Unit, came ashore with the Winnipeg Rifles. Although the landing craft came under heavy fire, Grant dashed onto the beach, bullets sweeping all around him. Grant loved to be in the thick of it. Later, while covering the attack on Carpiquet airfield, he showed the same disregard for his personal safety when he and his driver came under heavy mortar fire. His driver, who was assisting him, was killed. Grant made several attempts under heavy fire to reach his driver's body but was soon wounded himself.

MC Lt
RefScs: DHist 713 625 (D2)

After the war I worked with Don as a reporter with the *Windsor Star*. He continued to seem oblivious to danger. He had to get that picture, if it meant climbing up a ladder to get a shot of a fire, or squeezing under a wrecked truck. He treated each assignment as an adventure, not to mention a challenge. One of his classic wartime pictures was that of David Currie during the Falaise Gap.

North of Caen
July 5

WOODWARD James Crawford

"Fought off Tanks, Infantry, Attacked Trucks"

At twenty minutes past seven in the morning, the platoon commanded by James Woodward of the Cameron Highlanders of Ottawa was attacked by six German tanks accompanied by infantry. As the tanks drew within 150 yards of the Highlanders, Woodward rallied his men bringing to bear four machine guns, a Bren gun and a PIAT antitank weapon on the enemy vehicles. During the 30-minute engagement, Woodward directed the battle from open ground despite heavy German mortar and gun fire. One tank was destroyed and numerous casualties were inflicted on the enemy. As the remaining five tanks withdrew, Woodward led an attack on several German trucks carrying infantry causing the vehicles to leave the road, badly damaging them and resulting in casualties.

Bar to MC (Immediate)   Lt
RefScs: DHist 713 065 (D2)

Buron
July 8

ANDERSON John MacMorran

"Drove Jeep through Fire to Rescue Wounded"

During the attack on this town Anderson spent the day rescuing wounded from the front line. Time and again he drove his jeep in the middle of the battle disregarding German mortar fire, shelling and machine-gun bullets. His actions saved many lives of those who would otherwise have been left on the field.

MC (Immediate)   Capt
RefScs: DHist 713 065 (D2)

VERSON
July 15/16

SMITH John Alfred

"Continued Evacuating Wounded despite Shelling"

On his way to the Royal Regiment of Canada field dressing station, the jeep driven by stretcher-bearer John Smith broke down. Smith continued on foot, found another jeep and returned for his patients. By this time Verson had come under heavy shelling and he was advised to wait until it ended. However, knowing there were many cases needing to be evacuated, he went back to his abandoned vehicle, repaired it and continued to bring back the wounded.

MM (Immediate) Pte
RefScs: DHist 713 065 (D1)

LOUVIGNY
July 18/19

DRURY Charles Mills

"Future Deputy Defence Minister Took Command of Battle"

As artillery representative of the 4th Canadian Infantry Brigade headquarters for the attack on Louvigny, "Bud" Drury went beyond the infantry points to spot the German positions. During the battle he stayed at a forward observation post in spite of snipers and mortar and shellfire, personally directing the artillery on the enemy. When the brigade commander became wounded he took charge of the fighting until relieved.

By war's end Drury had attained the rank of Brigadier. Following WW2 he was deputy minister of national defence from 1948 to 1955.

DSO (Immediate) Lt/Col
RefScs: CE   DHist 713 065 (D2)

CORBETT James Robert

"Reconnaissance Bonus — Captured Enemy Soldier"

When the carrier in which Jim Corbett, a member of the Royal Regiment of Canada headquarters staff, was riding was blown up by a land mine, he continued his reconnaissance in the darkness on foot despite being injured and badly shaken up. Proceeding through enemy fire he not only acquired the tactical information he had been ordered to obtain, but captured a German soldier enroute.

MM   Sgt
RefScs: DHist 713 065 (D1)

ETAVAUX
July 23

LACOURSE Benoit

"Fait d'Armes"

During the afternoon Benoit Lacourse of Le Régiment de Maisonneuve led four of his men in destroying three German machine-gun posts using hand grenades. This *fait d'armes* enabled his company to reach its objective, an action which would otherwise have been jeopardized by the enemy gun nests.

DCM   Sgt
RefScs: DHist 713 065 (D1)

ST. ANDRÉ-SUR-ORNE
July 24

YOUNG Hugh Andrew

"Brigade Commander Directed Battle from Forward Post"

During the attack on the village in its first major action, heavy German resistance and counterattacks disrupted 6th Infantry Brigade communications; companies and battalions became separated from one another. To maintain cohesion the brigade commander, Hugh Young, went forward to personally supervise the redisposition of the units and to ensure that enemy counterattacks were repelled. When his brigade major was killed and another of his staff officers wounded, Young continued to direct the battle until it was successfully concluded two days later.

DSO Brig
RefScs: DHist 713 065 (D2)

Orne River
July 25

Barron Robert Duff

"Medical Officer in Two Heroic Actions on the Same Night"

At nine o'clock in the evening, an ammunition truck caught fire and exploded causing a number of casualties among troops in the vicinity. In spite of the danger, Robert Barron of No 7 Field Ambulance rendered medical attention to the many wounded while shells exploded all around him. Then, between eleven o'clock and midnight, the regimental headquarters was bombed and strafed by German aircraft. Barron left his shelter to tend to those injured in the raid ignoring the fact that a bomb blew down part of the HQ and shattered several vehicles. And although the streets were machine gunned and bombed, Barron evacuated all wounded personnel as well as assisting in recovering the bodies of those killed.

MC (Immediate) Capt
RefScs: DHist 713 065 (D2)

Verrières

Sawyer Harold Victor

"Daring Attack Wiped Out Four Enemy Machine-Gun Posts"

As the company of the Royal Hamilton Light Infantry in which Harold Sawyer was a section leader neared a line of hedges to the north of the town, the troops came under heavy fire from German tanks on their right flank and machine guns also to their left. This made it impossible for the company to advance. Leading a party of three men, Sawyer attacked in the face of volleys of fire. They took out four of the machine-gun posts. This daring action, in which Sawyer was wounded, allowed the company to advance and reach its objective.

DCM   Cpl
RefScs: DHist 713 065 (D1)

The Falaise Gap
August 7 - 22, 1944

As General George Patton's 3rd and 1st armies swept around from the south, the First Canadian Army was ordered to capture Falaise along the line of the pocket's opening. By August 7 the town was under siege by Lieutenant-General Guy Simond's Second Corps. The attack began before midnight and the defence lines were soon overrun, but then in the face of stiff resistance and due to errors in Allied bombing, the momentum floundered. Simonds launched a second assault, this time in daylight under the cover of smokescreens, and by August 17 Falaise had fallen to the Canadians. Meanwhile, a corps of Patton's had penetrated from the south to Argentan. The German 7th Army was trapped

Fusiliers Mont-Royal supported by Sherman tank during hunt for sniper. Falaise, 1944. (PA 132719)

in a vice between the forces of Simonds and Patton. By August 22 the Battle of Normandy was over for the Wehrmacht. Three days later when the Americans marched into Paris, the Allies reported that the Germans had lost 400,000 men killed and wounded, 200,000 of whom were prisoners of war. In addition, 1,300 tanks, 20,000 vehicles, 500 assault guns, and 1,500 field guns and heavier artillery pieces had been captured or destroyed.

FONTENAY-LE-MARMION
August 7/8

HANSON Albert

"Cleared Path and Positions for Guns in Darkness and under Fire"

The job of Albert Hanson's platoon of Royal Canadian Engineers was to clear a safe path for the antitank carriers to support newly won positions by the Queen's Own Cameron Highlanders. The only practical approach was littered with derelict German vehicles, studded with mines, and under constant artillery fire.

Despite relentless enemy fire and mounting casualties, Hanson led his men forward, clearing a three-mile route to battalion headquarters and picking locations for each antitank gun. Still in darkness and under continuous harassing fire, he also directed his men in clearing mines from each of the proposed sites.

MC (Immediate)   Lt
RefScs: DHist 713 065 (D2)

QUILLY
August 8

FRECHETTE Louis

"Single-Handed Attack Took Out German Gun Crew"

During the attack on the village, Louis Frechette's platoon of Le Régiment de Maisonneuve was pinned down by a German machinegun nest. With one other member of the unit, Frechette made his way forward to the front line, spotted the enemy post and worked his way in behind it.

When one of the enemy gun crew saw him, he coolly killed the man with a single shot then dashed forward to neutralize the other two. One of them was about to throw a hand grenade but Frechette fired, exploding it and blowing the German up with it. That was too much for the remaining crew member; he put up his hands in a gesture of surrender.

CdeGwbs (Fr)   Cpl (A/Sgt)
RefScs: DHist 713 065 (D1)

BRETTEVILLE
August 9

COOK William Matthew Bruce

"Led Daring Attack on Enemy Trench"

While attacking the village, the leading section of the Calgary Highlanders became subjected to heavy machine-gun and rifle fire from German slit trenches in a bank 50 yards ahead.

Bill Cook, in spite of the terrifying volley of fire, ran forward over open ground exchanging bursts with the enemy as he charged ahead. When he was a few yards from the German trench he stood up, firing his Bren gun from the hip. This so completely demoralized the enemy that one German officer and five other ranks surrendered to him.

MM (Immediate)   Pte
RefScs: DHist 713 065 (D1)

QUESNAY WOODS
August 10

SPRINGER Charles

"Injured Himself, Stayed to Evacuate Wounded"

During the attack on the woods, though injured himself, Charles Springer of the North Shore Regiment worked unceasingly under German fire for five-and-a-half hours evacuating the wounded. His diligence, determination and courage did much to raise the morale of the unit at the time.

MM (Immediate)   Pte
RefScs: DHist 713 065 (D1)

PIERRE-SUR-DIVES
August 13

HOGARTH Robert Ernest

"Saved Tanks from Being Wiped Out"

Coming to an open hill just before the Quesnay Woods, tanks of the Fourth Canadian Armoured Division headquarters group suddenly came under a heavy concentration of German fire. The brigade commander was badly wounded and his tank was knocked out. But although the vehicle in which Robert Hogarth, representing the Royal Canadian Artillery, was riding was also hit, he realized the entire group was in danger of being wiped out and immediately took charge.

Leading the remaining tanks to shelter he took control of the rescue and care of the wounded. Then when it turned dark he led the tanks to a harbour area where the rest of the brigade headquarters had been set up.

CdeGwp (Fr)   Maj
RefScs: DHist 713 065 (D2)

MONTBOINT
August 14

AYER Donald Holman

"Led Courageous Tank Assault"

During an attack across the Laison River, Don Ayer of the 7th Canadian Reconnaissance Regiment surveyed the area by himself before leading his section of six carriers to high ground. Then, although severely wounded in the chest by machine-gun fire, he refused to leave the position until his small force became sufficiently organized to hold it. His action enabled the entire regiment to cross the river free from the harassment of heavy enemy fire.

MC (Immediate) Lt
RefScs: DHist 713 065 (D2)

LOUVIÈRES-EN-AUGE
August 15

McGOWAN Douglas

"Instrumental in Recovering and Repairing Knocked-Out Tanks"

On this second day of the thrust to Falaise, the 22nd Canadian Armoured Regiment had been reduced in strength to one Stuart tank and 21 Sherman tanks. Taking it upon himself to search for recoverable tanks damaged in the battle, Doug McGowan frequently had to leave his scout car to deal with German snipers. And there was always the danger of mines. But on one occasion he returned with six prisoners. Working throughout the night under shaded lights, he personally directed and assisted fitter crews so that nine of the recovered tanks were battleworthy next day for the regiment's advance to the north of Trun to begin sealing off the gap.

MC Capt
RefScs: DHist 713 065 (D2)

PIERRE CANIVET
August 16

BRUNSTRON Terrence

"One-Man Reconnaissance Pinpointed German Positions"

Reconnoitering in advance of the Royal Winnipeg Rifles during an attack down the road to Falaise, Terry Brunstron of the 7th Canadian Reconnaissance Regiment came to a standstill due to heavy German antitank and machine-gun fire. Brunstron dismounted from his vehicle to search out the enemy positions on foot. Opening fire on suspected posts, he drew fire enabling him to pinpoint the nests. Once his task was accomplished, by prearranged signal his driver fired off smoke bombs to allow him to withdraw.

    MC (Immediate)   Lt
    RefScs: DHist 713 065 (D2)

CAEN
August 9-18

KNIGHT Dorothy Melrose

"Fought Fatigue to Stay at Her Post"

At times during the battle of Falaise, Dorothy Knight, a nursing sister with the Royal Canadian Army Medical Corps, was so weary she could hardly stay on her feet. But despite the fact that all the other nursing sisters took rest breaks, Knight refused to leave her unit at this time. On two occasions she worked 22 hours non-stop. Both patients and operating surgeons applauded her continuous presence, conscientiousness and endurance during a very trying period.

    ARRC   Lt
    RefScs: DHist 713 065 (D2)

ST. LAMBERT-SUR-DIVES
August 18-20

CURRIE David Vivian

"Kept the Gap Closed"

Dave Currie played a key role in keeping the Falaise Gap closed. As commander of the 29th Canadian Armoured Reconnaissance Regiment, a mixed force of tanks, self-propelled antitanks guns and infantry, he was instrumental in cutting off a major part of the German army. He thus prevented it from escaping from the pincers of the Ca-

Dave Currie (PA 140875)

nadian, Polish and American forces. When, on August 18, 1944, his unit was held up by stiff enemy resistance at St. Lambert-sur-Dives, that evening Currie entered the village alone on foot to reconnoitre the defences. Early next morning, he led an attack on the town and by noon had successfully seized and consolidated a position within the town. Then, for the next 36 hours, the Germans hurled one counterattack after another at the Canadians. Throughout the onslaught Currie not only displayed a contemptuous defiance for the enemy as he led his men against the repeated assaults, but took part in the battle himself. On one occasion he personally directed the fire of his command tank onto a German Tiger tank knocking it out. During a subsequent attack he used a rifle from his gun turret to kill enemy snipers. Another time, even though his unit's artillery fire was falling within 15 yards of his tank, because of its devastating effect on the Germans, he ordered it continued. Throughout the engagement his unit suffered such heavy casualties — all of his officers were either killed or wounded — that Currie had virtually no respite or time to rest. On August 20, after a final assault in which the Germans were routed, Currie ordered a counterattack. That completed the capture of the town, conclusively denying the Cambois-Trun escape route to the remaining Germans caught in the Falaise pocket. His regiment was quickly relieved but by then Currie was so exhausted he fell asleep on his feet and collapsed. The yield to the regiment was enormous for a single unit: seven enemy tanks; 12 88mm guns and 40 vehicles destroyed; 300 Germans killed, 500 wounded and 2,100 captured. Currie's bravery throughout the three days and nights of fierce fighting earned him the Victoria Cross. One of his NCOs summed up his valiant behaviour in a manner no citation could describe: "We knew at one stage it was going to be a fight to the finish but he was so cool about it, it was impossible for us to get excited."

Born in Sutherland, Sask., Currie enlisted in the Moose Jaw militia before WW2 broke out. From 1939 to 1942 he served at various training camps until joining the 29th CARR (South Alberta Regiment). He and his unit were shipped overseas and landed on the Normandy beaches on D-Day. Following the war Currie held several senior executive positions with industrial firms in Quebec City and Montreal. In 1960 he became sergeant-at-arms for the Canadian House of Commons at which post he remained until his retirement in 1978.

VC CM STM   Maj   Born July 8 1912
RefScs: CVC 184-5   DHist 713 065 (D2)   VM 188-9

One of my favourite war pictures is that of the Germans surrendering to Dave Currie and his regiment. Currie stands to the left, pistol in hand, looking tired and grimy, but alert, while a German officer, well dressed and militant with hands raised, confronts a Canadian infantryman. Tanks and buildings are smouldering in the background. As one historian put it: "This is as close as we are ever likely to come to a photograph of a man winning the VC." The picture was taken by Don Grant of the Canadian Film and Photo Unit. (See page 243.)

BREAKOUT
Clearing the Channel Ports
September 17 - 22, 1944

Following the victory at Falaise, the First Canadian Army was assigned the job of clearing the coastal areas and opening the Channel ports to supplies. On the left flank of the Allied forces the Canadians pushed rapidly eastward through France and into Belgium. September began with the Second Canadian Divison being welcomed at Dieppe. Bolougne, Calais and Cap Gris Nez were also captured, and by the end of the month the Channel coast had been cleared. The exception was Dunkirk which was by-passed to allow the troops to concentrate on clearing the Scheldt Estuary of the enemy and allow shipping into the Belgian port of Antwerp. During the brief campaign, the hardest nut to crack had been Boulogne.

MONT LAMBERT
September 17

FORBES Donald

"Led Dismounted Troops in Spectacular Attack"

During the assault on Mont Lambert, the ground at the foot of the position was so badly cratered that the troops of the North Nova Scotia Highlanders had to dismount from their carriers. But their commander Donald Forbes organized them so effectively that in the subsequent attack 40 German concrete pillboxes were captured and 400 enemy were taken prisoner.

DSO (Immediate)   Lt/Col
RefScs: DHist 713 065 (D2)

Boulogne

GINGELL Harold David

"Cut Off, Continued Transmitting"

As artillery observation post signaller, Harry Gingell of Le Régiment de la Chaudière was one of a party assigned to find a suitable observation post to direct fire on the enemy. At one point the party was cut off from their own troops. But although without food, water or protection, and going without sleep, Gingell continued to operate his radio equipment allowing the 8th Canadian Infantry Brigade to maintain its attack on the German defences.

MM (Immediate)   Gr
RefScs: 713 065 (D1)

OUELLET Joseph Etienne

"Made Attack on Machine-Gun Nest Alone when Rest of Platoon Wounded"

When all members of the leading platoon of Le Régiment de Chaudière were either killed or wounded in an assault on a slope in front of Denacre, northeast of Boulogne, where 100 Germans had positions knitted together by trenches and protected by land mines, Joe Ouellet continued the attack by himself. In the process, though injured by a hand grenade, he took out a machine-gun nest and wounded three of the enemy. This made possible the establishment of a toe-hold by his company.

MM (Immediate)   Pte
RefScs: DHist 713 065 (D1)

September 18

KIRK Andrew James

"Led Supply Column through on Four Occasions"

During the assault on Boulogne on this date, Andrew Kirk led the fuel and ammunition column of the 10th Canadian Armoured Regiment to the front through mortar and shell-fire on four different occasions. This was typical of Kirk's determination, efficiency and bravery throughout the European campaign.

NBC Sgt
RefScs: 713 065 (D1)

THOMAS Maurice Pollock

"Broadcasts Netted 210 Prisoners in Two Days"

On this day at Mont Lambert, Maurice Thomas of the 3rd Canadian Public Relations Group was credited with the surrender of 150 Germans. His method was to go forward in a scout car as far as he dared and broadcast an appeal to them to lay down their arms and give themselves up. It was dangerous work often in the face of enemy fire in broad daylight. On this occasion his vehicle was hit by shrapnel, his driver was wounded in the foot, and Thomas himself was injured in the neck. But the action succeeded. In fact, on next day by employing the same tactic he took 60 more of the enemy prisoner.

MC Capt
RefScs: DHist 713 065 (D2)

September 19

BASSET James

"Led Audacious Assault over River Bridge"

James Bassett, in charge of the leading platoon of the Highland Light Infantry of Canada, led the assault across the Liane River. Though the bridge was partially destroyed, it was strongly defended by the Germans. When Bassett's platoon got across the bridge, it attacked the enemy machine-gun posts enabling the rest of the company to get across with only light casualties.

DCM   Sgt
RefScs: DHist 713 065 (D2)

September 20-22

BAUGH Rupert Donald

"Daring Artillery Spotting Ensured Success in Final Assault"

In one of the final operations to capture Boulogne, on the afternoon of September 20 the Queen's Own Rifles with Le Régiment de la Chaudière to their right were bogged down by German small-arms fire, light artillery and four 88mm guns. Rupert Baugh, forward artillery officer attached to the QOR, went ahead alone and established an observation post to the rear of the enemy strongpoint where he could direct fire against it.

All through the night he stayed there under constant German fire until daylight when he was able to direct his own artillery guns to put all the German heavy guns out of action. He then took command of a group of Bren gunners and, in a subsequent attack, directed them against the remaining enemy gun posts. As a result of this action the attack on Fort de la Creche, which ended the defence of the Boulogne garrison north of the Liane River, was made the following morning without harassment from any flanking fire.

MC (Immediate)   A/Capt
RefScs: DHist 713 065 (D2)

THE CANADIAN CAMPAIGN IN ITALY (3)
The Rugged Route to Rimini
August 25 - September 30, 1944

By the end of the summer of 1944 the Canadians had moved back to the Adriatic front. Their objective: the east end of the formidable German Gothic Line that separated them from the Po Valley and Lombardy Plain. Running roughly between Pisa and Pesaro, this defence line was composed of machine-gun posts, antitank guns, and mortar and assault positions, tank turrets set in concrete, plus mines, wire obstacles and antitank ditches.

The attack began in the last week of August with the objective of capturing Rimini. By August 30 the Canadians had crossed the Metauro River and the attack on the line itself began. By September 2 they had breached the fortifications and had started advancing towards Rimini. However, they met stiff resistance from the secondary line of German defences. This resistance coupled with steady rains that soaked the battlefield prevented them from reaching their objective until three weeks later.

Breaking the Gothic Line
August 25 - September 2, 1944

The advance began on the night of August 25 when the Canadians crossed the Metauro River. For the next four days the Germans fell steadily back to their vaunted Gothic Line three miles to the north. On Wednesday afternoon of August 30, the Canadians crossed the Fogliu River to attack the fortification. This crossing marked the start of a bitterly fought three-day battle to breach it. That night one regiment broke through and the next day the breach was slowly widened until by dusk on August 31 the Canadians had opened a hole more than a mile wide and two miles deep. Next day marked the climax of the battle with the capture of the key position of Monte Peloso. By September 2 the Gothic Line had been shattered. But the cost had been heavy: 219 Canadian soldiers dead and another 519 wounded.

BORGO SANTA MARIA
August 30

WILMOT Laurence Frank

"Padre Directed Evacuation of Wounded from Minefield"

The West Nova Scotia Regiment had walked into a nightmare, a minefield between Osteria Nuova and Borgo Santa Maria. Schu-mines, designed to maim rather than kill, blew off their feet. S-mines, *Schrapnellium*, scattered ball-bearings and scrap metal for two hundred yards in all directions. It was carnage made more suicidal by German machine-gun and artillery fire. The dead and wounded lay everywhere, and the wounded had little hope of being evacuated.

Frank Wilmot, regimental chaplain for the West Nova Scotia Regiment, refused to be daunted. He cheerfully and coolly entered the minefield and began directing the evacuation of the wounded, at the same time talking to them, keeping up their spirits. He searched the minefield for other wounded and, when he came to a casualty, marked the spot for the stretcher-bearers. Despite the danger of the mines themselves, as well as enemy fire, Wilmot stayed to assist and organize the rescue parties until all of the wounded had been taken from the field. He was the last to leave when the two West Nova companies were forced to withdraw. His very presence not only boosted morale, but without his efforts many wounded, who desperately needed medical attention, would have been left to die.

MC (Immediate)   H/Capt
RefScs: DHist 713 065 (D2)

MONTECCHIO
August 30

BRANNEN Lindsay Eaton

"Repelled Two Counterattacks, Single-Handedly Overcame Machine-Gun Post"

Having almost reached the height of his objective, Lindsay Brannen's platoon of Cape Breton Highlanders was pinned down by heavy German machine-gun fire. Leading a flanking movement to the top, the unit ran into strong enemy fire and a counterattack which Brannen successfully repelled. Staying at the post without any cover, he calmly directed fire from another platoon on a second counterattack. Then, although his gun had jammed, he single-handedly attacked a camouflaged enemy machine-gun nest and took three German prisoners.

MC (Immediate)   Lt (A/Capt)
RefScs: DHist 713 065 (D2)

TOD William

"Alone, Captured House, Took 11 Prisoners"

While moving through the town, heavy and accurate enemy machine-gun fire coming from a group of houses had checked all forward movement of the Irish Regiment of Canada. On his own initiative, Bill

Tod worked his way forward to the first house and threw every hand grenade he had into it. He then rushed into the bulding and, with only his Thompson machine gun for armament, took 11 German gunners prisoner. His speedy, daring action wiped out the enemy resistance allowing the battalion to continue its advance.

MM (Immediate) Sgt
RefScs: DHist 713 065 (D1)

FOGLIA RIVER
August 31

GLOVER Frank Alexander

"Lost Tank, Fought Innovative One-Man Battle for Survival"

During the advance, the tank in which Frank Glover was riding received a direct hit. He and his gunner were blown clear but the driver was killed and the co-driver fatally wounded. Though injured himself and badly shaken by the explosion, he climbed up a slope in full view of the enemy and under heavy shell-fire to find a reconnaissance tank to evacuate his gunner who had been seriously wounded.

Unable to find one, he returned to his tank, collecting an assortment of small arms on the way, and dug three slit trenches uphill from the vehicle. When the Germans attacked that night he fired his weapons from one slit trench, then dashed into another, firing again, to give the illusion of a strong defence. Three times he warded off enemy attacks until he was eventually relieved and the tank recovered.

MM (Immediate) Sgt
RefScs: DHist 713 056 (D1)

MONTE PELOSO
September 1

DARLING William

"CO Was Everywhere"

The Princess Louise Dragoon Guards were not only new to infantry fighting, they had a new commanding officer, Bill Darling, who led his green troops in a charge against fierce crossfire. Casualties mounted but Darling continued to ignore the German snipers and machine-gun bullets flying about, rallying his men to keep moving ahead. By the time they reached the foot of Monte Peloso there were only 40 survivors left in his two assault companies. Now tanks of the Lord Strathcona's Horse moved up the hillside firing as they went, knocking down every house in their path. Darling and his men followed. Only 15 made it to the top with him and for the last 50 yards they were literally on their hands and knees. But the victory had been gained; the Gothic Line had been smashed, and in suitable celebration the surviving "Plugs" passed round a bottle of whisky that miraculously appeared.

DSO   Lt Col
RefScs: DHist 713 065 (D2)   TDD 319-20

Slog to the San Fortunato Ridge
September 2 - 22, 1944

The chase began on the night of September 2, but although the Canadians crossed the Conca River the following morning just nine miles short of Rimini on the Adriatic coast, and with the Marecchia River running to it, it would take 18 days to cover the nine miles to reach it. By September 5 the Canadians had reached Riccione, Santa Maria de Scaciano and Coriano; the next day the rains came that for days got steadily worse turning the battlefield into a quagmire. But the advance continued slowly and surely. On September 13 the Dominion troops stormed the Coriano Ridge and secured it the following day. On September 15 they crossed the Marano River and captured Lorenzo and Corregiano, and three days later forded the Ausa River. By September 21 the Marecchia River had been reached, the San Fortunato Ridge taken, and the Germans had evacuated Rimini which was in ruins from bombing and shelling. Next day the First Canadian Division was withdrawn for a rest.

MARANO RIVER
September 15

TELLIER Henri

"Aggressiveness Disrupted Enemy Defenders"

At first light crossing the river, company commander Henri Tellier of the Royal 22nd Regiment led his men through intense enemy machine-gun and small-arms fire and then engaged in fierce hand-to-hand fighting with the German defenders. His aggressiveness so unnerved the enemy that it disrupted their defences, allowing the Van Doos to establish the first bridgehead across the waterway.

> DSO   Maj
> RefScs: DHist 713 065 (D2)

AUSA RIVER
September 18

HESLER William Charles

"Heroic Effort during River Crossing"

When the infantry became pinned down by enemy machine guns during an attempt to establish a bridgehead across the river, Bill Hesler of the 7th Canadian Anti-tank Regiment climbed into a self-propelled gun carrier and, leading three others, began an advance towards the German gun positions.

However, a Tiger tank blocked the way and opened fire disabling two of the SPs and wounding several of the crewmen. Unable to engage the tank due to the lay of the land, Hesler herded the remaining SPs into a nearby house. He then returned to assist in getting the wounded into the building, no easy feat with enemy fire all around them.

By this time the Canadian infantry were forced to give ground and Hesler began supervising the evacuation of his crews and SPs. To draw fire away from them and onto himself he fired his revolver at the tank. By thus diverting the tank's attention, the men and machines were able to withdraw to cover.

Hesler remained in the area despite heavy enemy mortar fire to direct artillery to bring fire on the tank. That accomplished he then retired from the field.

MC (Immediate)   Lt
RefScs: DHist 713 065 (D2)

SAN FORTUNATO RIDGE
September 19

ALLARD Jean Victor

"Triple DSO Winner First French-Canadian Chief of the Defense Staff"

Jean Allard had one of the most colourful and distinctive careers of any Canadian soldier. On this date, as commanding officer of the Royal 22nd Regiment, it was his task to sieze the southern part of the ridge, an area defended by the Germans in great strength. Despite this determined opposition, Allard managed to secure a foothold. From there he directed his men with such skill and resolution that they destroyed one German detachment after the other until the entire area was completely rid of the enemy. During the fighting, 56 Germans were killed and 249 taken prisoner. In addition, large quantities of equipment including 20 mortars, 15 heavy machine guns and 100 rifles were captured. One tank, a Mark IV Special, was destroyed and the Germans were forced to demolish one of their own infantry guns. For the action Allard was awarded a Bar to a DSO he had received earlier. And later in the war he would earn a second Bar.

In Korea, as commander of the 25th Canadian Infantry Brigade, he was awarded the American Legion of Merit. He also served as military attaché to Russia. He then became the first French-Canadian Chief of the Defence Staff and was responsible for establishing French-language units in all sectors of Canadian military activity.

DSO and 2 Bars   LoM(Am)   CdeG(Fr)   NBL   Lt/Col (Gen)   Born June 12 1913   Author *Allard*
RefScs: DHist 713 065 (D2)

I feel it is appropriate to quote Jean Allard as follows because it fits into most any context concerning the military in Canada:

"The great majority of Canadians, in peacetime, is utterly indifferent towards military affairs. We are a nation that will 'participate' if necessary without demanding preparation from the government."

Aftermath

Stiff German resistance and heavy rains dashed all Canadian hopes for a speedy romp across the plains of Lombardy to Bologna and the Po River. Streams turned into raging torrents. Mud replaced the powder dust, and tanks bogged down in the swamplands of the Romagna. All further advance came to a temporary standstill.

NORTH OF RIMINI ON THE ADRIATIC COAST
September 23 - October 1

TURNER Sydney Allen

"Week of Clandestine Activity behind Enemy Lines Paid Dividends"

On the night of September 23/24, Sydney Turner, commanding a party of six, was landed by the Italian navy on the Adriatic coast behind enemy lines with the objective of observing German positions and traffic, and directing artillery fire. At the time the plan was to relieve the group at the end of a week by the advancing Canadian forces.

During the first day Turner and his party hid out near the shore where he made contact with Italian partisans. That night they established themselves inland in an attic of one of the patriot's houses. There the men remained all week long, gathering information about enemy strength, equipment and morale, directing artillery fire by radio, the latter causing innumerable German casualties, as well as considerable damage to enemy equipment and positions.

By week's end, because the Canadian advance had bogged down, they were ordered to make their own way out through the front lines. On the night of September 30, they returned to the beach where they had landed to begin the journey south. Throwing their equipment into the sea, they proceeded down the coast offshore, chest-deep in the water, clinging to a rope to ensure that they stayed together.

But due to a heavy surf their progress was slow and the men soon tired. As a result, Turner abandoned this method and the party returned to the shore and the men made their way on foot. By this means, however, they ran the danger of passing enemy positions and sentries enroute. Inevitably, as they reached the front lines, they were fired upon. Turner, among others, was wounded.

It was a remarkable exercise and an example of doggedly brilliant leadership on Turner's part in that it was executed without any fatalities. And the information gained was invaluable when the Canadians renewed their advance.

MC (Immediate) Capt
RefScs: DHist 713 065 (D2)

FREEING THE PORT OF ANTWERP
September 5 - November 28, 1944

*B*y the time the 2nd British Army captured Antwerp on September 4, the Allied supply lines had been stretched to the limit — all the way back to Normandy — and their offensive had ground to a halt. It now became critical that this Belgian inland seaport, the second largest in Europe, be opened to Allied shipping as quickly as possible to enable the advance to continue. But the pause at this stage allowed the German 15th Army, six divisions comprising 86,100 men and their equipment, to escape and take up defensive positions in the Scheldt Estuary on either side of the river entrance. This effectively denied Allied shipping access to the harbour, prolonging the war for at least six months. (And incidentally gave the Germans time to launch their Ardennes offensive with Antwerp a prime target.) Clearing the enemy fortifications in the area had become vital, a lot that befell the First Canadian Army — on the double.

It was a twin-pronged assignment. East of Antwerp it called for an advance north across the Netherlands border, then a sharp left turn through the Beveland Isthmus into the peninsula proper which led to a causeway onto Walcheren Island. Directly south the Canadians had to ford the Leopold Canal on the Belgian mainland to capture the small port of Breskens on the north shore of the river, an escape route for the Germans to Walcheren. Finally, that island itself had to be taken before the harbour could be freed.

At the beginning of October, the Second Canadian Infantry Division advanced north of Antwerp and by the 24th of the month had sealed off the Beveland Isthmus. Simultaneously, the Third Canadian Infantry Division moved forward behind devastating fire and massed flame-throwers to cross the Leopold Canal. But there they met determined resistance until Breskens fell on November 3. To the northeast, with the Beveland Peninsula secured, only the German fortress of the Walcheren Island remained. The sole land approach along the deadly, narrow, open causeway at Sloedam called for a supporting adjunct. After alerting the civilian population, the RAF bombed the dykes flooding the countryside and the German positions. An Allied amphibious attack from the rear strained the German defences. Following a week of ferocious fighting German resistance finally collapsed. Now the channel was cleared of mines and, on November 28, the first Allied convoy entered Antwerp.

The Battle of the Scheldt had cost the Canadians 6,370 casualties, losses magnified by the Conscription Crisis at home that sent untrained reinforcements into battle. And the end of the war was still a long way off.

Advance to the Dutch Border

By the beginning of October, east of Antwerp, Canadian troops had crossed the Albert and Turnhout canals and by the 5th of the month were poised near the Dutch border. There the 4th, 5th and 6th Canadian Infantry Brigades stood ready to plunge into Holland and seal off the South Beveland Peninsula at Woensdrecht.

CROCKETT George Robert

"Daring Defence on the Albert Canal"

On the night of September 27, George Crockett was one of eight members of the Calgary Highlanders who had volunteered to cross the footbridge at Wommelgehm along the sniper-infested Albert Canal and set up an advance bridgehead. As they reached the north bank, swinging across the bridge hand-over-hand, they were suddenly challenged by a German sentry. Crockett quickly silenced the man with his knife. Then two machine guns opened up on the band. In quick order Crockett put both out of commission with his PIAT antitank gun. For his action Crockett was recommended for the VC but instead received the DCM.

DCM Sgt
RefScs: DHist 713 065 (D1)   TOW 157-8

ADAMS Albert Edwin

"Directed Artillery under Vicious Enemy Fire"

At Putte on the main road north from Antwerp to Holland, Albert Adams was artillery forward observation officer for the Essex Scottish Regiment's attack on the town. Success was vital to prevent the Germans from cutting the main route of the Second Canadian Infantry Division advancing from the south.

On the night of October 5, 150 yards from the enemy position in the face of severe shell, mortar and small-arms fire, Adams directed the Essex Scottish artillery fire for 20 minutes inflicting such heavy casualties on the Germans that they were unable to take offensive action.

MC (Immediate)   Capt
RefScs: DHist 713 065 (D2)

Woensdrecht

With the main objective now to seal off the South Beveland Peninsula, the capture of Woensdrecht by the Canadian Second Division was essential. A small farming village in peacetime, it dominated the isthmus through which the main road and rail line passed to South Beveland and westward beyond to Walcheren Island. Time and time again it was assaulted but the German defences, shielded by well-entrenched guns behind them, held firm.

On October 13, known as "Black Friday," the Black Watch of Canada suffered horrible casualties when 183 men were lost, 56 of them killed. Then at three-thirty on the morning of October 16, under a barrage of 168 guns, 500 infantrymen of the Royal Hamilton Light Infantry began a renewed assault that lasted five more days before the dreaded guns of Woensdrecht were finally silenced.

DEARDON Ernest Hughes

"Badly Wounded Twice, Led His Men in Securing Objective"

On the morning of October 18 during the attack on Woensdrecht, Ernest Deardon, a platoon leader with the Royal Hamilton Light Infantry, was severely wounded in the arm but refused to be evacuated. Under heavy enemy mortar and machine-gun fire, he continued to lead his men and on reaching their objective was wounded again, this time in the legs by hand grenades. In intense pain he still refused to be evacuated and only when the position was secure consented to receive first aid. On reaching the regimental aid post he fainted from weakness and loss of blood.

MM Sgt
RefScs: DHist 713 065 (D1)

PIGOTT Joseph Michael

"Beat Off Enemy Counterattack, Led Charge despite Wounds"

At five o'clock in the morning of October 16, Joe Pigott, a company commander with the Royal Hamilton Light Infantry, paced up and down inside the farm cottage that served as his headquarters overlooking the main road to Woensdrecht. He was well aware that his platoons were too spread out to form a proper defence if the Germans counterattacked.

Five hours later he had the disconcerting experience of having to pull his revolver and force men, who had fled the field, back into battle at gun point. By then an enemy counterattack was fully underway. At this stage Piggot's platoons were so disorganized he had no choice but to call a "Victor Target," a concentrated artillery barrage on his position regardless of the risk of being mutilated by his own guns.

The barrage succeeded but Pigott was wounded. Nevertheless, he proceeded to lead his men over 100 yards of open ground under heavy machine-gun fire, and personally maneuvered an antitank gun into position from which it destroyed an enemy self-propelled gun. The Germans were then forced to withdraw and the counterattack was halted.

DSO Maj
RefScs: DHist 713 065 (D2)   TOW 190-5

Closing the Breskens Pocket

*B*y the end of September the Germans had been forced to withdraw to a line of defence along the Leopold Canal which formed a barrier below the port of Breskens on the south shore of the Scheldt facing Walcheren Island. To make the area as impassable as possible, the Germans opened the dykes to flood the land. Adding to the quagmire were the October rains. At the beginning of the month, the commander of the Third Canadian Infantry Division, Major General Dan Spry, had been informed that to clear the pocket would take only a matter of days; there were only 6,000 poorly equipped, demoralized German troops at the most to contend with. In fact, the battle, one of the filthiest, most treacherous of the war, lasted 29 days. In its duration the Canadians took more than 12,000 prisoners.

In mid-September the first attack to cross the canal had failed. A second attempt launched on October 6 succeeded in establishing a small bridgehead but resulted in a stalemate. The answer to breaking the deadlock was an amphibious landing launched on October 9 by the 9th Brigade of the Third Division commanded by Brigadier John Rockingham, through the back door of the pocket across the Braakman Inlet to the east of Breskens. After a mud-slogging mile-by-mile advance, Breskens, the last remaining German line of retreat from the mainland, fell to the Canadians on October 22. By November 4, the battle was over but the Third Division had lost 314 dead, 2,077 wounded, with 231 men missing in action.

JOHNSTON Merritt Elmer

"Bold Assault Cleared Canal of Machine-Gun Nests"

During the first attack on the Leopold Canal on September 18, near the tiny Belgian village of Moerkerke, one Canadian outpost occupying a house on the canal bank became pinned down by enemy machine-gun fire from both sides of the waterway. Merritt Johnston of the Algonquin Regiment was despatched with a patrol of 10 men to root the enemy out. As he approached one of the machine-gun nests, his troops encountered a German patrol blocking their path. Johnston quickly turned his Bren gun on the enemy killing four and taking one prisoner. His fast action forced the rest of the German gunners surrounding the area into beating a hasty retreat.

MM (Immediate) Sgt
RefScs: DHist 715 065 (D2)

GOEPEL Ruston Herbert

"Determined to Keep Going"

During the initial assault on the Leopold Canal, Ruston Goepel had already distinguished himself by leading his tank troop from the 28th Canadian Armoured Regiment against a heavily fortified German entrenchment knocking out two antitank guns and an enemy pillbox. Not content with that achievement, together with a platoon of infantry he then charged 500 yards into enemy territory destroying two more antitank guns and in the process captured more than 60 prisoners.

Those exploits well behind him, during the Rhineland campaign in the following February of 1945, Goepel added to his laurels. In a furious fire-fight against overwhelming odds, with all his tanks shot out or bogged down, and the leader of the accompanying infantry troop killed, Goepel took charge and, for five frantic hours, in and out of his vehicle, he warded off countless German counterattacks from mortar and shell-fire, untill relief finally arrived. (Look ahead to "Clearing the Rhineland.")

MC Capt
RefScs: DHist 713 065 (D2)

Rubber rafts ferry soldiers of the Chaudières across the canal at Zutphen. (PA 133331)

OOSTHOEK

SCHJELDERUP Vilhelm Roger

"Fought to the Last to Prevent Enemy Breakout"

On October 7 in this village near Aardenburg, C Company of the 1st Canadian Scottish Regiment, commanded by Roger Schjelderup, who had been awarded the MC for exploits on D-Day, was completely surrounded by 150 Germans who overran the company HQ. But Schjelderup was determined to fight to the last to prevent an enemy breakout to the Leopold Canal. Not until their ammunition was exhausted and the building was burning to the ground around them, did the Canadians surrender. But during the train trip to Germany and to imprisonment, Schjelderup and his companions managed to escape. On January 6, 1945, after a harrowing trek over ice and through snow, they finally reached the Canadian lines bringing with them valuable information on German movements and positions. For these actions Schjelderup received the DSO.

DSO MC   Capt
RefScs: DHist 713 065 (D2)

ADAMS Homer

"Impulsive, Daring Quick Thinking Saved Company's Position"

During a German counterattack near Moerhuizen on October 8 along the Leopold Canal, a German soldier tossed a stick of five hand grenades tied together into a trench serving as headquarters for the Regina Rifle Regiment. Without hesitation and with total disregard for his own safety, Homer Adams picked up the bundle and threw it back killing and wounding several of the enemy and disrupting their attack so completely that the rest of the Germans fled in disorder. Had the enemy not been repulsed at this stage, consolidation of this part of the bridgehead would have been impossible.

MM (Immediate)   Rfn
RefScs: DHist 713 065 (D1)

KENT Hubert Ernest

"Consolidated Brigade Bridgehead"

Through his efficiency and daring during the initial stage of the amphibious landings on the northeast Breskens pocket, Hubert Kent of the Cameron Highlanders of Ottawa was instrumental in consolidating the 9th Canadian Infantry Brigade bridgehead. Though his platoon suffered heavy casualties in men and equipment from enemy shell-fire, he held his ground in spite of incessant counterattacks and continued to direct his company's mortar fire.

MC (Immediate)   Capt
RefScs: DHist 713 065 (D2)

ROWLEY Roger

"'Special Kind of Cat' Caused Last Scheldt Mainland Bastion to Fall"

Roger Rowley, who once said "You've got to be a special kind of cat to be a good infantryman," led the advance that finally captured Beskens, the last retreat on the mainland to the German garrison of Walcheren Island. It had not been easy or without cost.

During Operation Switchback, the initial role of Rowley's Stormont, Dundas and Glengarry Highlanders — the "breakout battalion" — was to break from the right flank of the bridgehead and out along the coastal seawall to the small port of Hoofplaat. As they advanced, the Highlanders came under increasingly violent German counterattacks that had to be driven off by supporting Canadian artillery. Then, once the objective was reached, the regiment found itself all alone well beyond the range of its own artillery, and with its left flank fully exposed. For three days the Highlanders were surrounded by Germans. From October 9 to 11, 15 men were killed and 46 wounded.

When reinforcements eventually arrived the Glengarries again advanced capturing one coastal town after another. Finally they were assigned the task of taking the port of Breskens, cutting off the German escape route by water from Walcheren. "What we did," Rowley later reported, "was to go in on a one-man front. We went along the seawall and used kapok bridging equipment which got to us over the antitank ditch . . . the Germans never believed that anybody would be so foolish to put in an attack from there, so we got in with very few casualties."

Roger Rowley (far right). (PA 130177)

Bresken's capture sealed the fate of the Germans on the Scheldt mainland. But before Antwerp could be opened to Allied shipping to allow the advance to the Rhine to continue, Walcheren Island still had to be taken.

DSO & Bar (Bar: Immediate) Lt/Col
RefScs: DHist 713 065 (D2)   TOW 217 224 229 280 292-3 300-3

Walcheren Island

*B*y the end of October, the Second Canadian Infantry Division had cleared the 40-kilometre-long Beveland Peninsula, and with the Breskens pocket overrun, the stage was set for conquering Walcheren Island. It proved a tough nut to crack even though the communications

Walcheren Island family evacuates. (Imperial War Museum)

had been flooded when the RAF bombed the dykes, and the major gun batteries had been softened by further air attacks. On the last day of October and the first of November, three almost simultaneous assaults on the island took place. The first was by the 5th Canadian Infantry Brigade on the east side of the island. But when it was discovered that the Sloe Channel separating Beveland from the island rose only twice a day, plans for an amphibious attack were scrapped in favour of crossing the causeway. This proved to be so hotly defended it took the attackers four days to get across the channel. Meanwhile, two British commando and infantry troops under the command of the First Canadian Army landed at Flushing on the mouth of the Scheldt River and Westkapelle on the east coast. The fighting was heavy and deadly but by November 5, to all intents the battle for the island was over. The cost had been high, however. Canadian losses since October 1 numbered 6,432 killed, wounded and missing.

SKAROTT Walter Cameron

"Coolly Provided Covering Fire to Allow Infantry to Cross Causeway"

At the start of the attack on the Beveland-Walcheren causeway the Calgary Highlanders, who were in the vanguard, were held up by intense German fire. Leading a platoon of the Toronto Scottish Regiment in support, Walter Skarott deployed his troops along the top of the dykes where they came under close enemy scrutiny and sweeping gun fire. Yet in spite of this resistance, under his leadership Skarott's platoon coolly provided covering fire until all enemy positions were silenced allowing the Calgary infantry to cross the causeway.

DCM   CQMS
RefScs: DHist 713 065 (D1)

GILLESPIE Alan Charles

"Skill in Silencing Gun Posts Opened Way to Advance"

During the battle for the Beveland-Walcheren causeway, Alan Gillespie's platoon of The Royal Regiment of Canada was assigned to clear German machine-gun nests and pillboxes during which they simultaneously mopped up four army barracks. One of the machine-gun nests, in plain sight, was protected by 20 feet of barbed-wire. Gillespie inched his men slowly forward, cutting a hole in the entanglements and at the same time covering surrounding land mines with steel helmets. These maneuvers were executed so quickly and quietly that the German gunners never heard the Canadians approach. As a result they were instantly overcome without a single Canadian casualty during the entire engagement. Once their objectives had been achieved and their position secured, Gillespie's men now found themselves confronted with a German counterattack. But despite their shortage of ammunition by this time, and with the platoon reduced to 12 men, Gillespie's force repulsed the enemy leaving the rest of the company's flank fully protected so the advance could continue.

MC   Lt
RefScs: DHist 713 065 (D2)

LALOGE Jean Emile

"One-Man Display of Valour Ensured Success of Entire Company"

On the early morning of November 1, a platoon of the Calgary Highlanders led by Emile Laloge had fought its way to within 25 yards of the enemy's end of the Walcheren-Beveland causeway when it became pinned down by severe machine-gun and 20mm-cannon fire. Laloge despatched a runner back to company headquarters to request artillery support, but the runner never made it. Accordingly Laloge made his own way back through heavy machine-gun fire and arranged an artillery barrage himself. That accomplished, the platoon and the rest of the company then proceeded onto its objectives.

At times the right flank of Laloge's own unit came dangerously close to the enemy's position. Three times he had to pick up German hand grenades that virtually landed at his feet and throw them into the water. Then, when one of his Bren gunners was killed and his weapon damaged, Laloge repaired it and manned the gun until another of his men could take over.

Later, when a German counterattack began to develop, Laloge called for fire from his PIAT gunner only to find the man had been so badly wounded that he could no longer handle the heavy antitank weapon. Laloge immediately took over, deploying the gun with such accuracy and determination that he broke up the entire enemy assault in no time flat.

As a result of his action and leadership, sometimes against overwhelming odds, his company accomplished its task and in the process took 60 of the enemy prisoner, killed and wounded dozens of others and also knocked out two machine guns and a 20mm cannon.

DCM (Immediate)   Sgt
RefScs: DHist 713 065 (D1)   TOW 328

Market Garden
September 17 - 26, 1944

*I*n late August, Field Marshal Bernard Montgomery conceived a plan designed to deliver a final, paralyzing blow against Germany that would cut off an enemy retreat and shorten the war by months. Airborne troops would seize a series of bridges over the principal waterways of Holland and gain control of key points along the north-south line of Arnhem-Nijmegen-Eindhoven. At the same time, ground troops would advance from the south to Eindhoven, then Nijmegen and finally the last link, Arnhem, from which point the Allies would turn eastward and take the Ruhr. This bridge was assigned to the British 1st Airborne Division supported by a Polish brigade.

The southern objectives were comparatively more quickly accomplished. But at Arnhem the airborne troops met stiff resistance and the ground forces which became bogged down were unable to reach them. After a week of bloody fighting the order was given for the airborne division to withdraw what forces it had left. Their rescue was in the hands of the 23rd Field Company of the Royal Canadian Engineers.

Evacuation from Arnhem

At nine-thirty on the night of September 25, the RCE sappers began crossing the Rhine from an apple orchard just east of Driel. The 40 stormboats that ferried the troops were driven by unreliable 50-horsepower engines; 20 feet in length and six feet in beam, they were capable of carrying 15 soldiers. In fact, in some cases as many as 36 men crowded into them. Immediately as the operation began the Germans started lobbying mortars and shells into the orchard and the river, then raging at high tide. Many of the boats were hit, some sunk. Most disconcerting of all were the engines that kept cutting out. All night long the boats ferried the Arnhem survivors, many of them wounded, back to the orchard. Then, as dawn broke, the airborne troops began fighting for the last places in the boats. They had to be stopped at gun point. By early morning the Canadian engineers had saved 2,100 men from capture, the last of the contingent of 10,000 that had been dropped from the air. The remainder were either killed or taken prisoner.

TUCKER Michael Lovett

"Worked Tirelessly under Heavy Enemy Fire to Rescue Survivors"

As commanding officer of the 23rd Field Company, Michael Tucker was solely responsible for the organization of the rescue of the British airborne troops. His planning ability and contempt for danger while exposed to the heaviest concentration of enemy fire were cited as "a magnificent example to all those present." Tucker continued his efforts to evacuate the survivors even after daylight. He was finally ordered to retire by a senior officer on the scene. For his feat Tucker received the DSO.

DSO Lt/Col
RefScs: DHist 073 065 (D1)   GGA 90 91-4 203-4 218

THE CANADIAN CAMPAIGN IN ITALY (4)
The Final Phase: October 1, 1944 - February 25, 1945

In October the defences of the Savio River were breached but the Canadians were thrown back by a fierce German counterattack. Meanwhile, the Americans' progress in the west forced the enemy to transfer two crack divisions from the Adriatic area allowing the Canadian advance to continue. The Canadian Corps was then withdrawn for a rest. In the meantime, two major changes had been implemented: Lieutenant General Charles Foulkes took over command of the First Corps and Major-General Harold Foster succeeded Chris Vokes as commander of the First Division, the latter leaving for Europe to take over the Fourth Canadian Armoured Division. When the Corps returned to battle on December 1, it faced a bloody month of river crossings as it fought through to the Senio River. By January 1945 this position had been stabilized as the Winter Line. That was the Canadians' last action in Italy. In February the First Corps moved to Europe to be united with the First Canadian Army.

A total of 92,757 Canadians served in the Italian campaign, a long hard-fought battle from start to finish. Casualties came to 5,764 dead, 19,486 wounded and 1,004 captured.

The Savio River
October 19 - 28, 1944

*B*y October 19, having crossed the Salto, Fuicimino and Pisciatello rivers, the Canadians reached the Savio, the biggest obstacle they had so far encountered in northern Italy. One hundred yards wide, the embankment on the far side had been cleared to allow the German gunners a clear field of vision. Next day, in the first attempt to cross it, two companies were decimated by fire from the far bank. On October 21, although a toe-hold had been made by the Canadians, the situation from enemy artillery had become critical. That night another crossing was made and by daylight a bridgehead had been established a mile wide and 1,400 yards deep. But bringing across tanks or supplies was impossible. In two hours the river rose three feet, the current so strong it swept men off their feet and downstream. Then another bridgehead was formed at Borgo de Rolto. But the situation remained desperate. By October 23, however, the Canadians had crossed the river at Cesena on the left flank at the foot of the mountains making further German defence of the Savio untenable. But as they withdrew, the Germans fought every inch of the way. To add to the Canadians' problems, the river kept rising sweeping away the hastily erected Bailey bridges and widening the waterway to 200 feet. Respite came just in time when, on October 28, the Canadians were relieved and pulled out of the line for a short rest.

October 21/22

SMITH Ernest Alvia "Smoky"

"Destroyed a Tank and Two Self-Propelled Guns; Routed Enemy Infantry Single-handedly"

Weather conditions that night for the Seaforth Highlanders of Canada to spearhead an attack across the Savio River and establish a bridgehead could hardly have been worse. Torrential rains had caused the river to rise six feet in five hours. The soft vertical banks made it impossible to take tanks or antitank guns across the raging stream. But despite these obstacles the Highlanders managed to stabilize a foothold, only to be attacked suddenly by three German Mark V Panther tanks. Supported by two self-propelled guns and about 30 infantry, the situation looked hopeless. But, under heavy fire from the approaching Panthers, Smoky Smith led his PIAT antitank gun team across an open field to a roadside ditch which offered the cover and close range he needed. Leaving one man with a PIAT, Smith crossed the ditch with a companion and obtained another gun. Almost immediately an enemy tank came rattling down the road firing machine guns into the ditches.

His comrade was wounded but, at a range of 30 feet, Smith fired the PIAT and scored a direct on the tank, knocking it out of action. Ten German infantry jumped off the back and charged him with Schmeissers and grenades. Smith moved out onto the road and fired his Tommy gun at point-blank range. His aggressive stand killed four of the Germans and drove the rest back. Then another Panther opened up and more enemy infantry closed in. Smith reloaded his machine gun and fought them off until they fled in disorder. But another tank now swept the area with gun fire, from a far greater range, however, than the other. Still, it created a dangerous situation. Yet, in spite of it, Smith helped his wounded comrade to a nearby building where he received medical attention. Smith then returned to his post to ward off any further attacks. None developed, however, and thanks to Smith's earlier efforts the battalion was able to consolidate the bridgehead. This was vital to the success of the eventual capture of San Giogio di Cesena which allowed the Canadian advance to continue. For his dogged determination and gallantry in the face of danger, Smith was awarded the Victoria Cross.

Born in New Westminster, B.C., after leaving school Smith engaged in contracting work. Following the war, he was employed at a photographic studio in his native city. Later he reenlisted in the Permanent Force, serving at British Columbia Army Command Headquarters in Vancouver before he retired.

VC   Pte Sgt (PF)   Born May 3 1914
RefScs: CVC 186-7   DHist 713 065 (D2)   TDD 364 VM 190-1

Smoky Smith shrugged off the action that won him the VC as "It was a job to do, and you did it. And I was scared the whole time. Who wouldn't be?" Of the decoration itself: "A nice Christmas present to take home to Mom." He also got a week's leave in Rome.

The Last Operation
December 3, 1944 - January 7, 1945

The final campaign for the Canadians — Operation Chuckle — in Italy began on the third day of December with the Allied objective of capturing Bologna. The designated start-line was the Santerno River and to get there the Montone, Lamone, Fosso Vecchio, Fosso Munio and Serno rivers — "rivers of blood" — had to be crossed. Both Canadian divisions were committed to the battle. The Fifth on the right flank swung through San Pancrazio and Rodo to cut Route 16 and capture Ravenna. The First meanwhile drove toward Russi. It was hard slogging all the way, through rain-swollen streams, irrigation ditches and canals, while the major rivers flowed between high flood banks giving the Germans deadly vantage observation positions.

It took five days alone to ford the 35-foot-wide Lamone. The Canadians finally stormed across on December 10. The next obstacle was the Canale Navaglio, site of the last full-scale battle in which Canadians took part in Italy, which began on December 12. As the Canadians strove to consolidate a bridgehead on the far side of the canal, the Germans continuously counterattacked. By Christmas they had at last established themselves along the Senio River.

The nine-mile advance had been costly. The Canadians lost 548 men killed, 1,796 wounded and 212 taken prisoner. The campaign now staggered to a standstill, characterized by small-scale actions mopping up enemy pockets. The exception was a German counterattack aimed at gaining lost ground around Granarolo, but it soon lost momentum.

CANAL NAVIGLIO
December 13

WICKLOW Donald Charles

"Led Daring Tank Assault to Save Bridgehead"

That morning German infantry, two Panther tanks, and several self-propelled guns were threatening a bridgehead held by the Carlton and York Regiment. Under intense crossfire, Donald Wicklow of the 9th Canadian Armoured Regiment led his troops across the canal completely surprising the enemy. His tanks' concentrated fire on the nearest Panther quickly destroyed it. The other German tank, the SPs, and the infantry quickly withdrew and the bridgehead was restored.

MC Lt
RefScs: DHist 713 065 (D2)

SHAW Roderick Finley

"Wrested Wounded Man from Burning Truck"

At three-thirty in the afternoon, the area north of Santa Leonardo came under particularly heavy shelling and mortar fire. One bomb came so close to Roderick Shaw of the Carlton and York Regiment that it blew him out of the slit trench in which he was lying. Terribly dazed, he was about to scramble back in when he noticed a radio truck burning a short distance away. Despite bombs and shells falling all around, he ran to the vehicle to find the wireless operator badly wounded. With the help of two others he wrested the man from the truck and into a slit trench. He then ran off in search of a stretcher-bearer, which he found, to help take the man to the regimental aid post.

MM Sgt
RefScs: DHist 713 065 (D1)

Russi
December 16

McCANN Margaret

"Ignored Shelling while Attending to Her Patients"

Margaret McCann of No 5 Field Ambulance was dressing a patient's leg that had been amputated above the knee, when a large shell crashed into the ward of the Advanced Surgical Centre in Russi to which she was attached. Though the shell narrowly missed her she calmly finished the dressing and then coolly directed her patient to another ward.

This action was typical of Nursing Sister McCann's conduct — her capability, courage and exemplary manner during the bitter December battles.

MBE Lt
RefScs: DHist 713 065 (D?)

BETWEEN RUSSI AND BAGNACAVALLO

BRAY Joseph Albert

"Wounded, Led Assault on Enemy Buildings"

On this morning a company of the 48th Highlanders of Canada attacked a group of buildings called Casa Boschi that were strongly held by the Germans. Ignoring heavy machine-gun and rifle fire, Joe Bray's section advanced steadily towards a brick shed. The section leader received a wound in the neck, disabling him. But although Bray was injured — in the stomach by a bullet from a German Schmeisser — he immediately took command. Charging the position he killed two Germans with his Bren gun. He had no sooner returned to the shed when a dozen Germans counterattacked. Without hesitation Bray moved into the open, killed two of the enemy and dispersed the rest. The Germans then reorganized and attacked again. Bray, though wounded a second time by a bullet that broke his leg, kept firing until the Germans were once more driven off.

DCM (Immediate)   Pte
RefScs: DHist 713 065 (D1)

SENIO RIVER
December 22/23

PITRE Benoit

"Firing From the Hip, Destroyed Machine-Gun Nest"

During a night advance to clear a section of the bank of the river, a platoon of the Cape Breton Highlanders became pinned down by a German machine-gun nest. Assessing that unless some immediate action was taken further advance was impossible, Benoit Pitre abandoned the comparative safety of his trench and raced across 75 feet of open ground. Firing his Bren gun from his hip, he ran into the face of the full force of enemy machine-gun fire. Undeterred, Pitre kept closing in until, when only a few yards from the position, he finally succeeded in killing all four of the German gun crew. As a result the advance resumed.

MM (Immediate)   Pte
RefScs: DHist 713 056 (D1)

1945

CANALE NAVIGLIO, WEST OF RUSSI
January 4

KING John Thomas

"Leadership and Gallantry Beat Off German Counterattack"

Having crossed the canal during the night, at one o'clock in the morning a platoon of the Princess Patricia's Canadian Light Infantry was ordered to capture two houses ahead of the regiment's position which were strongly defended by the enemy. By two o'clock the objective was attained and the platoon moved into the buildings, one of which acted as its headquarters. Fifteen minutes later the Germans launched a strong counterattack supported by a self-propelled gun and machine-gun and mortar fire. Because the platoon commander was out checking on the position of his sections, John King was left in charge. The headquarters house was hit and set on fire, and in addition a haystack outside the building was also set ablaze. By this time the SP gun was 50 yards from the house while 35 yards away German infantry was overrunning one of the platoon's sections.

King ran out and across open ground, which was completely illuminated in the SP's line of fire to the menaced section. There he rallied the men, so effectively directing their fire that the German attack in that sector was beaten off. Eight Germans were killed, King accounting for three of them.

King then returned to his headquarters again across fire-swept ground, carrying one of his men who had been critically wounded. Upon reaching the house he found that his platoon commander had been killed. Taking charge, under heavy machine-gun fire and shelling, he ran to the forward section and led it in an attack that wiped out the infiltrating enemy party. He then moved from section to section exhorting his troops who under his leadership and direction beat off the counterattack, forcing the enemy to withdraw and leave their SP behind. As a result the position was stabilized.

DCM Sgt
RefScs: DHist 713 065 (D1)

January 7

GODFREY William George

"Heavily Attacked, Refused to Abandon Observation Post"

Having got across the canal the night before, next morning the Carleton and York Regiment was attacked by German tanks and infantry. Despite the heavy hail of fire, William Godfrey of the 1st Field Regiment remained at his forward observation post to direct harassing fire against the enemy. This action held up the Germans for several hours until they made a determined thrust to split the Canadian forces in the bridgehead. But again Godfrey refused to leave his post which was hit five times by tanks. Godfrey now directed fire from one of his own 6-pound guns so successfully that one German tank was destroyed, another damaged and one other forced to withdraw. Godfrey's efforts resulted in the stabilization of the bridgehead.

MC Capt
RefScs: DHist 713 065 (D2)

CLEARING THE RHINELAND
February 8 - March 19, 1945

*T*o deliver the death knell to Hitler's Third Reich, the primary objective of the First Canadian Army, along with the British and U.S. armies, was to force the enemy out of the area west of the Rhine. The task called for capturing the Reichwald Forest, breaking the Siegfried Line, and seizing the Hochwald Forest defences. It was a slogging, inch-by-inch battle fought on mud and flooded ground and through water three-feet deep. But by February 21, the Canadians and their allies, mainly the British Corps, under command of the First Canadian Army, had cracked the Siegfried Line. However, the formidable defences about the Hochwald Forest and the Balberger Heights still barred the way to the Rhine. The assault on these positions was launched on February 26 by the Second and Third Canadian Infantry Divisions and the Fourth Armoured Division. Fighting under the same conditions as the Reichswald Battle, as well as in heavy rains and against fierce enemy counterattacks, it took the Canadians until March 4 to accomplish both objectives. Resistance ended on March 10 when the Germans blew up the Wesel bridges and withdrew to the east bank of the Rhine. Canadian losses during the month-long campaign totalled 5,304 killed, wounded and missing.

The Moyland Wood

*T*he first step in the Rhineland Battle was the capture of the road and rail town of Goch. A pivotal point in the Germans' Siegfried Line defences, it opened the way to the next phase in the advance southeast: Operation Veritable and its follow-up under Guy Simonds, commander of the Second Canadian Corps. The "Blockbuster" starting point was to be the holding of the Goch-Calcar Road. In the process it was necessary to take the formidably defended Moyland Wood.

ADOLPH Milton Eugene

"Saved Comrades from Burning Vehicle"

*O*n the afternoon of Sunday February 18, Milton Adolph, a crew member with a carrier platoon of the Regina Rifle Regiment, was returning from the attack when his section commander's vehicle struck a mine causing it to overturn and catch on fire. Adolph leaped from his carrier and with a fire extinguisher ran back to put out the flames. There he found the driver dead, the gunner seriously wounded and the commander trapped. But despite enemy mortar shelling and small-arms fire, he got the fire under control and extricated the gunner. Then, when the pair was unable to free the commander, Adolph dug the earth out from under the carrier with his hands and dragged the commander from the burning vehicle.

He then loaded the two men into his own carrier and drove them back to an aid station. That completed, he returned to the mined area to provide support for the follow-up assault until his fuel was again exhausted and his section put out of action.

MM (Immediate) Cpl
RefScs: DHist 713 065 (D1)

AUSTIN James Gordon

"Rescued Wounded under Relentless Fire"

Three days later on February 21, James Austin, a regimental sergeant-major with the Royal Winnipeg Rifles, organized the evacuation of casualties, frequently going into the heavily wooded area under severe enemy fire to assist the overworked stretcher-bearers. Towards the end of the day, due to heavy shelling and mortaring, his A company had lost all of its officers and Austin took command. He was praised not only for his leadership and energy, but for setting an example to other members of his battalion.

MC WO1
RefScs: DHist 713 065 (D1)

Blockbuster

The purpose of this part of Operation Veritable was to open a 16-mile corridor to the Rhine. It had been calculated that with the overwhelming force at hand a quick, sharp victory was assured. But the February thaw, the quagmire that clogged roads, and cloud cover that limited air support, turned the campaign into a nightmarish 13-day struggle that claimed 3,638 Canadian killed and wounded, 214 alone slaughtered on February 26, the first day of the battle.

COSENS Aubrey

"Routed Enemy from Three Strongholds Unaided"

On the night of February 25/26, 1945, during the Rhineland fighting, 23-year-old Aubrey Cosens from Latchford, Ont., single-handedly routed out enemy soldiers from three different strongpoints before being killed by a sniper's bullet. That night his regiment, the Queen's Own

Aubrey Cosens (PA 166764)

Rifles of Canada, had launched an attack on the hamlet of Mooshof. Cosen's platoon, with two Sherman tanks in support, was twice beaten back by fire from German troops holed up in three farm buildings they had turned into strongholds. Most of the platoon was killed including its commander, and one of the tanks was put out of action. Cosens immediately took charge of the four survivors of the platoon whom he ordered to cover him as he dashed across open ground under heavy mortar and shell-fire. Stationing himself behind the turret of the remaining tank, he directed its fire. The tank then rammed the first building knocking a hole in the side and Cosens, supported by the other four infantrymen, charged through it, bricks falling all around them. Going from room to room he killed several of the defenders and took the rest prisoner. He then single-handedly stormed the other two buildings killing or capturing the occupants. The strongpoints overcome, his regiment was able to continue its advance. Cosens was on his way back to report to his company commander when he was cut down by an enemy bullet and died almost instantly. For his daring, initiative and determined leadership, Cosens was awarded the Victoria Cross.

Born in 1921, Cosens' family moved to Porquois Junction, Ont., shortly afterward and there he received his education. In 1940 he enlisted in the army. He is buried in Groesbeck Canadian War Cemetery at Nijmegen in Holland.

VC   Sgt   Born May 21 1921   KIA Feb 26 1945
RefScs: CVC 188-9   RH 198-9 200 205   VM 192-3

DUNKLEMAN, BEN   SRC: CAN'S AT WAR
         DSO   p 132

RODGERS David Muncie

"Single-Handedly Cleared Two Houses of Enemy Snipers"

Soon after crossing the Goch-Calcar Road start-line on the night of February 25/26, the armoured troop carriers of the Queen's Own Cameron Highlanders of Canada ran into heavily mined soft ground necessitating a change of maneuver. Leading the flotilla, David Rodgers pushed to within a hundred years of the final objective to find it infested with snipers hidden in houses and slit trenches. Ignoring the hail of fire he leaped from his vehicle and dashed forward clearing two houses, killing four of the defenders and taking 12 prisoners. He then rallied his platoon and cleared a third house killing more German soldiers and taking additional prisoners.

For his action which took place less than a mile from where Aubrey Cosens had won his VC, Rodgers was recommended for the same decoration. But when the commendation reached General Bernard Montgomery's desk, the 21st British Army Group Commander blue-pencilled it, approving instead a DSO.

DSO (Immediate) Major
RefScs: DHist 713 065 (D2)   RH 205-6

The Hochwald Gap

*H*aving cracked the vaunted Siegfried Line, the Canadians still had to breach the formidable defences around the Hochwald Forest and the Balberger Heights that barred the way to the Rhine. The assault against these positions to break through a corridor along the Goch-Xanten railway line was launched on February 26 by the Second and Third Canadian Infantry Divisions and the Fourth Armoured Division. Handicapped by rain and mud, and faced with fierce German counterattacks, it took until March 4 to clear the enemy from the defences.

Tank of the 4th Canadian Armoured Division during the advance towards the Hochwald Forest, February 1945. (PA 133675)

STOCK Robert Burns

"Wounded, Continued to Direct Fire"

Without waiting for the rest of his company to form up, on the night of February 26/27, Robert Stock of the Algonquin Regiment, having reached the high ground of the Hochwald Forest, led a company of tanks on foot against enemy positions heavily protected by mortar fire and shelling. By first light the tanks had reached their objective but shortly afterwards the Germans brought down heavy mortar fire on the position and Stock was wounded.

Despite his intense pain, he refused to be evacuated and for the next 12 hours directed artillery fire onto enemy positions. So effective were his directions that his small force of 32 men was able to repel continuous counterattacks. Only when relief arrived did Stock relinquish his post.

DSO (Immediate) Maj
RefScs: DHist 713 065 (D2)

FREEMAN Laurence Frederick

"Led Daring Tank Assault"

On that same night, under cover of darkness, Laurence Freeman, commander of a troop of tanks from the South Alberta Regiment, on reaching his position in the Hochwald Gap destroyed one German Tiger tank and drove off three others. A short time later under difficult ground conditions he maneuvered his tank into position to engage another Tiger tank, disabling it so severely that the crew was forced to abandon it.

MM Sgt
RefScs: DHist 713 065 (D1)

WIGLE Frederick Ernest

"Severely Wounded, Staved Off Countless Enemy Counterattacks"

During a series of German counterattacks in the Hochwald Gap that began at dawn on February 28, Fred Wigle, in command of a force of the Argyll and Sutherland Highlanders of Canada, was severely wounded. Nevertheless, he remained at his post and directed defence after defence against continuous assaults inflicting heavy casualties on the enemy. As a result of his tireless efforts, after 40 hours his company's position had been consolidated.

DSO (Immediate)   Lt-Col
RefScs: DHist 713 065 (D2)   RH 225

TILSTON Frederick Albert

"Hero of the Hochwald Forest"

On March 1, Fred Tilston of the Essex Scottish Regiment, though severely wounded three times, put on a whirling-dervish performance of bravery, leadership and sheer guts seldom seen on any battlefield anywhere. As part of the Second Canadian Division the unit was assigned to breach the defence line northeast of Udem and clear the northern half of the Hochwald Forest. This was vital to capturing Xanten, the last German bastion west of the Rhine protecting the Wesel bridge escape route. The attack began at 7:15 a.m., but due to the softness of the ground it proved impossible to support the advance with tanks as originally planned. Tilston led his company across 500 yards of flat open country close behind his own creeping barrage to ensure maximum coverage from the bombardment. Although wounded in the head, Tilston continued to lead his men through a belt of 10 feet of barbed-wire to the enemy trenches, shouting orders and encouragement, and firing his Sten gun as he advanced. When a platoon on the left came under intense fire from a machine-gun post, he dashed forward and silenced it with a grenade. First to reach the enemy position he was also the first to take a prisoner. Ordering the reserve platoon to mop up, he pressed forward with his main force to the second line of German defences at the edge of the woods. As he approached them a piece of flying shrapnel struck him in the hip and he fell. Despite the severity of his wound he struggled to his feet shouting to his men to keep going. When they reached the defences they found an elaborate system of underground dugouts and heavily manned trenches. After bitter hand-to-hand combat with the enemy, the redoubt was cleared and two German company headquarters were overrun. But by this time Tilston's company had been reduced to only 26 men, a quarter of its original strength. And now the enemy counterattacked in strength with a hail of mortar and machine-gun fire. Moving from platoon to platoon Tilston organized his defences, directing fire at the onrushing Germans. Despite the ferociousness of the assault the Highlanders held on. When their ammunition ran out, Tilston braved the bullet-swept ground between his own company and one on his right to replenish it, carrying grenades and rifle and machine-gun ammunition back to his troops. In the process he also replaced a damaged radio set to reestablish contact with his battalion headquarters. Tilston made at least six such trips, each time crossing a road dominated by German machine-gun posts. On his last errand he was wounded for a third time; in this instance, in the leg, and was unable to proceed further. Found in a shell-hole beside the road, although in serious condition and barely conscious, he refused medical aid until he had given complete instructions for consolidating his company's position and had ordered his one remaining officer to take charge with the epigraph: "We held!" It was an incredible display of gallantry, one that cost Tilston parts of both legs which had to be amputated. He was awarded the Victoria Cross.

Tilston was born in Toronto, where he graduated from the Ontario College of Pharmacy. Prior to enlisting in the Canadian army in 1940 he was sales manager of one of Canada's leading drug manufacturers with head office in Windsor, Ont. After the war he returned to his former job eventually rising to become president and chairman of the board, and making his home in Aurora, Ont.

VC   Maj   Col(R)   Born June 11 1906   Died Sept 23 1992
RefScs: CVC 190-1   RH 236-42   VM 194-5

In 1945 I was fortunate enough to be one of the newspaper reporters who covered Fred Tilston's return to Windsor. He struck me as a paradox, being one of the most benign yet determined individuals I have ever had the pleasure of meeting. Warm and friendly with a sense of humour, nothing stood in his way. Exactly a year after his injuries on the battlefield he was back in action at his old job on civvie street.

CLEVE

YOUNG McGregor

"Skill as Artillery Officer Earned Him the DSO"

"Mac" Young, who commanded the 4th Canadian Field Regiment Royal Canadian Artillery, was regarded as one of the army's most brilliant and knowledgeable artillerymen. During the battle south of Cleve, which culminated in the clearing of the Hochwald Forest and the capture of Xanten, Young frequently had several regiments of artillery under his command as well as his own. On several occasions, in order to maintain proper control of these units, he remained at his wireless for as long as 48 hours without rest. Whenever a lull in the battle occurred he used the opportunity to visit his observers with the forward battalions to encourage them and ensure that the artillery support for the advance troops was as strong and effective as possible. While carrying out these excursions he exhibited a coolness under fire and a complete disregard for his personal safety. McGregor was cited for his "sound tactical judgement and thorough knowledge of artillery . . . [which] instilled great confidence in all those who worked with him."

DSO   Lt/Col
RefScs: DHist 713 065 (D2)

COULAS Melvin Louis

"Slaughtered Enemy in Counterassault"

After retreating from the Hochwald Forest, on the night of February 4/5 the Germans manned a ridge 700 yards south of it on rising ground. While attacking the position, when his platoon commander was killed, Melvin Coulas of the Stormont, Dundas and Glengarry Highlanders took charge. Upon reaching the ridge his force came under such heavy counterattack that one of his sections had to retire. Coulas then led the his remaining force in a charge in which he killed eight German soldiers and wounded another 15. In the resulting enemy confusion his platoon secured the position.

MM (Immediate)   Cpl
RefScs: DHist 713 065 (D2)

JULL Frank Reginald

"Despite Wounds, Burns, Continued Charge against Enemy Gun Post"

On March 6, a platoon of the Highland Light Infantry of Canada was assigned the task of capturing a group of houses near Sonsbeck. At the head of a section Frank Jull was hit in the thigh with a rifle bullet, but continued to lead his men in clearing the first set of buildings. Having had his wound dressed, he led an assault on an enemy gun post in an adjacent orchard. Then a bullet struck his webbing pouches, igniting two phosphorous grenades that burnt his battle dress and scorched his skin. In spite of these severe burns he continued to lead the charge until the German position was overrun and his own objective reached.

MM (Immediate)   Cpl
RefScs: DHist 713 065 (D2)

CROSSING THE RHINE
March 25 - 30, 1945

*A*t eleven o'clock on the night of March 23, 1945, Allied troops began crossing the Rhine on a 27-mile front between Rees to the north and Rheinberg to the south. It was the start of Operation Plunder, the landing of a million-and-a-half Canadian, British and American troops in Germany for the final assault against the Reich. Among those participating in the initial crossing was the 9th Canadian Infantry Brigade.

Twelve hours later, on the morning of March 24, troops of the 1st Canadian Parachute Battalion took part in Operation Varsity, the airborne landings east of the river near Wesel. Several days later the Canadian Third Division crossed the Rhine fighting its way to Emmerich to open up a gateway to the liberation of the Netherlands and the Canadian-Polish advance into east Germany across the Ems River.

(l. to r.) Generals Harold Crerar, Alan Brooke, Guy Simonds; Prime Minister Winston Churchill; General Bernard Montgomery (PA 143952)

TOPHAM Frederick George

"Last Canadian To Be Awarded the VC"

Frederick Topham was the last Canadian to be awarded the Victoria Cross (see PA below). As a medical orderly he had jumped with the 1st Canadian Parachute Battalion during Operation Varsity. That morning, while treating casualties from the drop, he heard a cry for help from a wounded man exposed to enemy fire. Two other orderlies from

Fred Topham (PA 143952)

a field ambulance had gone to his aid in succession but the Germans killed them both as they knelt beside the man. Topham, who had witnessed the scene, rushed forward to replace them. As he attended the wounded parachutist he was shot in the nose. Bleeding profusely and in agonizing pain, he nevertheless carried the man through continuous enemy fire to the shelter of a wood. There, for the next two hours, he refused all medical aid for his wound and, disregarding heavy and accurate German fire, continued to bring in casualties from the field. Only after all wounded had been cleared did he consent to have his own wound treated. He was told to evacuate but insisted in remaining at his post. Then, on his way back to his company, he came across a motor-carrier that had received a direct hit. Mortars were dropping all around and the vehicle was on fire, its own ammunition exploding. Despite orders not to approach it, Topham ran on alone and rescued its three occupants, all of whom were suffering from severe injuries. Although one of them died shortly afterwards, Topham helped evacuate the other two to safety. For six hours, all of it spent in great pain, Topham was responsible for saving the lives of many members of his battalion, an action that won him the VC.

A native of Toronto, before WW2 Topham worked in the mines at Kirkland Lake, Ont., before enlisting in the army. Following his discharge from the service, he was employed by Toronto Hydro.

VC Cpl Born Aug 10 1917
RefScs: CVC 192–3 VM 196–7

The title of this anecdote is based on the date the VC was actually awarded, not when it was won. Topham was the second-to-last Canadian to win the decoration, the last being Robert Hampton Gray (Lt) of the Royal Navy Fleet Air Arm on July 28, 1945.

KING Joseph Charles
WINHOLD Lloyd Christmas

"Two Actions to Expand North Rhine Bridgehead Earned Immediate DSOs"

On March 24, the day after they had crossed the Rhine by Buffalo craft, Joseph King of the Highland Light Infantry of Canada, and Lloyd Winhold of the North Nova Scotia Highlanders, in the face of withering machine-gun and mortar fire, consolidated the key town of Bienen allowing for expansion of the Rees bridgehead.

King led his company across a thousand feet of open ground during which two of his platoon commanders were killed and a third wounded. Although his troops faced fire from three German tanks as well as machine guns and mortars, his attack succeeded in clearing a group of buildings in the village of Speldrop. The result was that next day he was able to lead the capture of several other buildings in the town of Bienen.

Winhold took his company through 500 yards of enemy fire and mounted one of the supporting tanks from which position he directed their fire. That night the Germans counterattacked with self-propelled-gun-equipped tanks. Once again Winhold climbed on top of one of his own tanks and directed its fire. In the furious armoured fire-fight that followed, one of his supporting tanks and an enemy tank were knocked out. This resulted in the rest of the German tanks withdrawing allowing the troops to occupy Bienen.

King
DSO (Immediate) Maj
RefScs: DHist 713 065 (D2)

Winhold
DSO (Immediate) Maj
RefScs: DHist 713 065 (D2)

GOMEZ Darrow

"Saved Key Breakout Position"

On the morning of March 30 at Emmerich, gateway to the Canadian breakout, Darrow Gomez of the 3rd Canadian Anti-Tank Regiment repeatedly repelled German counterattacks against the Royal Winnipeg Rifles, two of them self-propelled gun assaults. At 11a.m., having reconnoitered an enemy position in the face of intense fire, Gomez maneuvered his 17-pound self-propelled Valentine gun into position, knocking out the enemy's comparable fire-power.

Gomez then made a further reconnaisance locating another German position that had an entire company of infantry pinned down. Despite the fact that the infantry commander had been killed, and his own driver was badly wounded, Gomez placed his Valentine gun in such a suitable position that, with a single blow, he demolished the enemy's self-propelled firearm.

Shortly afterwards, when a large German patrol attacked his own position, Gomez manned his machine gun, killed one of the enemy soldiers, took seven prisoners, and forced the rest to retreat.

DCM Sgt
RefScs: DHist 65 (D1)

LIBERATION OF THE NETHERLANDS
March 23 - May 5, 1945

During the final phase of the Allied campaign in Europe, the Canadian army's role was to open up the supply route to the north through Arnhem, then clear the northeastern Netherlands, the coastal belt of Germany eastwards to the Elbe River, and western Holland. At this stage the First Canadian Army was a formidable force, especially since the First Canadian Corps, which had fought so long in Italy, had been transferred to Northwest Europe. Now for the first time two Canadian Corps fought side by side. In the western Netherlands the First Canadian Corps, under Lieutenant-General Charles Foulkes, was responsible for the liberation of the area north of the Maas River. This area included such cities as Amsterdam, Rotterdam and the Hague. The Second Corps, commanded by Lieutenant-General Guy Simonds, cleared the northeastern Dutch coast and the German coast, then extended its drive into Western Germany. On May 5, all German troops in Holland, as well as those on the Second Corps' front, surrendered to the Canadians.

Western Holland

In the western Netherlands the First Canadian Corps, comprised of the First Canadian Infantry and the Fifth Canadian Armoured Divisions under Foulkes, was responsible for the liberation of the area north of the Maas River and the cities Amsterdam, Rotterdam and the Hague.

The assault of Arnhem began on April 12, and after fierce house-to-house fighting the town was cleared two days later. The Fifth Armoured then dashed northwards to Ijsselmeer some 30 miles away to cut off the Germans defending against the First Division at Apeldoorn which the Canadians occupied on April 17. By April 28 the enemy in west Holland had been driven back to a line running roughly between Wageningen through Amerstoff to the sea, known as the Grebbe Line. On that date a truce was arranged to allow food and medical supplies to be flown in for the starving Dutch.

Doetinghem
April 1

SHERRING William John Henry

"Paved the Way for Advance in Face of Fierce Fire"

On this Sunday around one o'clock in the early afternoon, a Calgary Highlanders platoon was pinned down in a damp crawl trench by German machine-gun and mortar fire. Another platoon was ordered to move into a position where it could clear the way ahead. One section led by William Sherring rounded a corner to be confronted by enemy fire from an orchard 300 yards away. Sherring steered his section from one building to another, flushing the Germans out as he advanced and taking several prisoners. Although fired upon constantly, he led his section to a crossroads, charged across alone and established a foothold in a building from where he was able to cover the advance of the rest of the infantry.

NBL Cpl
RefScs: DHist 713 065 (D1)

Westervoort
April 12/13

SIMPSON James McLean

"Slaved throughout the Night under Fire to Ready Ferry Launching Site"

During the night the 14th Canadian Field Company of the Royal Canadian Engineers was assigned the task of bringing up two rafts to operate a ferry service to carry tanks across the Ijssel River to Arnhem. On reaching Westervoort, James Simpson, in charge of the advance party, spent the night sweeping the approach road of mines and carried out reconnaisance of the riverbank, all the while under heavy German mortar and shell-fire.

Early the next morning, fresh troops arrived to relieve the party, but Simpson continued with his work to prepare the landing site. Only at noon with the job all but finished, after labouring for over 13 hours continuously under enemy fire, and suffering a painful back injury, did Simpson finally agree to withdraw for rest.

MM Sgt
RefScs: DHist 713 065 (D1)

"Let's Go Canada." Poster designed for Director of Public Information urging Canadians to take up arms. (C 87120)

APELDOORN
April 13

TAMBLYN Glen Owen

"Risked His Neck to Save Crewmen, Wiped Out Resistance"

Proceeding along the road to the town, the Carleton and York Regiment's advance suddenly ground to a halt when it encountered heavy German machine-gun and sniper fire coming from three different directions. Disregarding the threat of bazookas known to be in the area, Glen Tamblyn of the 6th Canadian Armoured Regiment, who were in support, drove his tank ahead of the infantry. He had already taken out two of the small-arms posts when his vehicle was hit by a mortar which set it on fire. Two of the crew were badly wounded and trapped in the burning tank. Under machine-gun and sniper fire, Tamblyn lifted his two comrades to safety.

He then took over another tank, and with the same disdain for his own safety drove forward again and by bold and skillful maneuver reached a position from which he was able to eliminate the remaining machine gun and clear out the last enemy resistance. As a result of Tamblyn's actions the infantry was able to resume its advance and reach its objectives.

MC (Immediate)   Lt
RefScs: DHist 713 065 (D1)

HOVEN AND ZUTPHEN
April 14

STONE James Riley

"Leadership Earned Bar to DSO"

Jim Stone's leadership qualities in battle during the Italian campaign had become something of a legend — and he wore the ribbons, DSO and MC, attesting to it. Here in Holland this morning, as CO of the Loyal Edmonton Regiment, he had been ordered to capture two bridges intact, one north of Hoven and another at Zutphen. The assignment needed all of Stone's brand of command to achieve it. The Germans were firmly entrenched along a railway embankment some 200 yards in front of the bridges. This defence proved so formidable that one company assaulting the position suffered such heavy casualties and became so disorganized it was compelled to withdraw.

Stone, who had knack of knowing when and where to be at the right time, went forward instilling fresh confidence in his men and reorganizing them. The result was that a fresh assault on the position succeeded with many of the enemy killed. The bridges were seized before the Germans could blow them. For this action, and a previous battle in Italy, Stone was awarded a Bar to his DSO.

DSO & Bar MC   Lt/Col
RefScs: DHist 713 065 (D2)

ARNHEM

MUNRO James Hay

"Kept Enemy at Bay with Pistol and Hand Grenades"

During an attack on a fortified house, both the 75mm gun and the machine gun on James Munro's tank jammed. But the 11th Canadian Armoured Regiment trooper calmly climbed out of the turret and onto the back deck of his vehicle and kept the Germans inside the house engaged with his pistol and hand grenades until the tank weapons could be cleared. In a sense this was a climax to two years of combat for Munro who had already distinguished himself earlier in tank battles in Italy.

MM   Sgt
RefScs: DHist 713 085 (D2)

APELDOORN
April 15

FRASER William

"In Face of Danger Brought in Critical Supplies"

By the time C Company of the 48th Highlanders reached its objective on the east bank of the canal running through the town, by the evening of the 15th casualties in men and equipment had been high. Rations and ammunition were in dangerously short supply. And with the Germans only 40 feet away across the canal, movement was virtually impossible. Despite the danger, William Fraser led his carrying party to each of the company's three platoons, delivering the necessary arms, equipment, food and rum, at all times exposed to enemy fire. By his action a critical situation had been relieved that allowed the regiment to maintain its positions.

NBC   CQMSgt
RefScs: DHist 713 065 (D1)

ARNHEM
April 15

JONAH Howard Labaren

"Heroic Action Rescued Crewmen, Destroyed Antitank Guns"

Four miles to the north of the town, the tank in which Howard Jonah was gunner received a direct hit from a German antitank gun. The blast killed the driver, wounded three of the crew and set the vehicle on fire. Jonah remained at his gun, firing back at the enemy even though he knew that at any minute fire might reach the fuel tanks. Finally he pulled the co-driver, who was so badly hurt he was unable to help himself, from the tank and carried him to a covered position where the other wounded had been assembled, all the time under German machine-gun fire. Jonah grabbed a Bren gun and, exposing himself still further, sought out the location of the antitank gun that had knocked out his vehicle. Spotting a party of 20 Germans advancing on his tank, he opened fire killing 12 of them and forcing the rest to surrender. Then Jonah found the antitank positions, reported their location to his squadron and directed its fire with his incendiary bullets. Both guns were subsequently destroyed enabling the unit to again move forward.

MM (Immediate)   L/Cpl
RefScs: DHist 713 065 (D1)

APELDOORN TO SOEST
April 16-22

JOHNSON Frank William

"Kept Infantry Supplied despite Lack of Communications"

In the push to the Eem Canal, it was the job of the 12th Canadian Armoured Regiment commanded by Frank Johnson to keep the advancing 3rd Infantry Brigade supplied with ammunition and fuel supplies as well as passing on vital tactical information. Normally this could have been facilitated by radio communication, but due to the speed of the advance, the distance between Johnson's headquarters and the "fluid" front ruled out clear wireless transmission/reception most of the time. Johnson overcame this problem by making his way forward himself to the advance positions, frequently risking he life from deadly enemy crossfire and shelling on the way to and fro. However, his bold action during the advance allowed the infantry to proceed without interruption and reach the Soest-Baarn area on schedule.

    DSO (Immediate) Maj
    RefScs: DHist 713 065 (D2)

IN THE NORTHWEST NETHERLANDS
April 28

LEATHERBARROW Robert Wilson

"Exposed to Enemy, Directed Fire at Antitank Guns"

With only a week to go before the end of the war in Europe, Robert Leatherbarrow of the 2nd Canadian Armoured Regiment had lost none of his zeal for coming to grips with the enemy. On this date, while advancing over ground under severe shell and heavy mortar bombardment, he suddenly detected the tell-tale flash of a German 88mm antitank gun cunningly concealed on the left flank of his troop. Leatherbarrow calculated that unless the weapon was taken out of action the Canadian advance would bog down. Without hesitation he wheeled his tank into the open where, although badly exposed, he could place his fire accurately. Twice the tank shuddered under the impact of a hit, but in each case the blows were only glancing since the enemy gunners, seeing the tank approach, were firing in haste. Leatherbarrow continued to press forward and with his own devastating fire soon neutralized the German weapon allowing his troop to continue its advance.

MM (Immediate) Sgt
RefScs: DHist 713 065 (D1)

Northeastern Holland

The Second Canadian Corps' northern drive rapidly gained momentum, and as the troops crossed into Holland they were greeted by enthusiastic demonstrations by a liberated Dutch people. On the right the Fourth Canadian Armoured Division under Chris Vokes crossed the Twente Canal and pushed forward to capture Amelo on April 5, before curving eastward into Germany. In the centre, the Second Division crossed the Shipbeck Canal and advanced in a virtually straight line to Groningen in northern Holland which it reached on April 16. The Third Division on the left flank was charged with clearing the area adjoining the Ijssel River, and after several days of stiff fighting, occupied Zutphen. Then it pushed forward to capture Deventer, Zwolle and Leeuwarden, reaching the sea on April 18.

The operations of the Second Corps were then extended from eastern Holland into western Germany. The Fourth Division crossed the Ems River at Meppen, and combined with the 1st Polish Armoured Division in thrusts on Emden, Wilhemshaven and Oldenburg. The Third Division also moved on Emden while the Second Division advanced from Groningen to the area of Oldenburg.

TWENTE CANAL
April 3

ELDRIDGE Garnet William

"Captured Position, Beat Off Counterattacks"

Having crossed the Twente Canal, a platoon of the Royal Regiment of Canada, led by Garnet Eldridge, reached a railway crossing where it came under a deadly hail of German machine-gun fire soon intensified by bazooka explosions and mortar bombs. Undaunted, and with little concern for his own safety, Eldridge led his men over the fire-swept ground right up to the muzzles of the enemy machine guns and bazookas, spraying the positions with his Sten gun. Though badly outnumbered in men and weapons, he pressed forward, thoroughly demoralizing the Germans who fled leaving many casualties behind.

Once his position had been consolidated the platoon then came under enemy counterattack and had to be beaten back with small-arms fire since artillery support had not had time to cross the canal. But despite this inexpediency, with coolness and expertise Eldridge rallied his troops and repelled the assault inflicting heavy losses. After two hours reinforcements arrived to fully consolidate the bridgehead.

DCM Sgt
RefScs: DHist 713 065 (D1)

ZUTPHEN
April 3

BLACKBURN George Gideon

"Bold Attack Secured Bridgehead"

Around the same time as Eldridge's valiant action, a few miles to the east of Zutphen on the Twente Canal another fierce fight was taking place. Here it was essential that a bridgehead be held by a company of the Royal Regiment of Canada against enemy attack so that a bridge could be built to ford the waterway with armour. At seven-thirty that evening, the Germans brought a single tank supported with infantry to bear on the position. Attacking vigorously, the tank knocked out both of the Royal Regiment's antitank guns. It then moved forward and fired two rounds into a house where George Blackburn, the forward observation officer, was stationed on the top floor. The shells landed just below him and the tank advanced to within 300 yards of the house. At this point the situation had become critical; the tank was neutralizing the Canadian troops and the German infantry was fast pressing in. But in spite of direct fire from the tank, Blackburn remained at his post directing artillery shelling on the German infantry with such accuracy that the enemy broke and withdrew. Seeing the hopelessness of the situation, the tank also retreated leaving the bridgehead fully secured.

MC (Immediate) Capt
RefScs: DHist 713 065 (D2)

April 6

JEAN Gerard

"Supervised River Crossing for Four Hours under Fire"

On this date Le Régiment de la Chaudière attacked the town of Zutphen, a garrison occupied by determined Hitler Youth. At the outset encountering an antitank ditch, Gerard Jean led his men forward under intense German machine-gun, mortrar and artillery fire, and started the preliminary work of having the sappers clear the area of mines and demolition charges before the bridge on the road to Zutphen, the enemy had had time to blow it up. Jean, again under heavy fire, reconnoitered the stream until he found a shallow spot where tanks could get across. But first the nearby enemy positions had to be overcome. Jean gathered a handful of men, attacked the German outposts and succeeded in routing them. One enemy soldier was killed and another wounded, and one light machine gun was abandoned by the retreating Germans.

It was now necessary to fell enough trees to reinforce the crossing area with timber. This took four hours during which Jean and his men worked under constant enemy fire. But their determination paid off and the tanks were able to proceed on to their objective. For his action Jean was recommended for an immediate DSO although it was later commuted to an MC.

MC (Immediate) Lt
RefScs: DHist 713 065 (D2)

DEVENTER
April 10

RIGBY Arthur

"Determined One-Man Tank Attack Broke Enemy Resistance"

At eleven o'clock in the morning, the 8th Canadian Infantry Brigade and the Canadian Scottish Regiment were pinned down by two German self-propelled 75mm guns and a wall of small-arms fire. Because their position was so close to the enemy, the supporting artillery did not dare bring its guns on the target.

Guiding his tank to the left flank of the Canadian infantry, Arthur Rigby of the 27th Canadian Armoured Regiment began searching the ground ahead for the enemy guns when one of the self-propelled weapons opened up on him revealing its position. From 500 yards away Rigby returned the fire and knocked out the enemy SP. Then he spotted the second moving into a position to engage him. But before it could do so, Rigby fired accurately and put it out of action. Now the remaining Germans who had been dug into well-entrenched positions dropped their weapons and began to run. With his high explosive and .30-caliber guns, Rigby fired on them. Forty of the Germans surrendered allowing the Canadian infantry to reorganize and, later on, to approach the outskirts of Deventer before fog settled in for the night.

MM (Immediate) Sgt
RefScs: DHist 713 065 (D1)

SOGEL
April 11

PORTEOUS Conrad de Lotbiniere

"Dashing Battle with 15 Paratroopers Earned Him the MC"

"C on" Porteous, a liaison officer with the 4th Canadian Armoured Brigade Headquarters, had been ordered to proceed to Sogel where the Lake Superior Rifles were engaged in clearing the town of the Germans. While driving through the middle of it in a Humber scout car, he noticed 15 enemy paratroopers trying to escape on bicycles. Porteous and his driver charged forward, Porteous firing his Sten gun from the turret cutting down three of the Germans. Then his rifle jammed so he drew his pistol. By this time he was in the midst of the paratroopers who had dismounted and taken up firing positions. Porteous ordered three of them to surrender and loaded them into the back of his scout car. At this point two of the enemy began to engage the Canadians with *Panzerfausts*, forcing them to withdraw. Then three German prisoners were killed by their own comrades' fire and Porteous' driver was wounded. He then took over the driving, proceeding onto the Lake Superiors' HQ, obtained the information he had been ordered to get, and returned with it to brigade HQ. Appended to the commendation for a MC for his

Con Porteous (Courtesy Bud Porter)

action was a handwritten note from Chris Vokes which read: "The dash, enterprise, and courage of this officer has been brought to my attention on several occasions."

MC Capt
RefScs: DHist 713 065 (D2)

Con exhibited "dash" in other ways, too. After he and fellow liaison officer Bud Porter had been out on the town, Porter awoke to find his roommate gone and his own shoes missing. Porteous had gone downtown and sold them because he "needed some cash."

DEVENTER

NICOL Frederick James

"Kept Enemy at Bay at Close Range with Mortar Fire"

At six-thirty in the morning, by the time the fog had begun to lift, the 3rd Mortar Platoon of the Canadian Scottish Regiment, which had reached the outskirts of the town the night before, found itself entirely cut off by the enemy. Then, at this point, the Germans attacked with tanks and infantry. Gunner Frederick Nicol refused to be daunted, however. Stubbornly staying at his post, he opened fire on the enemy with his mortar from 100 yards' range. While this had a telling effect on the attackers, it also placed Nicol's own life in peril since shrapnel from a mortar bomb was deadly at 200 yards. Nevertheless, Nicol persevered and his stoic stand broke up the attack enabling his platoon to take 30 prisoners as well as killing and wounding a number of others. Nicol's action not only saved his battalion but helped clear the way into Deventer

NBL Cpl
RefScs: DHist 713 065 (D1)

April 13

GALLANT Ivan Gregory

"Although Wounded, Brought Six Others to Safety"

During the evening around eight o'clock, the West Nova Scotia Regiment, upon reaching the outskirts of the town, became subjected to heavy German shell-fire in which 12 men were wounded, six of them seriously. A call went out to the regimental aid post to send a vehicle though it seemed impossible that one could ever get through due to the intensity of the enemy's shelling. Nevertheless, Ivan Gallant volunteered to drive the carrier. On his way forward he was struck in the head by a piece of shrapnel which momentarily knocked him out. However, on regaining consciousness he proceeded to the forward position, collected the six severely wounded infantrymen and drove them back to the aid post.

NBL Pte
RefScs: DHist 713 065 (D1)

ASSAM
April 13

ARMSTRONG Richard John Wesley

"Dismantled Bridge Demolition Charges while under Fire"

At 10:00 a.m., the leading battalion of the 4th Canadian Infantry Brigade was held up at the bridge over the Noord Willems Kanaal, the last important canal crossing on the thrust to the business and intellectual centre of Groningnen in northern Holland. Heavily defended by German machine gunners and snipers on either side, its capture was essential for the rapid advance of the Canadian spearhead before the enemy could blow it up.

When Richard Armstrong of the Royal Canadian Engineers surveyed the situation at first hand, he realized that any attempt to move the demolition charges installed by the enemy would be strongly opposed. Knowing the hazard he would be working under, he called for covering fire and made a dash to the bridge. At the other end, the German engineer set to pull the igniters was instantly killed, allowing Armstrong to remove the charges on top. He then leapt into the water and disconnected the rest of the charges under the girders. The whole operation took 15 minutes during which Armstrong was under relentless enemy fire. His brave action allowed the division to cross the canal, the last natural obstacle in the path to the objective, at least 24 hours earlier than would otherwise have been possible.

MC (Immediate)   Lt
RefScs: DHist 713 065 (D2)

ZWOLLE
April 14

ARSENAULT Wilfrid

"Gave His Life to Root Out Enemy Position"

To save as many lives as possible, Le Régiment de la Chaudière, deployed to the south and east of Zwolle, had to ascertain the exact location of enemy defences. With one other soldier, Wilfrid Arsenault, while on reconnaissance, found an enemy outpost manned by four Germans near the town. Ordering his companion to take cover he charged the position alone. Though mortally wounded he kept firing until he ran out of ammunition, killing two of the Germans and wounding another before he died. His sacrificial action rooted out the post and served as an inspiration to the capture of the village the following morning without a single civilian casualty.

NBL   Cpl
RefScs: DHist 713 065 (D1)

GRONINGEN
April 14

BEAULIEU Jean Marie

"Daring Solo Dash to Capture Bridge"

To secure a bridge on a canal dominating the Canadian line of advance into the centre of the town, Jean Beaulieu of Le Régiment de Maisonneuve took matters into his own hands. As the leading section leader of his company, he led his unit to within 75 yards of the crossing which he found heavily guarded by two German 20mm guns as well as machine guns on the other side of the canal, making any further advance impossible.

With complete disregard for his own safety, Beaulieu sprang to his feet and rushed across the bridge. In spite of withering fire he turned his Sten gun on the first 20mm gun. Outflanked, the gun crew surrendered whereupon Beaulieu engaged the second enemy weapon. During the fight, his section raced across the bridge and secured a bridgehead. The way was clear for the Calgary Highlanders to enter this town.

DCM (Immediate)   Cpl
RefScs: DHist 713 065 (D1)

KUSTEN
April 17

ALLISON Millard Jasper

"One-Man Tank Regiment"

During the early stage of the breakout from the Kusten Canal bridgehead in western Germany, as he eased his tank onto the railway embankment, Millard Allison of the 28th Canadian Armoured Regiment and his crew came under high-velocity enemy fire and heavy shelling. Realizing he could not take evasive action due to the softness of the ground, but knowing that it was vital to eliminate all opposition if the Canadian advance was to continue, he hit upon the zany idea of shunting a railway goods truck along the rails ahead of his tank. Not as crazy as it might have seemed. The ruse worked so well that the Germans concentrated all their guns on the truck instead of the tank, enabling Allison to methodically dispose of all posts along a 2,500-yard route along which he killed 50 of the enemy.

However, when he abandoned his truck-shield at the end of the line, the German infantry, armed with their deadly *Panzerfaust* antitank weapons, closed in. Unable to depress his tank guns low enough to deal with his attackers, he stood up in the turret, fully exposed to the most merciless small-arms fire, holding the enemy off with hand grenades and a pistol. Then, by the time he reached his objective, he saw that his troop commander's tank, some distance behind him, had been hit, its burning hull blocking the rest of the squadron.

Without hesitation Allison scrambled out of his tank and worked his way through fierce automatic-weapons fire to find that his troop commander and another of the crew had been wounded, with the other two dead. After carrying the commander to temporary shelter in a farm building he returned to the blazing vehicle and rescued the other wounded man, sustaining painful burns in the process. He ran the gauntlet of fire back to his own tank where, for the next 48 hours, he beat off repeated counterattacks. During that time he eliminated two German self-propelled guns, an armoured troop carrier, and mowed down a number of German infantrymen — all in a day's work.

DCM (Immediate) Cpl
RefScs: DHist 713 065 (D1)

APPINGDAM
April 23

RYAN Francis Jerimia Thomas

"Protected Company's Flank in Face of Heavy Fire"

That morning, prior to the attack on this Dutch town north of Groningen, Francis Ryan, in charge of a carrier section of the Royal Winnipeg Rifle Regiment, went out ahead of the company to make a reconnaissance of German positions. As his section approached a group of buildings it was met with furious fire from two *Panzerfaust* antitank guns and a machine gun. Ryan personally silenced the machine gun and the section neutralized the rest of the enemy post taking several prisoners.

Later, with an extra section under his command during the direct attack on the town, his job was to protect the battalion's right flank. Occupying several buildings, both of his sections came under heavy shell-fire. Disregarding it, Ryan ran from house to house positioning his Bren gunners until he was confident the flank was fully protected. During the afternoon enemy patrols tried to penetrate his position but all were repulsed. The sections contined to come under shell-fire and late in the afternoon Ryan was so seriously wounded he had to be evacuated. His efforts had proved instrumental in the success of the day's operation.

MM (Immediate) Sgt
RefScs: DHist 713 065 (D1)

BUILD-UP TO CAPITULATION
April 26 - May 5, 1945

WEENER
April 26

DAVIS Milton David

"Found Way Through and Around Minefields"

In the assault on the strongly fortified German defence line at Ween in Germany, tanks of the 27th Canadian Armoured Regiment were held up by mines and demolitions. Milton Davis, a scout driver with A Company of the battalion, volunteered to reconnoitre a route through the minefield. Dismounting from his scout car and, despite small-arms fire and the inevitable antipersonnel mines, he successfully found a route through which the tanks could proceed and personally led them on foot.

Later in the day when the tanks were again held up by mines, Davis drove his scout car to look for a route by-passing the danger zone. This took him down streets and through back alleys where fighting was in progress. Then just as he had completed his reconnaissance his car struck a mine and he was severely wounded. His daring efforts had contributed greatly to the speed of the Canadian attack.

MM (Immediate)   L/Cpl
RefScs: DHist 713 065 (D1)

NEAR WEENER

RADLEY-WALTERS Sydney Valpy

"Courageous Leader, Inspiration to His Men"

On D-Day "Rad" Walters landed in Normandy as second-in-command of a platoon of the 27th Canadian Armoured Regiment. Within two weeks he was given command of the unit. In mid-August he distinguished himself in a tank battle with German Panthers and was awarded the MC. On this April day near the end of the war his squadron was in support of an attack by the North Shore Regiment which was held up by a minefield. Riding on top of his scout car, Radley-Walters made a reconnaissance through the mined field and, although his vehicle struck one of the explosives wounding his driver, he continued on foot. When he returned he led his platoon of tanks through the field without a single loss. The DSO was added to the MC. The commendation read in part: "His squadron has been led with great aggression and tenacity. Above all, he had been a courageous leader, an inspiration to not only his junior officers and senior non-commissioned officer, but to every man in his platoon."

DSO MC   Maj
RefScs: DHist 713 065 (D2)

Shortly after D-Day, when I was stationed at B-4 airfield at Beny-sur-Mer, Rad drove up in his jeep to say hello and took me on a tour of the beaches, at this point crowded with men and equipment as well as German prisoners. He had lost none of his poignancy of speech I remembered from our days at school together. Pointing to a church, which is a landmark in the area, he said, "On D-Day it stood out like a phantom and a guide. With all that shelling and so on it still stood there."

Last Remembrance Day Rad was quoted in the press as saying "Remembrance Day to me is walking through our cemeteries in Europe. [It] is a day when Canadians can remember where they came from and what they did."

LEER
April 28

WEBBER Kenneth Nelson

"Led Fierce Attack on One of Last Vestiges of Resistance"

In the attack on this strategic route to the East Friesland Peninsula in Germany, D Company of the North Nova Scotia Highlanders, commanded by Ken Webber, crossed the Leda River to land on the exposed right flank and cover the main assault by two other Canadian regiments. The Germans were firmly dug in on a 600-yard-long dyke, 75 yards from the riverbank with four 20mm guns covering it. Under a partial smokescreen the company landed and immediately rushed the dyke. In spite of intense enemy fire, Webber led his men until the whole of the position was taken and all of the enemy were either killed or captured.

Now the Highlanders faced heavy shelling, increased small-arms fire, and a counterattack. Personally directing the defence, Webber also called for artillery fire on a German battery that was shelling one of the other Canadian regiments. At the same time he conducted a mopping up operation along the right flank of his own position. Webber's leadership and disregard for his personal safety resulted in the flank being solidly established, allowing troops to go in and take the town of Leer.

DSO (Immediate)   Maj
RefScs: DHist 713 065 (D2)

Ken is reported to have said that he got his DSO for "getting lost and ending up at the vital spot."

Oldenberg State Forest
April 30

NELSON Ole

"Saved Platoon from Heavy Casualties by Heroic Action"

Five days before the Germans surrendered to the Canadians on two fronts, while the 6th Canadian Infantry Brigade advanced on the northern German city of Oldenberg, a company of the South Saskatchewan Regiment cleared the Oldenberg State Forest on the left flank. Ole Nelson had just begun to set up his machine gun when his platoon came under concentrated enemy fire 200 yards to the left. The gun crew and two others were taken out of action with severe wounds and the rest of the unit was pinned down.

Ignoring a hail of gun fire, Nelson ran to his weapon and began firing at the enemy position. Soon he ran out of ammunition. Still under heavy enemy fire he crawled over to the platoon's casualties, collected their magazines and bandoliers and returned to his gun. He then continued to engage the German machine-gun nests until he had wounded all but two of the enemy who finally surrendered to him.

Nelson's prompt action and boldness under intense fire prevented otherwise heavy casualties to his platoon and largely contributed to consolidating its position. This episode resulted in one of the last commendations for Canadian gallantry in the Second World War.

MM (Immediate) Cpl
RefScs: DHist 713 065 (D1)

Wageningen and Bad Zwischenahn
May 5

In the Hotel De Wereld in the Dutch town of Wageningen, Lieutenant-General Charles Foulkes, commander of the First Canadian Corps, accepted the surrender of all German forces in the Netherlands from General Johannes Blaskowitz, commander of the 25th Germany Army. Present at the signing of the peace terms was Prince Bernhard of Holland.

Surrender of the 25th German Army at Wageningen, May 5, 1945, Lieutenant-General Foulkes (left), GOC 1st Canadian Corps, accepts the surrender of General Johannes Blackowitz (second from right), commander of German forces in the Netherlands. Left foreground, H.R.H. Prince Bernhard. (PA 138588)

At the same time, at Bad Zwischenahn in northwest Germany, Lieutenant-General Guy Simonds, commander of the Second Canadian Corps, accepted the surrender of all German forces on that front.

These proceedings brought to an end the glorious chapter of the long journey of bravery and sacrifice shown by the Canadian soldier throughout World War Two.

KOREA

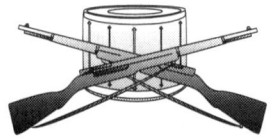

CANADIANS IN KOREA
June 25, 1950 - July 27, 1953

By the time Canadian troops went into action in Korea for the first time in mid-February 1951, the situation had changed dramatically since they had set sail from Seattle on November 25, 1950. At the time the war seemed to be near its end. On June 25 the North Korean army had invaded the south leading to the first policing action by the United Nations. Almost immediately the South Korean forces, bolstered by United States troops, were encircled in a perimetre around Pusan. But on September 15, the Americans landed at Inchon, the inland port of Seoul (the capital), and began a drive north across the 38th parallel which divided the north from the south to the Chinese border. Then at the end of October, six Chinese armies began crossing the Yalu River. By the time the Canadians reached Pusan, the UN forces were in retreat. At the beginning of the new year the enemy had recaptured Seoul and reached a line some 40 miles south of the city. Shortly afterwards the UN forces started a new drive towards the 38th parallel in which, by mid-February, the Canadians took part.

The Canadian Army Special Force, later designated the 25th Canadian Infantry Brigade, was made up entirely of volunteers, many of them WW2 veterans. The first contingent, the 2nd Princess Patricia's Canadian Light Infantry Battalion, sailed for Korea in November where it became part of the 27th Commonwealth Infantry Brigade. Gradually other second battalions of the Canadian army joined the force with which they fought for the next two years. On July 27, 1953, the Korean Armistice was signed bringing the war to an end. Altogether 26,792 Canadians served in the Korean conflict suffering 1,558 casualties. The names of 516 dead are inscribed in the Korean Book of Remembrance.

During the uneasy truce that followed the signing of the armistice, 7,000 Canadians were employed in a peace-keeping role setting an example for which the Canadian Forces have become internationally famous in trouble spots around the world.

ROCKINGHAM John Meredith

"Commander of the Canadians in Korea"

"Rocky" Rockingham had distinguished himself in WW2 during the campaign in Europe before he took over the Canadian Army Special Force. A native of Sydney, Australia, he emigrated to British Columbia as a youth. For his part in the European theatre he was awarded the Distinguished Service Order. In August 1944, he was given command of the 9th Canadian Infantry Brigade. At Boulogne he accepted the German surrender. His final military appointment was General Officer Commanding, Western Command, with headquarters in Edmonton. Rockingham's philosophy on war was best summed in by these words: "There is no peacetime job that can compare with the demands of wartime command. If you're really conscientious and really think about what you're doing, you're exposing the lives of thousands of men in everything you do. And they've got to follow you; they have no choice. So you'd better be right. In business, if you take a wrong decision, you lose a lot of money or get fired, but that's pretty easy compared to losing a lot of lives."

Rockingham retired to Qualicum Beach, B.C., and died in Vancouver General Hospital on July 24, 1987, at age 75.

CB CBE DSO USLM   Maj-Gen   Born 1911   Died July 24 1987
RefScs: DHist 713 065 (D2)   TOW 291

John "Rocky" Rockingham briefing platoon and company commanders of the 1st PPCLI. (PA 128875)

Kapyong
April 23 - 25, 1951

On April 23, the Commonwealth Brigade was in a blocking position in the valley of the Kapyong River. The 2nd Princess Patricia's Canadian Light Infantry was positioned on Hill 677 on the west side of the valley. Across from it, on another hill, was an Australian regiment with two British battalions positioned to the rear for support. The attack by the Chinese that night, which was aimed at capturing Seoul for a third time, overran the Australians who were forced to withdraw. This left the Canadians with no friendly troops on either side of them. As a result one company was moved to the flank exposed by the retreat of the Australians. On the evening of April 24 this company came under heavy mortar and machine-gun fire. It was then attacked by Chinese ground troops who also began moving on the battalion headquarters. Fire was held until the Chinese broke through the trees 200 metres away. Then 24 machine guns cut loose. Attacks on the PPCLI continued throughout the night. But the defenders had artillery support which drove the enemy back each time. By April 25 the battalion was surrounded and the supply route cut off. Supplies, dropped from the air, resupplied the Canadians who held their ground. That afternoon the regiment was finally relieved. Though the 2nd PPCLI inflicted heavy losses on the enemy, its own casualties of 10 killed and 23 wounded had been light. For its part in the battle the regiment was awarded the U.S. Presidential Citation.

A new supply of ammunition is passed over to Haida *at sea from a US destroyer, June 1953.* (PA 138197)

April 24

MITCHELL Wayne Robert

"Fought until He Nearly Dropped"

As soon as the Chinese attacks started, Wayne Mitchell was in action with his Bren gun and was largely responsible for repelling the enemy attacking his platoon. Wounded in the chest early in the battle, after having the injury dressed he continued to fight, firing from the hip and moving from fire-trench to fire-trench as the Chinese pressed towards the platoon headquarters. Though wounded again he failed to let this deter him and continued fighting right through the night. In the words of his commendation: "At daylight . . . Mitchell could hardly stand for loss of blood." He was subsequently evacuated by helicopter.

DCM Pte
RefScs: DHist Biof SB 77

HILLS John Graham Wallace

"Skillful Direction of Artillery Fire Repelled Attackers"

During the fighting, John Hills, a PPCLI company commander, seemed to be everywhere, rallying and encouraging his men. He directed the battle with such skill that the artillery fire he ordered time and again drove off the Chinese attacks.

MC Capt
RefScs: DHist Biof SB 78

STONE James Riley

"Heroic Leadership Earned Third DSO"

Throughout the battle the 2nd PPCLI commander James Stone, a WW2 veteran of the Italian and European campaigns in which he won the DSO and Bar, was an inspiration to his men. Cool-headed and cheerful, but determined, he simply refused to withdraw even though at times the heavily outnumbered enemy made the situation seem hopeless. Even when they were cut off and completely surrounded, he coolly requested that supplies be dropped by air. Heroic though his action was in setting an example and holding the position, had the Chinese persisted in their attacks and with greater numbers there was little doubt the PPCLI would have been overrun. Stone later admitted, "Our own troops show lack of basic training particularly in caring for weapons and equipment. Much 'scruff' that was hastily recruited has now been returned to Canada . . . [But] troops are very well led and the aggressiveness they display in attack under very difficult circumstances is a great credit to their officers."

Following the Korean conflict Stone became Provost Marshal. He retired from the army in 1960.

Second Bar to DSO   Lt/Col
RefScs: DHist Biof   SB 67

Kowang-Hi
November 23 - 25, 1951

*B*etween mid-October and the last week of November, the Chinese tried to regain as much territory as possible before November 27 since the front as it would then exist would become the truce talks' demarcation line in the event of an armistice within the next 30 days.

At this point the 2nd Regiment was ordered, along with two other battalions of the Commonwealth Brigade, to defend a front approximately four miles long in the Kowang-Hi region northeast of Sami-ch'on. On November 22, the R22R and an American unit adjacent to it came under heavy Chinese shelling. Next day during a heavy snowfall that made communications difficult, enemy artillery again pounded the two battalions. Then at 4:28 a.m. the Chinese, using rockets, began the anticipated offensive. The enemy, however, were greeted by a shower of grenades and sustained machine-gun fire from the Royal 22nd Regiment. A second attack was frustrated by artillery and mortar fire, but the Canadians did sustain some losses. Meanwhile, the Chinese had captured the hill position occupied by the Americans leaving the R22R exposed on both of its flanks.

That night was fairly quiet to begin with, then at 2:36 the following morning the Chinese could be seen readying for action. The assault lasted 20 minutes and was repulsed. At dawn, 450 Chinese attacked the Canadians' position but field guns and mortars turned the offensive into a retreat. By early morning the Americans had recaptured their hill position. Then, at 4:20 p.m. November 24, the enemy launched an assault

Soldier of PPCLI kneels at grave of fallen comrade in the United Nations Memorial Cemetery, Pusan, Korea. (PA 128813)

against the R22R from all directions. But the regiment held its ground all through the hours that followed. Next morning at 9:20 the Chinese made their fifth attack in three days. The battalion commander ordered artillery support and within minutes 3,500 shells rained down on the enemy. This bombardment broke the offensive. It also marked the last large-scale attack against the R22R in the fall of 1951. During the four days, the battalion had lost 16 men killed, 36 wounded, and two taken prisoner. Truce talks continued for the next two years while the battlefield turned into a virtual stalemate.

DEXTRAZE Jacques Alfred

"Cool-Headed Battle Commander Became Chief of the Defence Staff"

Through the five-day encounter, Jacques Dextraze remained imperturbable as he controlled the fighting from his battalion headquarters. During one of the toughest battles the regiment ever fought, at considerable risk to himself, Dextraze was constantly in touch with his forward posts. In a sense this action was a fitting climax to Dextraze's fighting career. In 1940 he joined Les Fusiliers Mont Royal as an infantry private. On August 1, 1944, he won an immediate DSO when leading the capture of the church of St. Martin in Normandy. Later he won a Bar to that decoration when he persuaded a German general to surrender the Dutch city of Groningen.

After WW2 Dextraze retired to civilian life but rejoined in 1950 to lead the Van Doos. Following his tour in Korea, Dextraze was attached to the Staff College in Kingston, Ont. After several senior positions he was appointed Chief of Staff of the United Nations Forces in the Congo. In 1970 he became Chief of Personnel of the Canadian Forces and in 1972 he was made Chief of the Defence Staff.

CBE DSO & Bar   Gen   Born 1918   Died May 10 1993
RefScs: CBS-K   DHist Bf   SB 126 153 158

LIBOIRON Real

"Despite Set-Backs Kept His Cool"

Company Commander Real Liboiron refused to be deterred by frequent set-backs. When the battle began he found that his field positions were much too crowded, and that some of the fire positions were built up instead of dug down, perfect targets for high-velocity weapons. He intended to adjust them but as he later said, "there never was time." Another problem was communications with battalion headquarters; frequently the phone lines were cut. Even this failed to phase him. Directing the battle against attack after attack he was just as cool-headed. As one of his officers put it: "He always seemed to be about two jumps ahead of the Chinese in his thinking."

DSO Capt (A/Maj)
RefScs: CBS-K   SB 153 155 157-8 160

MAJOR Leo

"Directed Fire So Effectively It Repulsed Four Counterattacks"

Leo Major had already distinguished himself in WW2 during which he was awarded the Distinguished Conduct Medal. Here in Korea he added to his laurels. At midnight on November 24/25, Leo Major headed up a section of 18 men to retake a position of Real Liboiron's forward platoon. Once stabilized, Major directed the artillery fire so expertly that the platoon was able to repulse four different counterattacks.

Bar to DCM   Cpl
RefScs: CBS-K SB 157-8

EPITAPH

"There is more truth in one sword than in ten thousand words."

The Koran

National War Memorial, Ottawa.

ABBREVIATIONS

DECORATIONS

BL(N) Bronze Lion (Netherlands)
CdeG Crois de Guerre - (Bel) Belgian (Fr) French
    (Wb) with Bronze Star
    (Wgc) with Clasp
    (WSS) with Silver Star
CB Commander of the Order of the Bath
CBE Commander of the Order of the British Empire
GC George Cross
CD Canadian Decoration
CGM Conspicuous Gallantry Medal
CM Crimean Medal
COON Dutch Command Order of Orange Nassau
DCM Distinguished Conduct Medal
DSO Distinguished Service Order
Ld'H Legion d'Honneur (Bel) Belgian (Fr) French
LoM(Am) American Legion of Merit
MBE Member of the Order of the British Empire
MC Military Cross
MiD Mentioned in Despatches
MM(Am) American Medal of Merit
MM(Fr) French Medal of Merit
NBL Netherlands Award Bronze Lion
OSA(Rus) Russian Order of St. Anne
SAM South African Medal
SM(Am) American Silver Medal
SS(Am) American Silver Star
VC Victoria Cross
VM Polish Virtuti Militari

DESIGNATIONS

ADC Aide-de-Camp
CO Commanding Officer
MD Military District
POW Prisoner of War
SHAEF Supreme Headquarters Allied Expeditionary Forces
WW1 World War One
WW2 World War Two

GENERAL

DNC Died of Natural Causes
DW Died of Wounds
KA Killed Accidentally
KIA Killed in Action

OdCWM On display at the Canadian War Museum, Ottawa

PA Personal Annotation
PIAT Projector, Infantry, Antitank
SP Self-propelled gun

RANKS

Act Acting
AS Assistant Surgeon
Bdr Bombadier
B/G Brigadier General
BSgt Brigade Sergeant-Major
Capt Captain
Col Colonel
Cpl Corporal
CSgt Company Sergeant-Major
Gen General
Gnr Gunner
Lt Lieutenant
Lt/Col Lieutenant-Colonel
Lt/Gen Lieutenant-General
Maj Major
M/Gen Major-General
MO Medical Officer
Pte Private
Rfn Rifleman
SG Surgeon General
Sgt Sergeant
Temp Temporary
Tpr Trooper
WO Warrant Officer

REFSCS: REFERENCE SOURCES

AEW G *An Encyclopedia of World History.* William L. Langer. Houghton Mifflin Company, Boston.
ANFIF *A Nation Forged in Fire.* J.L. Granatstein & Desmond Morton. Lester & Orpen Dennys Ltd., Toronto.
BIM *Battles of the Indian Mutiny.* Michael Edwards. B.T. Basford Ltd., London.
CAW *Canadians at War.* Leslie Hannon. McClelland & Stewart Ltd., Toronto.
CBS-K *The Canadian Battle Series: Korea.* Balmuir Book Publishing Ltd.
CE *Canadian Encyclopedia.* Hurtig Publishing, Edmonton.
CL Canadian *Legion* Magazine. Ottawa.

CSGWW *Canada's Sons and Great Britain in the World War.* Col. George G. Nasmith. Thomas Allen, Toronto.
CSKV *Canada's Sons on Kopje and Veldt.* T.G. Marquis. The Canada's Publishing Co., Toronto.
CVC *Canada's VC's.* Lt-Col. George Machum. McClelland & Stewart Ltd., Toronto.
DCMb *The Distinguished Conduct Medal.* David K. Riddle & Donald G. Mitchell. The Kirby-Malton Press, Winnipeg.
DHist Directorate of History, Ottawa. (JP) Jackson Papers (Field commendations: DHist 713 065 (D1) Other Ranks (D2) Officers.)
D *Dieppe.*
DSOb *The Distinguished Service Order.* Donald G. Mitchell. The Kirby-Malton Press, Winnipeg.
DTT *Dieppe: Tragedy to Triumph.* Denis & Shelagh Whitaker. McGraw-Hill Ryerson Limited, Toronto.
GM *The Globe and Mail*, Toronto.
FATB *Flames Across the Border.* Pierre Berton, McClelland & Stewart Ltd., Toronto.
GB *General Brock.* Lady Edgar. Morang & Co. Ltd., 1904.
JZ John Grodzinski Research
LD *Le Live D'Or of the Canadian Contingent in South Africa.*
MCb *The Military Cross.* David K. Riddle & Donald G. Mitchell. The Kirby Malton Press, Winnipeg.
MMb *The Military Medal.* David K. Riddle & Donald G. Mitchell. The Kirby-Malton Press, Winnipeg.
NRW *No Reason Why.* Carl Vincent. Canada's Wings Inc., Ottawa.
OEDSCC *Organization, Equipment Despatch Service of the Canadian Contingent during the War in South Africa.* S.E. Dawson. Queen's Printer, Ottawa.
OTC *Out of the Clouds.* John Willes.
RCMIYB *Royal Canadian Military Institute Year Book*, 1989.
RCMIC Royal Canadian Military Institute Collection
RH *Rhineland.* Denis & Shelagh Whitaker. Stoddart, Toronto.
SB *Strange Battle-Field.* Lt-Col Herbert Fairlie Wood. Queen's Printer & Controller of Stationary, Ottawa.
SIB *Sir Isaac Brock.* Hugh S. Eayrs. The MacMillan Company of Canada Ltd., 1924.
T *Tecumseh.* Ethel T. Raymond. Glasgow Brocke & Co., 1915
TCAW *The Canadians at War 1939/45.* The Reader's Digest Association (Canada) Ltd., Montreal.
TCW *The Crimean War.* Philip Warner. Taplinger Publishing Co., New York.
TGM *The Great Mutiny.* Christopher Hibberd. Penguin Books, Toronto.
TDD *The D-Day Dodgers.* Daniel G. Dancocks. McClelland & Stewart Ltd., Toronto.
TIOC *The Invasion of Canada.* Pierre Berton. McClelland & Stewart Ltd., Toronto.
TOW *Tug of War.* Denis & Shelagh Whitaker. Stoddart, Toronto.

TS *Toronto Star.*
TS & TG *The Shame and the Glory.* Terrence Robertson. McClelland & Stewart Ltd., Toronto.
TSOT *The Story of Tecumseh.* Norman S. Gurd. William Briggs, Toronto.
TTHWSA *The Times History of the War in South Africa.* L.S. Amery. Sampson Low, Marston and Co. Ltd., London.
TVC *The Victoria Cross.* Imperial War Museum, London.
TWO1 *The War of 1812.* Henry Coles. The University of Chicago Press.
V *Vanier.* Robert Speaight. Collins, Toronto.
VCGC *Illustrated Handbook of the Victoria Cross and George Cross.* Imperial War Museum, London.
VM *Valiant Men.* John Swettenham. Hakkert, Toronto.
VMS *Vokes Story.* John P. Maclean. Gallery Press, Ottawa.
W *Worthy.* Larry Worthington. MacMillan, Toronto.
WWIC *Who's Who in Canada.* Global Press, Toronto.

NAME INDEX

THE WAR OF 1812
Brock, Isaac 3-6
Tecumseh 6-9

CRIMEA
Dunn, Alexander Roberts 11-12

THE INDIAN MUTINY
Reade, Herbert Taylor 14-15

THE BOER WAR
Cockburn, Hampden Zane Churchill 18
Holland, Edward James Gibson 18-19
Richardson, Arthur Herbert Lindsey 17
Turner, Richard Ernest William 19-20

WORLD WAR 1
Adams, Read Thomas Payne 46
Affleck, John Ernest 112
Aitchison, John Miller 131
Algie, Wallace Lloyd 142-143
Allan, Robert James 53
Allen, Norman Burke 150
Allen, Ralph Fleton 146-147
Ames, Maurice Roland 67
Anderson, Alexander Davidson 83
Anderson, Sedley Cantrell 129
Anderson, William 137
Apperson, James McKee 132
Appleby, Edgar 127
Arnoldi, Frank Fauquier 151-152

Baker, Edwin Godfrey Phipps 132-133
Barron, Colin Fraser 84
Baverstock, William 55
Bellew, Edward Donald 25-26
Bent, Philip Eric 73
Berner, Adolph 147
Blair, Harold John 123
Biggs, Percy Armstrong 67-68
Bingham, Owen 77-78

Blackstock, George Grant 124
Blair, John Freeman 150
Blinko, Alfred Ralph 31
Boon, Charles Edward 58
Bradfield, Reginald Henderson 118-119
Bradley, Francis James 38
Brady, Michael Lewis 101
Brereton, Alexander Picton 105
Briggs, John Alfred 112
Brillant, Jean 100
Bristow, Albert Edward 43
Brown, Harry 60-61
Brown, Percy Wells 120
Brown, William Allen 68
Burns, George Herbert 42
Burrage, John Alfred Harcourt 41
Bucknam, Norral 85
Button, Edward William 85

Cairns, Hugh 147-149
Cameron, Herbert Thomas 29
Cameron, James Miller 40
Campbell, Glidden 78
Campbell, Frederick William 30-31
Campbell, Malcolm 73-74
Cantin, Alfred Henry 107
Carmichael, Dougall 133-134
Cartenach, James Sterling 48
Castle, Alfred John 45
Cave, Gerald Ricard 54
Chapman, Thomas Baird 53-54
Clarke, Leo 37
Clarke-Kennedy, William Hew 116-117
Clement, James Fergus 35
Cockeram, Alan 111
Combe, Robert Grierson 65-67
Cowling, Thomas 44
Croak, John Bernard 97-98
Curtis, Waller Basil 36

Deacon, Arthur Weymss 146
De Laurier, Melbourne Ross 46
De Wind, Edmund 89-90
Denman, Edward Percival 143
Dinesen, Thomas 105-106
Dunlop, William Waugh 133
Dunwoody, James Moore 140-141
Durnford, Harry George 59

Dryden, John Cameron 53

Eiler, Lorne Sinclair 69
Elliott, Onvil Ard 113
Emrey, Desmond Joseph 41
Evans, Walter Allen 72-73
Ewing, Royal Lindsay 112-113

Fisher, Frederick 23-24
Flowerdew, Gordon Muriel 90-91
Fyles, Charles Douglas 71

Gilbert, William McCombe 84-85
Good, Herman James 98-99
Goodwin, Leo Francis 88
Goodwin, Wilder Penfield 82
Grafftey, William Arthur 151
Graham, Edwin Ernest 122
Grant, Alexander Robert 70
Gregg, Milton Fowler 134-136

Hall, Frederick William 24
Hammert, Nathan Thomas 71
Hanson, Harold Stewart 113-114
Hanna, Robert 63-64
Hardy, John 70
Harvey, Frederick Maurice Watson 47
Hill, Cecil Henry 108
Hobson, Frederick 61-62
Hobson, George 32
Holmes, Waller John 40
Holmes, Thomas William 75
Honey, Samuel Lewis 129-131
Horie, Harold Wilson 47
Hoskins, Ernest Lawrence 52
Hutcheson, Bellenden Seymour 122

Ingles, Charles James 110-111

James, Robert Eustace 72
Jasper, Tate 56
Johnson, Ernest Charles 33

Keable, Joseph 93
Kerr, George Fraser 127
Kerr, John Chapman 39-40
Kinross, Cecil John 79
Knight, Arthur George 120
Knight, James Archibald 149
Konowal, Filip 64

Learmonth, Okill Massey 63
Livingstone, Andrew 131-132
Lyall, Graham Thomson 128

MacDonald, Cyril Hayden 35
MacDonald, Erik Whidden 88
MacDonald, Joseph Gerrard 83
MacDowell, Thain Wendell 52-53
MacGregor, John 138
MacKenzie, Hugh 78-79
MacLachlan, Roy Hansford 69
Marr, George 142
Matheson, Guy Maclean 34
McGibbon, Peter 33
McGuigan, Stewart Parrel 71-72
McKean, George Burden 92
McNeil, Hector 137
Meadows, Cecil Herbert 107
Merrifield, William 138-139
Metcalf, William Henry 119
Milne, James 117
Milne, William Johnstone 54
Miner, Harry Garnet Bedford 99-100
Mitchell, Coulson Norman 139-140
Montgomerie, James Baird
    Thorneycliffe 50
Morley, Leonard 51
Moses, Omand Forest 44
Mullin, George Harry 80

Nelson, Claude 32
Nunney, Claude Joseph Patrick 118

O'Kelly, Christopher Patrick John 77
O'Rourke, Marshall James 60

Pattison, George 56-58
Pearkes, George Randolph 80-82
Peck, Cyrus Wesley 121
Pyman, Colin Keith Lee 104

Rayfield, Walter Leigh 125-126
Richardson, James Cleland 43
Ricketts, Thomas 143
Rothesay, Frank 24
Rutherford, Charles Smith 109-110

Scrimger, Francis Alexander Carron
    26-27
Shankland, Robert 76-77
Sharpe, Henry Arthur 136

Sifton, Ellis Wellwood 55
Spall, Robert 106
Stanley, Frank Charles 51
Stanley, Harold Poole 51
Strachan, Harcus 86-87

Tait, James 101-102
Torrance, Harvie James 124

Vanier, Georges-Phileas 114-115

Wallace, William 56-57
Worthington, Frederick Frank 144-146

Young, John Francis 123

Zengel, Raphael Douglas 103-104

WORLD WAR 2

Adair, Robert William 237
Adams, Albert Edwin 269
Adams, Homer 273
Adolph, Milton Eugene 287-288
Allard, Jean Victor 265
Allison, Millard Jasper 315
Amero, Alfred John 207
Anderson, John MacMorran 244
Aris, James Edwin 237-238
Armstrong, Richard John Wesley 313
Arsenault, Wilfrid 313-314
Atkinson, Frederick Temple 163
Austin, James Gordon 288
Ayer, Donald Holman 251-252

Ballard, Norman Alexander 218
Barron, Robert Duff 247
Bassett, James 258-259
Baugh, Rupert Donald 259
Beaulieu, Jean Marie 314
Bell-Irving, Henry Pybus 194-195
Bernatchez, Joseph Paul Emile 201
Berthelot, Guy Bernard 171
Berube, Robert 181
Bishop, Wells Arnold 158-159
Blackburn, George Gideon 308
Blackwood, Thomas Alexander 159
Blaver, Collinson Alexander 160
Bond, Thomas 236
Bonneville, Hector 225
Brannen, Lindsay Eaton 261

Bray, Joseph Albert 284
Brunstron, Terrence 252
Buchanan, Norman Bruce 236
Buell, Donald Bowie 238
Burton, Alan 229

Carr-Harris, Peter Raymand Victor 221
Carson, Frederick Lyall 217
Charbonneau, Arnold James 199-200
Christie, Kathleen Georgia 166
Cloutier, Gerard 181
Conway, John Joseph 223
Cook, William Matthew Bruce 250
Corbett, James Robert 246
Cosens, Aubrey 289-290
Coulas, Melvin Louis 295
Crane, Robert Basil 211
Crockett, George Robert 268
Currie, David Vivian 253-256

Dalton, Charles Osborne 234-235
Dalton, Hume Elliot 234-235
Darling, William 262-263
Davis, Milton David 316-317
Deardon, Ernest Hughes 269-270
Demmy, William 202
Dicken, Leonard Lloyd 170
Donald, Archibald Scott 197
Dougan, John Alpine 197
Duchnicki, Frank Albert
Duddle, Joseph McPhee 222
Drapeau, Rene 195
Drury, Charles Mills 245
Dunkleman 290

Eby, Blair Stewart 200-201
Edkins, Roy Douglas 220-221
Eldridge, Garnet William 307
Ellis, Leslie George 175

Fetterley, James 240
Foote, John Weir 178-180
Forbes, Donald 256
Fraser, William 304-305
Frechette, Loius 249
Freeman, Laurence Frederick 292
Frost, Alfred Leo 230-240
Funk, Jacob Kippenstain 225

Galbraith, John MacNeill 209
Gallant, Ivan Gregory 312
Gardner, "John" Jack 187

Garneau, Marie-Edmond Paul 183-184
Gillespie, Alan Charles 277
Gingell, Harold David 257
Glover, Frank Alexander 262
Godfrey, William George 286
Goepel, Ruston Herbert 271-272
Gomez, Darrow 299
Grant, Donald Ian 243
Grayson, William David 237
Griffin, Peter Ryerse 239
Grigas, Joseph 187

Hanson, Albert 249
Hanson, John Philip 234
Harley, Donald Stuart 207-208
Hesler, William Charles 264-265
Hodkinson, Ernest 163-164
Hoey, Charles Ferguson 215
Hogarth, Robert Ernest 251
Hoffmeister, Bertram Meryl 192

Irvine, Alfred 221

James, James Alan 241
Jasperson, Frederick 182
Jean, Gerard 309
Johnson, Frank William 306
Johnston, Merritt Elmer 271
Jonah, Howard Labaren 305
Jones, James Harvey 204
Jones, Ralph Gordon 174
Jull, Frank Reginald 295

Kay, William 189
Kennedy, Albert Arnott 203-204
Kent, Hubert Ernest 274
Kidd, Edmund Andrew 222
King, John Thomas 285-286
King, Joseph Charles 298-299
Knight, Dorothy Melrose 253
Kingsmill, Hugh Anthony Galt 216
Kirk, Andrew James 258

Lacourse, Benoit 246
Laite, Uriah 164
Laloge, Jean Emile 277-278
Law, Andrew Thompson 172
Leatherbarrow, Robert Wilson 306
Low, John 195-196

Macey, Clifford Norman 226

Mahony, John Keefer 227-228
Matthews, Albert Bruce 193-194
McCann, Margaret 284
McGowan, Douglas 252
McLean, John 203
Merritt, Charles Cecil Ingersoll 168-170
Mitchell, George 187-188
Moorehead, Charles Hamilton 238-239
Munro, Hamish Coull 229
Munro, James Hay 304
Murphy, James 174-175

Nelson, Ole 319
Nicol, Frederick James 312
Nugent, William Francis 165

O'Hare, Howard Adolf 170
O'Neil, George Edward 210
Osborn, John Warren 161-163
Ouellet, Joseph Etienne 257

Pasfield, William 224
Peden, Donald Campbell 230
Pelly, Howard William 199
Perkins, Edward James 226
Philip, Robert William 159
Pitre, Benoit 285
Porteous, Conrad de Lotbiniere 310-311
Power, Francis Gavan 165
Prince, Thomas 212-213

Radley-Walters, Sydney Valpy 317-318
Rattray, Charles Gordon 209
Rigby, Arthur 309-310
Rix, Derek Everard 161
Robertson, Robert Frank 202
Rodgers, David Muncie 290-291
Ross, Norman Hugh 173
Rowley, Roger 274-275
Ryan, Francis Jerimia Thomas 316
Ryne, Stanley Edward 173

Sawyer, Harold Victor 247-248
Schjelderup, Vilhelm Roger 273
Shaw, Robert James 218-219
Shaw, Roderick Finley 283
Sherring, William John Henry 301
Simonds, Guy Granville 185-186
Simpson, James McLean 301-302
Sinclair, Carnet William 243

Skarott, Walter Cameron 276-277
Smith, Basil Henry 172
Smith, Ernest Avia "Smokey" 281-282
Smith, John Alfred 245
Smith, Lloyd Russell 223
Snell, Frederick William 221
Snodgrass, Henry James 244
Southern, Kenneth 190
Springer, Charles 250-251
Standish, Colin Alden 160
Stock, Robert Burns 292
Stone, James Riley 303
Sutcliffe, Bruce Albert 188

Tamblyn, Glen Owen 303
Taylor, Donald Clarke 217
Tellier, Henri 264
Thomas, Maurice Pollock 258
Thomson, Sydney Wilfred 210
Tilston, Frederick Albert 293-294
Tod, William 261-262
Topham, Frederick George 297-298
Triquet, Paul 205-207
Tubb, Charles Stuart Thorne 240
Tucker, Michael Lovett 279
Turner, Sydney Allen 266-267

Uruski, Angus Alvin 200

Vokes, Christopher 190-192

Walsh, Geoffery 190
Webber, Kenneth Nelson 318
Welsh, George Arthur 190
Whitaker, Denis 176-178
Wicklow, Donald Charles 283
Wigle, Frederick Ernest 292-293
Wilmot, Laurence Frank 260-261
Winhold, Lloyd Christmas 298-299
Woodward, James Crawford 244

Young, Hugh Andrew 246-247
Young, McGregor 294-295

Ziegler, William Smith 219-220

KOREA

Dextraze, Jacques Alfred 328
Hills, John Graham Wallace 325
Liboiron, Real 328
Major, Leo 329
Mitchell, Wayne Robert 325
Rockingham, John Meredith 323
Stone, James Riley 325-326